THE SAYINGS
of the
DESERT
FATHERS

The Sayings of the

DESERT
FATHERS

THE ALPHABETICAL COLLECTION

Translated, with a foreword by
Benedicta Ward, SLG

Preface by
Metropolitan Anthony of Sourozh

CISTERCIAN PUBLICATIONS

First published in 1975 by

Cistercian Publications, Kalamazoo
and
A. R. Mowbray, Oxford

Number 59 in the Cistercian Studies Series

ISBN (Mowbray) 0 264 66350 0
    (Cistercian) 0 87907 959 2

Cistercian Publications Inc
WMU Station
Kalamazoo, Michigan 49008

Revised edition, 1984

Printed in the United States of America

Contents

Contents

Contents

Preface

The Sayings of the Desert Fathers has been for centuries an inspiration to those Christians who strove for an uncompromising obedience to the word and to the spirit of the Gospel; yet the modern reader, used to an intellectual, discursive way of exposition and also to greater emotional effusions in mystical literature may find this direct challenge difficult to face and even more difficult to assimilate and to apply to everyday life. This prompts me to give here a few explanations and to try to bring out some of the features which seem to me essential in the attitude to life of these giants of the spirit.

The first thing that strikes a reader is the insistence in the stress laid on the ascetic endeavour. Modern man seeks mainly for 'experience'—putting himself at the centre of things he wishes to make them subservient to this aim; too often, even God becomes the source from which the highest experience flows, instead of being Him Whom we adore, worship, and are prepared to serve, whatever the cost to us. Such an attitude was unknown to the Desert, moreover, the Desert repudiated it as sacrilegious: the experiential knowledge which God in His infinite Love and condescension gives to those who seek Him with their whole heart is always a gift; its essential, abiding quality is its gratuity: it is an act of Divine Love and cannot therefore be deserved. The first Beatitude stands at the threshold of the Kingdom of God: 'Blessed are the poor in spirit, for theirs is the Kingdom of God'—blessed are those who have understood that they are nothing in themselves, possess nothing which they dare call 'their own'. If they are 'something' it is because they are loved of God and because they know for certain that their worth in God's eyes can be measured by the humiliation of the Son of God, His life, the Agony of the Garden, the dereliction of the Cross—the Blood of Christ. To be, to be possessed of the gift of life and to be granted all that makes its richness means to be loved by God; and those who know this, free from any delusion that they can exist or possess apart from this mystery of love have entered into the Kingdom of God which is the Kingdom of Love. What then shall be their response to this generous, self-effacing, sacrificial Love? An endeavour to respond to love for love, as there is no other way of acknowledging love. And this response is the ascetic endeavour, which can be summed up in the words of the Lord Jesus Christ: 'Renounce yourself, take up your Cross and follow Me'. To recognize one's own nonentity and discover the secret of the Kingdom is not enough: the King of Love must be enthroned in our mind and heart, take undivided possession of our will and make of our very bodies the Temples of the Holy Ghost. This small particle of the Cosmos, which is our soul and body must be conquered, freed by a lifelong struggle from enslavement to the world and to the devil, freed as if it were an occupied country and restored to its legitimate King. 'Render unto Cesar that which is Cesar's and to God that which is God's': the coins of the earthly kings bear their mark, Man bears the imprint of God's Image. He belongs to Him solely and totally; and nothing, no effort, no sacrifice is too great to render to God what is His. This is the very basis of an ascetic understanding of life.

Yet many will be surprised by the insistence of the Sayings on what seem to be incredible feats of physical endurance. Are these at the centre of a spiritual life? Why not tell us more about the secret, inner life of these men and women? Because the life of the Spirit cannot be conveyed, except in images and analogies which are deceptive: those who know do not need them, and those who do not know are only led by them to partake imaginatively, but not really, in a world which to many is still out of reach. Many can live either by the Word of God or by deriving his precarious existence from the earth, which ultimately will claim back what is its own; the more one is rooted in God, the less one depends on the transitory gifts of the earth. To describe to what degree the dwellers of the Desert were free from our usual necessities is the only way we possess to convey both how perfectly rooted they were in the life-giving realm of God, and also how different the world of the Spirit is from what we imagine it to be when we confuse the highest achievements of the psyche with the life which God the Holy Spirit pours into the soul and body of the faithful; 'among those born of women there has risen no one greater than John the Baptist, yet he who is least in the Kingdom of Heaven is greater than he'.

The men and women of whom the Sayings speak were Christians who received the challenge of the Gospel with all earnestness and wanted to respond to it uncomprisingly, as generously as God, with their whole selves. Some built their whole life on one Word of the Gospel, some on one glimpse of Eternity seen in the eyes, the behaviour, the whole personality of an Elder. Men of high rank in the world and of high culture came to monks without any worldly knowledge because 'they knew not the first letters of the book of Wisdom which the others possessed'.

We have a great deal to learn from their integrity and their unrelenting courage, from their vision of God—so Holy, so great, possessed of such a love, that nothing less than one's whole being could respond to it. These were men and women who had reached a humility of which we have no idea, because it is not rooted in an hypocritical or contrived depreciation of self, but in the vision of God, and a humbling experience of being so loved. They were ascetics, ruthless to themselves, yet so human, so immensely compassionate not only to the needs of men but also to their frailty and their sins; men and women wrapped in a depth of inner silence of which we have no idea and who taught by 'Being', not by speech: 'If a man cannot understand my silence, he will never understand my words.' If we wish to understand the sayings of the Fathers, let us approach them with veneration, silencing our judgments and our own thoughts in order to meet them on their own ground and perhaps to partake ultimately —if we prove able to emulate their earnestness in the search, their ruthless determination, their infinite compassion—in their own silent communion with God.

Anthony of Sourozh

The Foreword is taken from *The Wisdom of the Desert Fathers, Apophthegmata Patrum* (from the Anonymous Series) translated by Sister Benedicta Ward SLG, published by SLG Press 1975, and is reprinted here with permission.

Foreword

The historical background

The collections of the *Apophthegmata Patrum,* the *Sayings of the Fathers,* come from the very beginnings of Christian monasticism. In the fourth century, Egypt, Syria, Palestine, and Arabia were the forcing ground for monasticism in its Christian expression; every form of monastic life was tried, every kind of experiment, every kind of extreme. Monasticism is of course older than Christianity, but this was the flowering of it in its Christian expression and in many ways it has never been surpassed. The roots of western monasticism are in the East, and the wisdom of the desert, the understanding of this way of life, has formed a central, though often unidentified, source for Christian living through the centuries.

The great centre was Egypt. By A.D. 400 Egypt was a land of hermits and monks. There were three main types of monastic experiment there, corresponding very roughly to three geographical locations.

Lower Egypt—the hermit life. The prototype of the hermit life was St. Anthony the Great, a Copt and a layman. He was unlettered, the son of well-to-do peasants. One day in church he heard the saying of Jesus: 'Go, sell all you have and give to the poor and come and follow me', as a commandment addressed to himself. He withdrew from ordinary Christian society about 269, and later he went further and further into the solitude of the desert. Anthony died in 356 at the age of 105 and he is still regarded as the 'father of monks'. He had many disciples and many imitators, and it is from Anthony and this tradition that many of the *Sayings of the Fathers* come.

Upper Egypt—coenobitic monasticism. In a less remote part of Egypt, the radical break with society took a different form. At Tabennisi in the Thebaid, Pachomius (290–347) became the creator of an organized monasticism. These were not hermits grouped around a spiritual father, but communities of brothers united to each other in work and prayer. There are few *Sayings* that are preserved from this region, but the Pachomian experiment was of vital importance in the development of monasticism.

Nitria and Scetis—groups of ascetics. At Nitria, west of the Nile delta, and at Scetis, forty miles south of Nitria, there evolved a third form of monastic life in the 'lavra' or 'skete' where several monks lived together, often as disciples of an 'abba'. Nitria was nearer to Alexandria and formed a natural gateway to Scetis. It was a meeting place between the world and the desert where visitors, like John Cassian, could first make contact with the traditions of the desert. Here a more learned, Greek-influenced type of monasticism evolved around an educated minority of whom Evagrius Ponticus (345–399) is the most famous. Many *Sayings* come from here and are associated with the names of the great abbas such as Moses, Pambo, Abraham, Sisoes, John Colobos, and the two Macarii.

Syria. The Egyptian monks created an ethos of their own; they made a radical break with their environment and formed new groups to which the relentless round of prayer and manual labour was basic. In Syria, however, in the area around Edessa and Antioch, and especially in the mountains of Tur 'Abdin, the ascetic movement took a different form. The Syrian monks were great individualists and they deliberately imposed on themselves what is hardest for human beings to bear: they went about naked and in chains, they lived unsettled lives, eating whatever they found in the woods.

They chose to live at the limits of human nature, close to the animals, the angels, and the demons. Their most typical representatives in the fifth century were the 'Stylite' saints, men who lived for very long periods on the top of a pillar. The first to adopt this way of life was Simeon Stylites (from the Greek *stylos,* pillar) who lived for forty years on a fifty-foot column outside Antioch. Some *Sayings* of the Fathers come from this forbidding source, from the ascetics like Julian Saba, as well as the Stylites. The legend that Simeon Stylites converted and cured a blind dragon indicates both his approachability and his concern to communicate the wisdom to which his asceticism had given him access.

Asia Minor. In Cappadocia, where a more learned and liturgical monasticism developed in the heart of the city and of the Church, the key figure was St. Basil the Great (c. 330–379). He and his followers were known as theologians and writers rather than as simple monks of the Egyptian type.

Palestine. The great monastic centre in the fifth century was Palestine. In the Judean wilderness, and especially around the desert of Gaza, there were great spiritual fathers in the Egyptian tradition: Barsanuphius and John, Dorotheus, Euthymius, and Sabas. Many of the *Sayings* come from this source.

The Sayings of the Fathers

These experiments of fourth- and fifth-century monasticism, especially those in Egypt, produced a remarkable new literary genre in the records of the *Sayings of the Fathers (Apophthegmata Patrum).* Close to parable and folk-wisdom, their themes and anecdotes passed into the world of the Middle Ages and on into pre-revolutionary Russia. The *Vitae Patrum,* the *Lives* of various of the Desert Fathers, also exercised a great influence, especially the greatest of them, the *Life of St. Anthony* by St. Athanasius, but they were more sophisticated works. It is in the *Sayings* that we are closer to the wisdom of the desert as it was understood among the fathers of monasticism. One of the chief exponents of this tradition in the West was John Cassian.

Cassian (c. 360–435), according to one tradition, was a native of Scythia. As a young man he joined a monastery in Bethlehem, but soon left it and went to study monasticism in Egypt, where he was greatly influenced by Evagrius Ponticus. He was later a deacon of the Church in Constantinople. From there he was sent by St. John Chrysostom on a mission to Innocent I at Rome. He seems to have remained in the West, and about 415 he founded two monasteries near Marseilles. There he wrote two books, the *Institutes* and the *Conferences*, in which he presented what he had learned from the great Old Men of the desert in a series of sermons which he attributed to several of the famous Fathers. Though they crystallize much that he heard in the desert, he presents it in his own style, and with a consistency which is his rather than theirs. These works became classics in the West; quotations from them abound in the *Rule of St. Benedict*, and the *Conferences* were part of the reading before Compline each night in Benedictine monasteries.

The tradition of early desert monasticism reached the West chiefly through the writings of Cassian, though it was also known through the works of Jerome, Rufinus, and Palladius. These men knew the desert, and they knew, often at first-hand, the oral tradition of the *Apophthegmata*. They systematized it, interpreted it, and presented it as they understood it. Though their works, especially Cassian's, are of great merit and importance, it is not in them that the plain teaching of the desert is best seen.

For that, the *Apophthegmata Patrum*, the *Sayings of the Fathers*, are invaluable. These are short sayings originally delivered to individuals on specific occasions and written down later. Groups of monks would preserve the sayings of their founder or of some monks especially remembered by them, and this nucleus would be enlarged and rearranged as time passed. There is an *Alphabetical Collection* of sayings in Greek. There is another Greek collection of anonymous sayings, known as the *Anonymous Collection*. The collection best known in the West is the *Systematic Collection* in which the sayings have been grouped according to subject. The original form of the sayings was presumably Coptic or Greek; the records of the sayings are in Coptic, Syriac, Greek, Armenian; and, later, Latin and the Slavonic languages.

These sayings preserve the unstructured wisdom of the desert in simple language. These are records of practical advice given out of a long life of experience in monastic and ascetic discipline. For this reason they are not always consistent with one another and they always need to be read within the context in which they were given.

They are not abstract ideas to be applied indiscriminately, but instances of what was said in particular situations.

The teaching of the Apophthegmata

The essence of the spirituality of the desert is that it was not taught but caught; it was a whole way of life. It was not an esoteric doctrine or a predetermined plan of ascetic practice that would be learned and applied. The Father, or 'abba', was not the equivalent of the Zen Buddhist 'Master'. It is important to understand this, because there really is no way of talking about *the* way of prayer, or *the* spiritual teaching of the Desert Fathers. They did not have a systematic *way;* they had the hard work and experience of a lifetime of striving to re-direct every aspect of body, mind, and soul to God, and that is what they talked about. That, also, is what they meant by prayer: prayer was not an activity undertaken for a few hours each day, it was a life continually turned towards God.

Abba Agathon said, "Prayer is hard work and a great struggle to one's last breath'; and there is the story told about Abba Lot:

Abba Joseph came to Abba Lot and said to him: 'Father, according to my strength I keep a moderate rule of prayer and fasting, quiet and meditation, and as far as I can I control my imagination; what more must I do?' And the old man rose and held his hands towards the sky so that his fingers became like flames of fire and he said: 'If you will, you shall become all flame.'

When he was dying, Abba Pambo said:

From the time that I came into this solitude and built my cell and dwelt in it, I cannot remember eating any food that I have not earned with my own hands, nor speaking any word that I have been sorry for until now. And so I go to the Lord, as one who has not yet begun to serve God.

For Abba Arsenius, this was a rule for the whole of life: 'Be solitary, be silent, and be at peace.'

The spiritual father

In this context of a whole life of prayer, the role of the 'abba', the spiritual father, was *vital,* literally, that is to say, 'life-giving'. The abba was the one who, really knowing God in his own experience, could most truly intercede for his sons. He was the one who discerned reality and whose words, therefore, gave life. The key phrase of the *Apophthegmata* is, 'Speak a word, Father'. This recurs again and again, and the 'word' that was sought was not a theological explanation, nor was it 'counseling', nor any kind of a dialogue in which one argued the point; it was a word that was part of a relationship, a word which would give life to the disciple if it were received. The abbas were not spiritual directors in the later western sense; they were fathers to the sons whom they begot in Christ. A monk had only one abba, and he was not continually discussing his spiritual state with him. There is a great economy of words about the desert. A monk once came to Basil of Caesarea and said, 'Speak a word, Father'; and Basil replied, 'Thou shalt love the Lord thy God with all thy heart'; and the monk went away at once. Twenty years later he came back, and said, 'Father, I have struggled to keep your word; now speak another word to me'; and he said, 'Thou shalt love thy neighbour as thyself'; and the monk returned in obedience to his cell to keep that also.

The Coptic monks were simple men, and their understanding of this relationship is difficult to recapture in a sophisticated society. The Father was not the teacher or scholar. When Evagrius first came to Scetis he made the mistake of lecturing to the brethren during a discussion on some matter; they let him finish, and then one said, 'We know, Father, that if you had stayed in Alexandria you would have been a great bishop . . .'—after which Evagrius was understandably quiet. The great Arsenius, tutor to the emperor, came to Scetis, too. He talked with the unlettered Egyptians about himself; when someone asked him the reason, he said, 'I know Greek and Latin, but I have not begun to learn the alphabet of these peasants yet.' This awareness of the importance of the word spoken within a relationship made the monks very wary about books— perhaps too wary—but it was an emphasis we have lost and could well recover.

Many people, as well as their own monastic disciples, came to the fathers for their life-giving words. There were plenty of opportunities for theological discussion in the towns; it was for another kind of wisdom that they came to the desert. The Fathers, for their part, were shrewd enough to know that some of those who came to them were moved by curiosity rather than devotion, and they distinguished the genuine 'hearers' of the word, whom they called 'visitors from Jerusalem', from the superficial and curious, whom they called 'visitors from Babylon'. The latter were given a bowl of soup and sent away. The former were welcome to stay all night in conversation.

Radical simplicity and common sense

The Desert Fathers withdrew from ordinary society and sought the solitude of the desert. This was the first step in their 'spirituality'. Then they placed themselves under spiritual fathers. After that, the daily life was their prayer, and it was a radically simple life: a stone hut with a roof of branches, a reed mat for a bed, a sheep-skin, a lamp, a vessel for water or oil. It was enough. Food was reduced to the minimum; sleep also: 'One hour's sleep a night is enough for a monk if he is a fighter', they said. They had a horror of extra possessions: 'A disciple saw a few peas lying on the road and he said to his father, "Shall I pick them up?" but the old man said in amazement, "Why? Did you put them there?" and he said, "No." "Then why should you pick them up?" '

They tried many experiments, especially with fasting, but the final conclusion was, 'For a man of prayer, one meal a day is sufficient.' When a young monk boasted of fasting longer, they asked him searching questions about the rest of his life.

The ideal was not sub-human but super-human, the angelic life; but this was to be interpreted in the most practical and common-sense way. There is the story of John the Dwarf who announced to his brother that he was going off into the desert to live as an angel. After several days of acute hunger, his brother heard a knock at the door. He asked who was there, and when a voice said, 'John', he replied, 'John is now an angel and has no need of food and shelter'; but at last he took in the humbled John and set him to work again.

It was a life of continual 'striving', but not of taut effort the whole time. It was said of Anthony that one day he was relaxing with the brothers outside the cell when a hunter came by and rebuked him. Anthony said, 'Bend your bow and shoot an arrow', and he did so. 'Bend it again and shoot another', and he did—and again and again. The hunter said, 'Father, if I keep my bow always stretched it will break.' 'So it is with the monk', replied Anthony; 'if we push ourselves beyond measure we will break; it is right for us from time to time to relax our efforts.'

The result of this common-sense attitude is most beautifully illus-
trated in the story of St. Nilus and the harlot Pelagia: when she rode
naked through Antioch, all the clergy around Abba Nilus hid their
faces, but he 'gazed along and intently at her; then turning to the
rest he said, "Did not the sight of her great beauty delight you?
Verily, it greatly delighted me...." '

Charity

The aim of the monks' lives was not asceticism, but God, and the
way to God was charity. The gentle charity of the desert was the
pivot of all their work and the test of their way of life. Charity was
to be total and complete. To quote from a *Life*, rather than a *Saying*:
Abba Abraham had a niece, Mary, who became a harlot in Alexandria:

...and he dressed himself as a soldier and went to find her ... they feasted
together at the inn and he took her to his room to lie with her. 'Come close
to me, Mary,' he said and took her in his arms to kiss her ... but she
recognised him and wept and she said, 'Go before me and I will follow ...
for you have so loved me and grieved for me that you have come even into
this cess-pit to find me'; and so they went home.

Anthony the Great said, 'My life is with my brother,' and he
himself returned to the city twice, once to relieve those dying of
plague, and once to defend the faith against heresy. The old men
of the desert received guests as Christ would receive them. They
might live austerely themselves, but when visitors came they hid
their austerity and welcomed them. A brother said, 'Forgive me,
father, for I have made you break your rule,' but the old man said,
'My rule is to receive you with hospitality and send you on your
way in peace.'

There are innumerable stories about desert hospitality. One monk
was moved to question the difference between the monk who received visitors and the one who did not: the example he chose was
his visit to the austere nobleman, Arsenius, and to the reformed
robber, Moses. The former received him and sat down again to pray
in silence, until the brother felt uncomfortable and left. Moses came
out to greet him with open arms, and they talked all day with joy.
That night the monk had a vision; he saw Arsenius in a boat with

the Holy Spirit, sailing quietly along the river of life; and he saw
Moses in a similar boat with an angel, and they were eating honey-
cakes—so he knew that both ways were acceptable to God.

One of the marks of this charity was that the fathers did not
judge. Macarius, they said, was like God "who shields the world and
bears the sin of all; so he shielded the brethren and when anyone
sinned he would not hear or see it.' Moses, the black man who had
been a robber, heard one day that a brother was to be brought
before the council and judged; so he came also, carrying a basket
full of sand, and he said, 'How should I judge my brother when my
sins run out behind me like the sand in this basket?'

The place of asceticism

The desert was not a gigantic gymnasium where athletes vied
with one another in endurance tests. When one of the fathers went
in disguise to a monastery during Lent, he outdid all the monks in
asceticism. His name was Macarius the Egyptian and he was very
tough. At the end of a week, the abba led him outside and said, 'You
have taught us all a lesson, Father, but now please would you mind
going away, lest my sons become discouraged and despair? We have
been edified enough.'

The monks went without sleep because they were watching for
the Lord; they did not speak because they were listening to God;
they fasted because they were fed by the Word of God. It was the
end that mattered, the ascetic practices were only a means.

The cell was of central importance in their asceticism. 'Sit in your
cell and it will teach you everything,' they said. The point was that
unless a man could find God *here*, in this one place, his cell, he would
not find him by going somewhere else. But they had no illusions
about what it meant to stay in the cell: it meant to stay there in mind
as well as in body. To stay there in body, but to think about the
outside world, was already to have left it.

The Desert Fathers had a deep understanding of the connection
between man's spiritual and natural life: this gave them a concern
for the body which was part of their life of prayer. Much of their
advice was concerned with what to eat, where to sleep, where to
live, what to do with gifts, and—very specially—what to do about
demons. This aspect of warfare with the demons was a major con-

cern in the desert. The desert itself was the place of the final warfare against the devil, and the monks were 'sentries who keep watch on the walls of the city'. Monks were always meeting the devil face to face, and once the great Macarius asked him why he looked depressed, 'You have defeated me', he said, 'because of your humility'; and Macarius put his hands over his ears and fled. But most of the advice given was not about objective, personalized demons; nor was it about holy thoughts, or the pattern of the spiritual life, or the dark night of the soul. When it was not about ordinary Christian charity, it was about the vices. The knowledge of how to deal with the passions was learnt slowly, by long, hard living, but it was the great treasure for which men came to the desert from the cities. It was this aspect of warfare with demons that was called 'ascesis', the 'hard work' of being a monk. 'Abba Pambo came to Abba Anthony and said: "Give me a word, Father," and he said, "Do not trust in your own righteousness; do not grieve about a sin that is past and gone; and keep your tongue and your belly under control. . . ." '

Prayer

About prayer itself they had little to say; the life geared towards God was the prayer; and about contemplation, who could speak? Arsenius prayed on Saturday evening with his hands stretched out to the setting sun, and he stayed there until the sun shone on his face on Sunday. The usual pattern was to say the Psalms, one after another, during the week, and to intersperse this with weaving ropes, sometimes saying, 'Lord Jesus Christ, have mercy upon me.' The aim was *hesychia,* quiet, the calm through the whole man that is like a still pool of water, capable of reflecting the sun. To be in true relationship with God, standing before him in every situation —that was the angelic life, the spiritual life, the monastic life, the aim and the way of the monk. It was life orientated towards God. 'Unless a man can say, "I alone and God are here", he will not find the prayer of quiet.' It is the other side of the saying of St. Anthony, 'My life is with my brother.'

Conclusion

Abba Anthony said, 'Whatever you find in your heart to do in following God, that do, and remain within yourself in Him.' This personal integrity before God, without any disguises or pretentions, is the essence of the spirituality of the desert. All ascetic effort, all personal relationships, life in all its aspects, was to be brought slowly into the central relationship with God in Christ. All the means to this end were just that, means and no more; they could be changed or discarded as necessary. The *Sayings* of the Desert Fathers must be used in the spirit in which they were spoken, otherwise they will have less than their true value. They are not just for interest but for use. Radical simplicity and integrity is their aim and purpose. The literature of the desert might be called the essence of Christian monasticism; but as the monk is preeminently the one who seeks to live by the Word of God, it has a basic relevance for all Christian people. The *Sayings* of the Desert Fathers may help towards a valid interpretation of the Gospel in our own day; their words may come alive in contemporary life, whatever the particular setting. Evagrius described the monk as one who is separated from all and united to all; it is in that spirit that we have prepared this translation.

1979 BENEDICT WARD, S.L.G

TRANSLATOR'S NOTE

The text of the *Apophthegmata Patrum* presents a complicated problem among patristic texts. It is a literature that grew up in the fourth century among the monks in the deserts of Egypt, Syria and Palestine, first in oral form, then in written memorials of the tradition, in Coptic, Syriac and Greek, and later in Latin. The words and deeds of the pioneers of monasticism and of other celebrated spiritual teachers were recorded for the edification of later generations of monks. Since it was spiritual value that was the criteria, sayings were included from any time or place, from the great St. Anthony to the abbots of the sixth century. The literature thus formed is a genre of its own, and one which defies precise dating. The Sayings were more than words of advice or instruction; they were words given by a spiritual father to his sons as life-giving words that would bring them to salvation. They were remembered and passed on, other words were attached to them, they were attributed to

different fathers and given a new context. Copyists did not
regard themselves as bound to transfer any written material
that they had without change; they re-arranged and edited
their material. Each monastery or group of monks evolved
its own *Gerontikon* often around a nucleus of Sayings of
their founder or some other monk especially remembered
there. Anonymous sayings were recorded as well as those
associated with specific men, and there was cross-fertiliza-
tion. The preface given here to the Alphabetical Series shows
this process at work in one case: a monk collected material
from various sources and rearranged it in alphabetical order
of the names of the fathers to whom the sayings were attributed. He says he had added some anonymous sayings at the
end, either of each section or of the whole collection, it is
not quite clear which is meant. Another preface to a different collection, printed by P. Guy in *Recherches sur la
Tradition Greque des Apophthegmata Patrum* (p.8.) from a
colophon of an eleventh-century manuscript (Paris, Fonds
Grec, 1598) written about 1071–2 shows how this was done
in another situation.

Since the Paterikon of our monastery of the holy father
Saint Saba was getting very old, my holy fathers talked to
me about him, insignificant though I am. For his soul's
salvation, our most esteemed lord abbot, Johanikos, also
committed to writing an account of his death. I therefore
undertook this work as follows: I gathered together the
Paterikons of other monasteries and examined them to the
best of my ability; I arranged them in alphabetical order
making them into two books, twelve letters in one and
twelve letters in the other.

You who use this book, pray for our lord and master,
the most devout monk the lord Johanikos, for it was
through his diligence and initiative that this was accomplished. Year 6,580 from the creation of the world, in the
10th indiction.

Pray also for me, John the monk and elder, who wrote
it. Glory to God. Amen.

In both cases, the copyists were also editors. This freedom to improve and re-arrange material adds to the difficulty of tracing the sources of any of the Sayings. It is an essentially fluid and changing tradition.

The Alphabetical Collection seems to have been rearranged in its present form at the end of the sixth century, though the earliest Sayings it contains come from the early fourth century. The compiler may also be responsible for a collection of anonymous Sayings, which have become known as the *Anonymous Collection.* Among the many other collections, the most famous in the West is the *Systematic Collection* where the Sayings have been grouped according to the subject, in the Latin translation of Pelagius and John, this was known in the Middle Ages as the *Verba Seniorum.*

The text translated here is that of the *Greek Alphabetical Series,* printed in Migne's Patrologia Graeca, vol.65, col. 71–440. It was transcribed by Cotelerius from a twelfth-century manuscript, MS Paris Gr.1599. There is no doubt that the text is imperfect and needs re-editing. A reconsideration of various texts of the Apophthegmata is being undertaken by P. Guy and others, and it is hoped that a more reliable text will be produced; P. Guy has already discussed the problems involved in this matter in *Recherches sur la Tradition Greque des Apophthegmata Patrum.* In this book, he gives the text of some other Sayings which certainly belong to this collection, and these have been translated here with the Migne text. Where the text is obviously corrupt and therefore meaningless, I have tried to make sense of the Saying, without giving alternative translations. It has seemed right to make available in English the most complete text of Apophthegmata that is to hand, but this has given certain limitations to its value.

At the beginning of the Sayings attributed to each of the Fathers, notes have been given where possible to suggest an identification: these are of course tentative, and claim to be no more than a suggestion in many cases. The names used were very common in the desert and there is often no way, for instance, of being sure which of the many 'Johns' is meant. Nor is it certain that where a Father can be identified,

the Sayings attributed to him were really his; with the two
Macarii, for instance, there is certainly some confusion. It
would be rash, therefore, to deduce too much about a Father
from the Sayings under his name; but where there is other
evidence about them, in the *Lausiac History,* the *History of
the Monks of Egypt,* Cassian or Sozomen, this has been used.
A brief chronological table had also been included, to make
clear the background of the Sayings. The work of identify-
ing both monks and monasteries has been taken some way
by H. Evelyn White and Derwas Chitty; the maps used as end
papers owe much to their research.

One index has been prepared by subject, and another
index shows the relationship between the *Alphabetical* and
Systematic Series. For this, I am indebted to Sister Mary SLG
and Sister Christine SLG who prepared these indices, and to
P. Régnault OSB of Solesmes, who is preparing a complete
index of Apophthegmata and has generously offered us his
help and advice. A short glossary is included to explain
technical terms wherever there is no exact English equivalent,
and for this I am grateful to Dr. Kallistos Ware, for his help
in connecting this with his forthcoming translation of the
Philokalia, wherever similar terms are involved.

In preparing this translation I am conscious of my very
great dependence on other people: my own sisters, most of
all, for their patience and help within the monastic life of
prayer which is the setting of this book. I am especially
grateful to Sister Helen Mary SLG and Sr Agnes SLG for
their help with the text, as well as to my invaluable colla-
borator and critic, Sister Mary SLG. Sister Margaret Clare
OHP has typed the whole and provided the maps, and has
given constant encouragement by her enthusiasm for and
understanding of this genre. Among scholars, I also owe a
special debt of gratitude to Mr. Peter Brown for his generous
criticism and advice.

The dedication of this book to Gilbert Shaw and Mother
Mary Clare SLG expresses a debt which must be felt not only
by myself but by the whole church to a modern *abba* and
amma, who have done so much to restore the dimension of
the hermit life today.

To this I add a personal note of gratitude to Archbishop Anthony, who both inspired and moulded the work and provided the introduction out of his own wealth of experience within this tradition.

With such a 'cloud of witnesses' this book should be better than it is and its defects must be laid upon my own shortcomings and limitations.

Oxford 1975   Benedicta Ward, S.L.G.

THE SAYINGS
of the
DESERT
FATHERS

✦| PROLOGUE |✦

This book is an account of the virtuous asceticism and admirable way of life and also of the words of the holy and blessed fathers. They are meant to inspire and instruct those who want to imitate their heavenly lives, so that they may make progress on the way that leads to the kingdom of heaven. You must understand that the holy fathers who were the initiators and masters of the blessed monastic way of life, being entirely on fire with divine and heavenly love and counting as nothing at all that men hold to be beautiful and estimable, trained themselves here below to do nothing whatever out of vainglory. They hid themselves away, and by their supreme humility in keeping most of their good works hidden, they made progress on the way that leads to God.

Moreover, no-one has been able to describe their virtuous lives for us in detail, for those who have taken the greatest pains in this matter have only committed to writing a few fragments of their best words and actions. They did not do this to gain praise from men, but only to stir up future generations to emulate them. Thus there were many who have set down the words and deeds of the holy old men at various times in the way they told them, with simple and unstudied words. They had only one aim—to profit many.

Now, a narrative which is the work of many hands is confused, and disorderly, and it distracts the attention of the readers, for their minds are drawn in different directions and cannot retain sayings that are scattered about in the book. Therefore we have tried to gather them together in chapters, so that they will be in order and clear and easy to look up, for those who want to benefit by reading them. Thus, all that is attributed to Anthony, Arsenius, Agathon, and all those whose names begin with 'A' are listed under Alpha; Basil, Bessarion, Benjamin, under Beta, and so on to the end of the alphabet.

But since there are also some sayings and deeds of the holy fathers in which the name of him who said or did them does not appear, we have arranged them in chapters after the alphabetical sections.

We have investigated and gone through as many books as we could find, and we have placed the results at the end of the book, so that we may gather spiritual fruit from each one, and delighting in the words of the fathers which are sweeter than honey and the honeycomb (Ps. 19.10) let us live according to the vocation the Lord has given us and so gain His kingdom. Amen.

⋄| ALPHA |⋄

ANTHONY THE GREAT

Anthony the Great, called 'The Father of Monks', was born in central Egypt about A.D. 251, the son of peasant farmers who were Christian. In c. 269 he heard the Gospel read in church and applied to himself the words: 'Go, sell all that you have and give to the poor and come . . . .' He devoted himself to a life of asceticism under the guidance of a recluse near his village. In c. 285 he went alone into the desert to live in complete solitude. His reputation attracted followers, who settled near him, and in c. 305 he came out of his hermitage in order to act as their spiritual father. Five years later he again retired into solitude. He visited Alexandria at least twice, once during the persecution of Christians and again to support the Bishop Athanasius against heresy. He died at the age of one hundred and five. His life was written by Saint Athanasius and was very influential in spreading the ideals of monasticism throughout the Christian World.

1. When the holy Abba Anthony lived in the desert he was beset by *accidie*, and attacked by many sinful thoughts. He said to God,

'Lord, I want to be saved but these thoughts do not leave me alone; what shall I do in my affliction? How can I be saved?' A short while afterwards, when he got up to go out, Anthony saw a man like himself sitting at his work, getting up from his work to pray, then sitting down and plaiting a rope, then getting up again to pray. It was an angel of the Lord sent to correct and reassure him. He heard the angel saying to him, 'Do this and you will be saved.' At these words, Anthony was filled with joy and courage. He did this, and he was saved.

2. When the same Abba Anthony thought about the depth of the judgements of God, he asked, 'Lord, how is it that some die when they are young, while others drag on to extreme old age? Why are there those who are poor and those who are rich? Why do wicked men prosper and why are the just in need?' He heard a voice answering him, 'Anthony, keep your attention on yourself; these things are according to the judgement of God, and it is not to your advantage to know anything about them.'

3. Someone asked Abba Anthony, 'What must one do in order to please God?' The old man replied, 'Pay attention to what I tell you: whoever you may be, always have God before your eyes; whatever you do, do it according to the testimony of the holy Scriptures; in whatever place you live, do not easily leave it. Keep these three precepts and you will be saved.'

4. Abba Anthony said to Abba Poemen, 'This is the great work of a man: always to take the blame for his own sins before God and to expect temptation to his last breath.'

5. He also said, 'Whoever has not experienced temptation cannot enter into the Kingdom of Heaven.' He even added, 'Without temptations no-one can be saved.'

6. Abba Pambo asked Abba Anthony, 'What ought I to do?' and the old man said to him, 'Do not trust in your own righteousness, do not worry about the past, but control your tongue and your stomach.'

7. Abba Anthony said, 'I saw the snares that the enemy spreads out over the world and I said groaning, "What can get through from such snares?" Then I heard a voice saying to me, "Humility." '

8. He also said, 'Some have afflicted their bodies by asceticism, but they lack discernment, and so they are far from God.'

9. He also said, 'Our life and our death is with our neighbour. If we gain our brother, we have gained God, but if we scandalise our brother, we have sinned against Christ.'

10. He said also, 'Just as fish die if they stay too long out of water, so the monks who loiter outside their cells or pass their time with men of the world lose the intensity of inner peace. So like a fish going towards the sea, we must hurry to reach our cell, for fear that if we delay outside we will lose our interior watchfulness.'

11. He said also, 'He who wishes to live in solitude in the desert is delivered from three conflicts: hearing, speech, and sight; there is only one conflict for him and that is with fornication.'

12. Some brothers came to find Abba Anthony to tell him about the visions they were having, and to find out from him if they were true or if they came from the demons. They had a donkey which died on the way. When they reached the place where the old man was, he said to them before they could ask him anything, 'How was it that the little donkey died on the way here?' They said, 'How do you know about that, Father?' And he told them, 'The demons shewed me what happened.' So they said, 'That was what we came to question you about, for fear we were being deceived, for we have visions which often turn out to be true.' Thus the old man convinced them, by the example of the donkey, that their visions came from the demons.

13. A hunter in the desert saw Abba Anthony enjoying himself with the brethren and he was shocked. Wanting to show him that it was necessary sometimes to meet the needs of the brethren, the old man said to him, 'Put an arrow in your bow and shoot it.' So he did. The old man then said, 'Shoot another,' and he did so. Then the old man said, 'Shoot yet again,' and the hunter replied 'If I bend my bow so much I will break it.' Then the old man said to him, 'It is the same with the work of God. If we stretch the brethren beyond measure they will soon break. Sometimes it is necessary to come down to meet their needs.' When he heard these words

the hunter was pierced by compunction and, greatly edified by the old man, he went away. As for the brethren, they went home strengthened.

14. Abba Anthony heard of a very young monk who had performed a miracle on the road. Seeing the old men walking with difficulty along the road, he ordered the wild asses to come and carry them until they reached Abba Anthony. Those whom they had carried told Abba Anthony about it. He said to them, 'This monk seems to me to be a ship loaded with goods but I do not know if he will reach harbour.' After a while, Anthony suddenly began to weep, to tear his hair and lament. His disciples said to him, 'Why are you weeping, Father?' and the old man replied, 'A great pillar of the Church has just fallen (he meant the young monk) but go to him and see what has happened.' So the disciples went and found the monk sitting on a mat and weeping for the sin he had committed. Seeing the disciples of the old man he said, 'Tell the old man to pray that God will give me just ten days and I hope I will have made satisfaction.' But in the space of five days he died.

15. The brothers praised a monk before Abba Anthony. When the monk came to see him, Anthony wanted to know how he would bear insults; and seeing that he could not bear them at all, he said to him, 'You are like a village magnificently decorated on the outside, but destroyed from within by robbers.'

16. A brother said to Abba Anthony, 'Pray for me.' The old man said to him, 'I will have no mercy upon you, nor will God have any, if you yourself do not make an effort and if you do not pray to God.'

17. One day some old men came to see Abba Anthony. In the midst of them was Abba Joseph. Wanting to test them, the old man suggested a text from the Scriptures, and, beginning with the youngest, he asked them what it meant. Each gave his opinion as he was able. But to each one the old man said, 'You have not understood it.' Last of all he said to Abba Joseph, 'How would you explain this saying?' and he replied, 'I do not know.' Then Abba Anthony said, 'Indeed, Abba Joseph has found the way, for he has said: "I do not know." '

18. Some brothers were coming from Scetis to see Abba Anthony. When they were getting into a boat to go there, they found an old man who also wanted to go there. The brothers did not know him. They sat in the boat, occupied by turns with the words of the Fathers, Scripture and their manual work. As for the old man, he remained silent. When they arrived on shore they found that the old man was going to the cell of Abba Anthony too. When they reached the place, Anthony said to them, 'You found this old man a good companion for the journey?' Then he said to the old man, 'You have brought many good brethren with you, father.' The old man said, 'No doubt they are good, but they do not have a door to their house and anyone who wishes can enter the stable and loose the ass.' He meant that the brethren said whatever came into their mouths.

19. The brethren came to the Abba Anthony and said to him, 'Speak a word; how are we to be saved?' The old man said to them, 'You have heard the Scriptures. That should teach you how.' But they said, 'We want to hear from you too, Father.' Then the old man said to them, 'The Gospel says, "if anyone strikes you on one cheek, turn to him the other also." ' (Matt. 5.39) They said, 'We cannot do that.' The old man said, 'If you cannot offer the other cheek, at least allow one cheek to be struck.' 'We cannot do that either,' they said. So he said, 'If you are not able to do that, do not return evil for evil,' and they said, 'We cannot do that either.' Then the old man said to his disciple, 'Prepare a little brew of corn for these invalids. If you cannot do this, or that, what can I do for you? What you need is prayers.'

20. A brother renounced the world and gave his goods to the poor, but he kept back a little for his personal expenses. He went to see Abba Anthony. When he told him this, the old man said to him, 'If you want to be a monk, go into the village, buy some meat, cover your naked body with it and come here like that.' The brother did so, and the dogs and birds tore at his flesh. When he came back the old man asked him whether he had followed his advice. He showed him his wounded body, and Saint Anthony said, 'Those who renounce the world but want to keep something for themselves are torn in this way by the demons who make war on them.'

21. It happened one day that one of the brethren in the monastery of Abba Elias was tempted. Cast out of the monastery, he went over the mountain to Abba Anthony. The brother lived near him for a while and then Anthony sent him back to the monastery from which he had been expelled. When the brothers saw him they cast him out yet again, and he went back to Abba Anthony saying, 'My Father, they will not receive me.' Then the old man sent them a message saying, 'A boat was shipwrecked at sea and lost its cargo; with great difficulty it reached the shore; but you want to throw into the sea that which has found a safe harbour on the shore.' When the brothers understood that it was Abba Anthony who had sent them this monk, they received him at once.

22. Abba Anthony said, 'I believe that the body possesses a natural movement, to which it is adapted, but which it cannot follow without the consent of the soul; it only signifies in the body a movement without passion. There is another movement, which comes from the nourishment and warming of the body by eating and drinking, and this causes the heat of the blood to stir up the body to work. That is why the apostle said, "Do not get drunk with wine for that is debauchery." (Ephes. 5.18) And in the Gospel the Lord also recommends this to his disciples: "Take heed to yourselves lest your hearts be weighed down with dissipation and drunkenness." (Luke 21:34) But there is yet another movement which afflicts those who fight, and that comes from the wiles and jealousy of the demons. You must understand what these three bodily movements are: one is natural, one comes from too much to eat, the third is caused by the demons.'

23. He also said, 'God does not allow the same warfare and temptations to this generation as he did formerly, for men are weaker now and cannot bear so much.'

24. It was revealed to Abba Anthony in his desert that there was one who was his equal in the city. He was a doctor by profession and whatever he had beyond his needs he gave to the poor, and every day he sang the Sanctus with the angels.

25. Abba Anthony said, 'A time is coming when men will go mad, and when they see someone who is not mad, they will attack him saying, "You are mad, you are not like us." '

26. The brethren came to Abba Anthony and laid before him a passage from Leviticus. The old man went out into the desert, secretly followed by Abba Ammonas, who knew that this was his custom. Abba Anthony went a long way off and stood there praying, crying in a loud voice, 'God, send Moses, to make me understand this saying.' Then there came a voice speaking with him. Abba Ammonas said that although he heard the voice speaking with him, he could not understand what it said.

27. Three Fathers used to go and visit blessed Anthony every year and two of them used to discuss their thoughts and the salvation of their souls with him, but the third always remained silent and did not ask him anything. After a long time, Abba Anthony said to him, 'You often come here to see me, but you never ask me anything,' and the other replied, 'It is enough for me to see you, Father.'

28. They said that a certain old man asked God to let him see the Fathers and he saw them all except Abba Anthony. So he asked his guide, 'Where is Abba Anthony?' He told him in reply that in the place where God is, there Anthony would be.

29. A brother in a monastery was falsely accused of fornication and he arose and went to Abba Anthony. The brethren also came from the monastery to correct him and bring him back. They set about proving that he had done this thing, but he defended himself and denied that he had done anything of the kind. Now Abba Paphnutius, who is called Cephalus, happened to be there, and he told them this parable: 'I have seen a man on the bank of the river buried up to his knees in mud and some men came to give him a hand to help him out, but they pushed him further in up to his neck.' Then Abba Anthony said this about Abba Paphnutius: 'Here is a real man, who can care for souls and save them.' All those present were pierced to the heart by the words of the old man and they asked forgiveness of the brother. So, admonished by the Fathers, they took the brother back to the monastery.

30. Some say of Saint Anthony that he was 'Spirit-borne', that is, carried along by the Holy Spirit, but he would never speak of this to men. Such men see what is happening in the world, as well as knowing what is going to happen.

31. One day Abba Anthony received a letter from the Emperor Constantius, asking him to come to Constantinople and he wondered whether he ought to go. So he said to Abba Paul, his disciple, 'Ought I to go?' He replied, 'If you go, you will be called Anthony; but if you stay here, you will be called Abba Anthony.'

32. Abba Anthony said, 'I no longer fear God, but I love Him. For love casts out fear.' (John 4.18)

33. He also said, 'Always have the fear of God before your eyes. Remember him who gives death and life. Hate the world and all that is in it. Hate all peace that comes from the flesh. Renounce this life, so that you may be alive to God. Remember what you have promised God, for it will be required of you on the day of judgement. Suffer hunger, thirst, nakedness, be watchful and sorrowful; weep, and groan in your heart; test yourselves, to see if you are worthy of God; despise the flesh, so that you may preserve your souls.'

34. Abba Anthony once went to visit Abba Amoun in Mount Nitria and when they met, Abba Amoun said, 'By your prayers, the number of the brethren increases, and some of them want to build more cells where they may live in peace. How far away from here do you think we should build the cells?' Abba Anthony said, 'Let us eat at the ninth hour and then let us go out for a walk in the desert and explore the country.' So they went out into the desert and they walked until sunset and then Abba Anthony said, 'Let us pray and plant the cross here, so that those who wish to do so may build here. Then when those who remain there want to visit those who have come here, they can take a little food at the ninth hour and then come. If they do this, they will be able to keep in touch with each other without distraction of mind.' The distance is twelve miles.

35. Abba Anthony said, 'Whoever hammers a lump of iron, first decides what he is going to make of it, a scythe, a sword, or an axe. Even so we ought to make up our minds what kind of virtue we want to forge or we labour in vain.'

36. He also said, 'Obedience with abstinence gives men power over wild beasts.'

37. He also said, 'Nine monks fell away after many labours and were obsessed with spiritual pride, for they put their trust in their

own works and being deceived they did not give due heed to the commandment that says, "Ask your father and he will tell you." ' (Deut. 32.7)

38. And he said this, 'If he is able to, a monk ought to tell his elders confidently how many steps he takes and how many drops of water he drinks in his cell, in case he is in error about it.'

ARSENIUS

Arsenius was born in Rome about 360. A well-educated man, of senatorial rank, he was appointed by the Emperor Theodosius I as tutor to the princes Arcadius and Honorius. He left the palace in 394 and sailed secretly to Alexandria. From there he went to Scetis and placed himself under the guidance of Abba John the Dwarf. He became an anchorite near Petra in Scetis. He seems to have had only three disciples, Alexander, Zoïlus and Daniel. He was renowned for his austerity and silence and this combined with his learning made him seem somewhat forbidding to the Coptic monks. After the second devastation of Scetis in 434 he went to the mountain of Troë where he died in 449.

1. While still living in the palace, Abba Arsenius prayed to God in these words, 'Lord, lead me in the way of salvation.' And a voice came saying to him, 'Arsenius, flee from men and you will be saved.'

2. Having withdrawn to the solitary life he made the same prayer again and he heard a voice saying to him, 'Arsenius, flee, be silent, pray always, for these are the source of sinlessness.'

3. It happened that when Abba Arsenius was sitting in his cell that he was harassed by demons. His servants, on their return, stood outside his cell and heard him praying to God in these words, 'O God, do not leave me. I have done nothing good in your sight, but according to your goodness, let me now make a beginning of good.'

4. It was said of him that, just as none in the palace had worn more splendid garments than he when he lived there, so no-one in the Church wore such poor clothing.

5. Someone said to blessed Arsenius, 'How is it that we, with all our education and our wide knowledge get no-where, while these Egyptian peasants acquire so many virtues?' Abba Arsenius said to him, 'We indeed get nothing from our secular education, but these Egyptian peasants acquire the virtues by hard work.'

6. One day Abba Arsenius consulted an old Egyptian monk about his own thoughts. Someone noticed this and said to him, 'Abba Arsenius, how is it that you with such a good Latin and Greek education, ask this peasant about your thoughts?' He replied, 'I have indeed been taught Latin and Greek, but I do not know even the alphabet of this peasant.'

7. Blessed Archbishop Theophilus, accompanied by a magistrate, came one day to find Abba Arsenius. He questioned the old man, to hear a word from him. After a short silence the old man answered him, 'Will you put into practice what I say to you?' They promised him this. 'If you hear Arsenius is anywhere, do not go there.'

8. Another time the archbishop, intending to come to see him, sent someone to see if the old man would receive him. Arsenius told him, 'If you come, I shall receive you; but if I receive you, I receive everyone and therefore I shall no longer live here.' Hearing that, the archbishop said, 'If I drive him away by going to him, I shall not go any more.'

9. A brother questioned Abba Arsenius to hear a word of him and the old man said to him, 'Strive with all your might to bring your interior activity into accord with God, and you will overcome exterior passions.'

10. He also said, 'If we seek God, he will shew himself to us, and if we keep him, he will remain close to us.'

11. Someone said to Abba Arsenius, 'My thoughts trouble me, saying, "You can neither fast nor work; at least go and visit the sick, for that is also charity."' But the old man, recognising the suggestions of the demons, said to him, 'Go, eat, drink, sleep, do no work, only do not leave your cell.' For he knew that steadfastness in the cell keeps a monk in the right way.

12. Abba Arsenius used to say that a monk travelling abroad should not get involved in anything; thus he will remain in peace.

13. Abba Mark said to Abba Arsenius, 'Why do you avoid us?' The old man said to him, 'God knows that I love you, but I cannot live with God and with men. The thousands and ten thousands of the heavenly hosts have but one will, while men have many. So I cannot leave God to be with men.'

14. Abba Daniel said of Abba Arsenius that he used to pass the whole night without sleeping, and in the early morning when nature compelled him to go to sleep, he would say to sleep, 'Come here, wicked servant.' Then, seated, he would snatch a little sleep and soon wake up again.

15. Abba Arsenius used to say that one hour's sleep is enough for a monk if he is a good fighter.

16. The old man used to tell how one day someone handed round a few dried figs in Scetis. Because they were not worth anything, no-one took any to Abba Arsenius in order not to offend him. Learning of it, the old man did not come to the *synaxis* saying, 'You have cast me out by not giving me a share of the blessing which God had given the brethren and which I was not worthy to receive.' Everyone heard of this and was edified at the old man's humility. Then the priest went to take him the small dried figs and brought him to the *synaxis* with joy.

17. Abba Daniel used to say, 'He lived with us many a long year and every year we used to take him only one basket of bread and when we went to find him the next year we would eat some of that bread.'

18. It was said of the same Abba Arsenius that he only changed the water for his palm-leaves once a year; the rest of the time he simply added to it. One old man implored him in these words, 'Why do you not change the water for these palm-leaves when it smells bad?' He said to him, 'Instead of the perfumes and aromatics which I used in the world I must bear this bad smell.'

19. Abba Daniel used to tell how when Abba Arsenius learned that all the varieties of fruit were ripe he would say, 'Bring me some.' He would taste a very little of each, just once, giving thanks to God.

20. Once at Scetis Abba Arsenius was ill and he was without even a scrap of linen. As he had nothing with which to buy any, he received some through another's charity and he said, 'I give you thanks, Lord, for having considered me worthy to receive this charity in your name.'

21. It was said of him that his cell was thirty-two miles away and that he did not readily leave it: that in fact others did his errands. When Scetis was destroyed he left weeping and said, 'The world has lost Rome and the monks have lost Scetis.'

22. Abba Mark asked Abba Arsenius, 'Is it good to have nothing extra in the cell? I know a brother who had some vegetables and he has pulled them up.' Abba Arsenius replied, 'Undoubtedly that is good but it must be done according to a man's capacity. For if he does not have the strength for such a practice he will soon plant others.'

23. Abba Daniel, the disciple of Abba Arsenius, related this: 'One day I found myself close to Abba Alexander and he was full of sorrow. He lay down and stared up into the air because of his sorrow. Now it happened that the blessed Arsenius came to speak with him and saw him lying down. During their conversation he said to him, 'And who was the layman whom I saw here?' Abba Alexander said, 'Where did you see him?' He said, 'As I was coming down the mountain I cast my eyes in this direction towards the cave and I saw a man stretched full length looking up into the air.' So Abba Alexander did penance, saying, 'Forgive me, it was I; I was overcome by sorrow.' The old man said to him, 'Well now, so it was you? Good; I thought it was a layman and that was why I asked you.'

24. Another time Abba Arsenius said to Abba Alexander, 'When you have cut your palm-leaves, come and eat with me, but if visitors come, eat with them.' Now Abba Alexander worked slowly and carefully. When the time came, he had not finished the palm leaves and wishing to follow the old man's instructions, he waited until he had finished them. When Abba Arsenius saw that he was late, he ate, thinking that he had had guests. But Abba Alexander, when at last he had finished, came away. And the old man said to him, 'Have you had visitors?' 'No,' he said. 'Then why did you not come?' The other

replied, 'You told me to come when I had cut the palm-leaves; and following your instructions, I did not come, because I had not finished.' The old man marvelled at his exactitude and said to him, 'Break your fast at once so as to celebrate the *synaxis* untroubled, and drink some water, otherwise your body will soon suffer.'

25. One day Abba Arsenius came to a place where there were reeds blowing in the wind. The old man said to the brothers, 'What is this movement?' They said, 'Some reeds.' Then the old man said to them, 'When one who is living in silent prayer hears the song of a little sparrow, his heart no longer experiences the same peace. How much worse it is when you hear the movement of those reeds.'

26. Abba Daniel said that some brothers proposing to go to the Thebaid to find some flax said, 'Let us also take the opportunity to see Abba Arsenius.' So Abba Alexander came to tell the old man, 'Some brothers who have come from Alexandria wish to see you.' The old man answered, 'Ask them why they have come.' Having learned that they were going to the Thebaid to look for flax, he reported this to the old man, who said, 'They will certainly not see the face of Arsenius for they have not come on my account but because of their work. Make them rest and send them away in peace and tell them the old man cannot receive them.'

27. A brother came to the cell of Abba Arsenius at Scetis. Waiting outside the door he saw the old man entirely like a flame. (The brother was worthy of this sight.) When he knocked, the old man came out and saw the brother marvelling. He said to him, 'Have you been knocking long? Did you see anything here?' The other answered, 'No.' So then he talked with him and sent him away.

28. When Abba Arsenius was living at Canopus, a very rich and God-fearing virgin of senatorial rank came from Rome to see him. When the Archbishop Theophilus met her, she asked him to persuade the old man to receive her. So he went to ask him to do so in these words, 'A certain person of senatorial rank has come from Rome and wishes to see you.' The old man refused to meet her. But when the archbishop told the young girl this, she ordered the beast of burden to be saddled saying, 'I trust in God that I shall see him, for it is not a man whom I have come to see (there are plenty of those in our town), but a prophet.' When she had reached the old

man's cell, by a dispensation of God, he was outside it. Seeing him, she threw herself at his feet. Outraged, he lifted her up again, and said, looking steadily at her, 'If you must see my face, here it is, look.' She was covered with shame and did not look at his face. Then the old man said to her, 'Have you not heard tell of my way of life? It ought to be respected. How dare you make such a journey? Do you not realise you are a woman and cannot go just anywhere? Or is it so that on returning to Rome you can say to other women: I have seen Arsenius? Then they will turn the sea into a thoroughfare with women coming to see me.' She said, 'May it please the Lord, I shall not let anyone come here; but pray for me and remember me always.' But he answered her, 'I pray God to remove remembrance of you from my heart.' Overcome at hearing these words, she withdrew. When she had returned to the town, in her grief she fell ill with a fever, and blessed Archbishop Theophilus was informed that she was ill. He came to see her and asked her to tell him what was the matter. She said to him, 'If only I had not gone there! For I asked the old man to remember me, he said to me, "I pray God to take the remembrance of you from my heart." So now I am dying of grief.' The archbishop said to her, 'Do you not realise that you are a woman, and that it is through women that the enemy wars against the Saints? That is the explanation of the old man's words; but as for your soul, he will pray for it continually.' At this, her spirit was healed and she returned home joyfully.

29. Abba David related this about Abba Arsenius. One day a magistrate came, bringing him the will of a senator, a member of his family who had left him a very large inheritance. Arsenius took it and was about to destroy it. But the magistrate threw himself at his feet saying, 'I beg you, do not destroy it or they will cut off my head.' Abba Arsenius said to him, 'But I was dead long before this senator who has just died,' and he returned the will to him without accepting anything.

30. It was also said of him that on Saturday evenings, preparing for the glory of Sunday, he would turn his back on the sun and stretch out his hands in prayer towards the heavens, till once again the sun shone on his face. Then he would sit down.

31. It was said of Abba Arsenius and Abba Theodore of Pherme that, more than any of the others, they hated the esteem of other

men. Abba Arsenius would not readily meet people, while Abba
Theodore was like steel when he met anyone.

32. In the days when Abba Arsenius was living in Lower Egypt
he was continually interrupted there and so he judged it right to
leave his cell. Without taking anything away with him, he went to
his disciples at Pharan, Alexander and Zoïlus. He said to Alexander,
'Get up, and get into the boat,' which he did. And he said to Zoïlus, 'Come with me as far as the river and find me a boat which will
take me to Alexandria; then embark, so as to rejoin your brother.'
Zoïlus was troubled by these words but he said nothing. So they
parted company. The old man went down to the regions of Alexandria where he fell seriously ill. His disciples said to each other,
'Perhaps one of us has annoyed the old man, and that is the reason
why he has gone away from us?' But they found nothing with
which to reproach themselves nor any disobedience. Once he was
better, the old man said, 'I will return to my Fathers.' Going up-
stream again, he came to Petra where his disciples were. While he
was close to the river, a little Ethiopian slave-girl came and touched
his sheepskin. The old man rebuked her and she replied, 'If you are
a monk, go to the mountain.' Alexander and Zoïlus met him there.
Then, when they threw themselves at his feet, the old man fell down
with them also and they wept together. The old man said to them,
'Did you not hear that I was ill?' They answered, 'Yes.' 'Then,' he
continued, 'why did you not come to see me?' Abba Alexander said,
'Your going from us has not been good for us, and many have not
been edified by it, saying, "If they had not disobeyed the old man,
he would not have left them." ' Abba Arsenius said, 'On the other
hand, they will now be saying, "The dove, not finding anywhere to
rest, returned to Noah in the ark." ' So they were confronted and
he remained with them till his death.

33. Abba David said, 'Abba Arsenius told us the following, as
though it referred to someone else, but in fact it referred to himself.
An old man was sitting in his cell and a voice came to him which
said, "Come, and I will show you the works of men." He got up and
followed. The voice led him to a certain place and shewed him an
Ethiopian cutting wood and making a great pile. He struggled to
carry it but in vain. But instead of taking some off, he cut more
wood which he added to the pile. He did this for a long time. Going
on a little further, the old man was shown a man standing on the

shore of a lake drawing up water and pouring it into a broken receptacle, so that the water ran back into the lake. Then the voice said to the old man, "Come, and I will shew you something else." He saw a temple and two men on horseback, opposite one another, carrying a piece of wood crosswise. They wanted to go in through the door but could not because they held their piece of wood crosswise. Neither of them would draw back before the other, so as to carry the wood straight; so they remained outside the door. The voice said to the old man, "These men carry the yoke of righteousness with pride, and do not humble themselves so as to correct themselves and walk in the humble way of Christ. So they remain outside the Kingdom of God. The man cutting the wood is he who lives in many sins and instead of repenting he adds more faults to his sins. He who draws the water is he who does good deeds, but mixing bad ones with them, he spoils even his good works. So everyone must be watchful of his actions, lest he labour in vain."

34. The same abba told of some Fathers who came one day from Alexandria to see Abba Arsenius. Amongst them was the aged Timothy, Archbishop of Alexandria, surnamed the Poor and he refused to see them, for fear others would come and trouble him. In those days he was living in Petra of Troë. So they went back again, feeling annoyed. Now there was a barbarian invasion and the old man went to live in lower Egypt. Having heard this they came to see him again and he received them with joy. The brother who was with them said to him, 'Abba, don't you know that we came to see you at Troë and you did not receive us?' The old man said to him, 'You have eaten bread and drunk water, but truly, my son, I tasted neither bread nor water nor did I sit down until I thought you had reached home, to punish myself because you had been wearied through me. But forgive me, my brothers.' So they went away consoled.

35. The same abba said, 'One day Abba Arsenius called me and said, "Be a comfort to your Father, so that when he goes to the Lord, he may pray for you that the Lord may be good to you in your turn." '

36. It was said of Abba Arsenius that once when he was ill at Scetis, the priest came to take him to church and put him on a bed

with a small pillow under his head. Now behold an old man who was coming to see him, saw him lying on a bed with a little pillow under his head and he was shocked and said, 'Is this really Abba Arsenius, this man lying down like this?' Then the priest took him aside and said to him, 'In the village where you lived, what was your trade?' 'I was a shepherd,' he replied. 'And how did you live?' 'I had a very hard life.' Then the priest said, 'And how do you live in your cell now?' The other replied, 'I am more comfortable.' Then he said to him, 'Do you see this Abba Arsenius? When he was in the world he was the father of the emperor, surrounded by thousands of slaves with golden girdles, all wearing collars of gold and garments of silk. Beneath him were spread rich coverings. While you were in the world as a shepherd you did not enjoy even the comforts you now have but he no longer enjoys the delicate life he led in the world. So you are comforted while he is afflicted.' At these words the old man was filled with compunction and prostrated himself saying, 'Father, forgive me, for I have sinned. Truly the way this man follows is the way of truth, for it leads to humility, while mine leads to comfort.' So the old man withdrew, edified.

37. A Father went to see Abba Arsenius. When he knocked at the door the old man opened it, thinking that it was his servant. But when he saw that it was someone else he fell on his face to the ground. The other said to him, 'Get up, Father, so that I may greet you.' But the old man replied, 'I shall not get up till you have gone,' and in spite of much pleading he did not get up until the other had gone away.

38. It was told of a brother who came to see Abba Arsenius at Scetis that, when he came to the church, he asked the clergy if he could visit Abba Arsenius. They said to him, 'Brother, have a little refreshment and then go and see him.' 'I shall not eat anything,' said he, 'till I have met him.' So, because Arsenius' cell was far away, they sent a brother with him. Having knocked on the door, they entered, greeted the old man and sat down without saying anything. Then the brother from the church said, 'I will leave you. Pray for me.' Now the visiting brother, not feeling at ease with the old man, said, 'I will come with you,' and they went away together. Then the visitor asked, 'Take me to Abba Moses, who used to be a robber.' When they arrived the Abba welcomed them joyfully and then

took leave of them with delight. The brother who had brought the other one said to his companion, 'See, I have taken you to the foreigner and to the Egyptian, which of the two do you prefer?' 'As for me,' he replied, 'I prefer the Egyptian.' Now a Father who heard this prayed to God saying, 'Lord, explain this matter to me: for Thy name's sake the one flees from men, and the other, for Thy name's sake, receives them with open arms.' Then two large boats were shown to him on a river and he saw Abba Arsenius and the Spirit of God sailing in the one, in perfect peace; and in the other was Abba Moses with the angels of God, and they were all eating honey cakes.

39. Abba Daniel said 'At the point of death, Abba Arsenius sent us this message, "Do not trouble to make offerings for me, for truly I have made an offering for myself and I shall find it again." '

40. When Abba Arsenius was at the point of death, his disciples were troubled. He said to them, 'The time has not yet come; when it comes, I will tell you. But if ever you give my remains to anyone, we will be judged before the dreadful seat of judgment.' They said to him, 'What shall we do? We do not know how to bury anyone.' The old man said to them, 'Don't you know how to tie a rope to my feet and drag me to the mountain?' The old man used to say to himself: 'Arsenius, why have you left the world? I have often repented of having spoken, but never of having been silent.' When his death drew near, the brethren saw him weeping and they said to him 'Truly, Father, are you also afraid?' 'Indeed,' he answered them, 'the fear which is mine at this hour has been with me ever since I became a monk.' Upon this he fell asleep.

41. It was said of him that he had a hollow in his chest channelled out by the tears which fell from his eyes all his life while he sat at his manual work. When Abba Poemen learned that he was dead, he said weeping, 'Truly you are blessed, Abba Arsenius, for you wept for yourself in this world! He who does not weep for himself here below will weep eternally hereafter; so it is impossible not to weep, either voluntarily or when compelled through suffering.'

42. Abba Daniel used to say this about him: 'He never wanted to reply to a question concerning the Scriptures, though he could well have done so had he wished, just as he never readily wrote a

letter. When from time to time he came to church he would sit behind a pillar, so that no-one should see his face and so that he himself would not notice others. His appearance was angelic, like that of Jacob. His body was graceful and slender; his long beard reached down to his waist. Through much weeping his eye-lashes had fallen out. Tall of stature, he was bent with old age. He was ninety-five when he died. For forty years he was employed in the palace of Theodosius the Great of divine memory, who was the father of the divine Arcadius and Honorius; then he lived forty years in Scetis, ten years in Troë above Babylon, opposite Memphis and three years at Canopus of Alexandria. The last two years he returned to Troë where he died, finishing his course in peace and the fear of God. He was a good man "filled with the Holy Spirit and faith." (Acts 11.24) He left me his leather tunic, his white hair-shirt and his palm-leaf sandals. Although unworthy, I wear them, in order to gain his blessing.'

43. Abba Daniel used to tell this also about Abba Arsenius: 'One day he called my Fathers, Abba Alexander and Abba Zoïlus, and by way of humiliating himself, said to them, "Since the demons attack me and I do not know if they will not rob me when I am asleep tonight, share my suffering and watch lest I fall asleep during my vigil." Late at night they sat in silence, one on his right and the other on his left. My Fathers said, "As for us, we fell asleep, then woke again, but we did not notice that he had drowsed. Early in the morning (God knows if he did it on purpose to make us believe that he had slept, or whether he had really given way to sleep) he gave three sighs, then immediately got up, saying, 'I have been to sleep, haven't I?' We replied that we did not know." '

44. Some old men came one day to Abba Arsenius and insisted on seeing him. He received them. Then they asked him to say a word to them about those who live in solitude without seeing anyone. The old man said to them, 'As long as a young girl is living in her father's house, many young men wish to marry her, but when she has taken a husband, she is no longer pleasing to everyone; despised by some, approved by others, she no longer enjoys the favour of former times, when she lived a hidden life. So it is with the soul; from the day when it is shown to everyone, it is no longer able to satisfy everyone.'

AGATHON

Agathon was a young man when he came to the Thebaid, where he was trained by Poemen. His abba thought highly of him, and Poemen 61 shews Abba Joseph expressing surprise that Poemen should call such a young disciple 'abba'. Agathon went to Scetis, where he lived for a time with Alexander and Zoïlus, who were later disciples of Arsenius. He left Scetis, perhaps after the first devastation, with his disciple Abraham, and lived near the Nile, not far from Troë. He knew Amoun, Macarius, Joseph and Peter from the early days in Scetis.

1. Abba Peter, the disciple of Abba Lot, said, 'One day when I was in Abba Agathon's cell, a brother came in and said to him, "I want to live with the brethren; tell me how to dwell with them." The old man answered him, "All the days of your life keep the frame of mind of the stranger which you have on the first day you join them, so as not to become too familiar with them." The Abba Macarius asked, "And what does this familiarity produce?" The old man replied, "It is like a strong, burning wind, each time it arises everything flies swept before it, and it destroys the fruit of the trees." So Abba Macarius said, "Is speaking too freely really as bad as all that?" Abba Agathon said, "No passion is worse than an uncontrolled tongue, because it is the mother of all the passions. Accordingly the good workman should not use it, even if he is living as a solitary in the cell. I know a brother who spent a long time in his cell using a small bed who said, "I should have left my cell without making use of that small bed if no-one had told me it was there." It is the hard-working monk who is a warrior.'

2. Abba Agathon said, "Under no circumstances should the monk let his conscience accuse him of anything.'

3. He also said, 'Unless he keeps the commandments of God, a man cannot make progress, not even in a single virtue.'

4. He also said, 'I have never gone to sleep with a grievance against anyone, and, as far as I could, I have never let anyone go to sleep with a grievance against me.'

5. It was said concerning Abba Agathon that some monks came to find him having heard tell of his great discernment. Wanting to

see if he would lose his temper they said to him 'Aren't you that Agathon who is said to be a fornicator and a proud man?' 'Yes, it is very true,' he answered. They resumed, 'Aren't you that Agathon who is always talking nonsense?' 'I am.' Again they said 'Aren't you Agathon the heretic?' But at that he replied 'I am not a heretic.' So they asked him, 'Tell us why you accepted everything we cast you, but repudiated this last insult.' He replied 'The first accusations I take to myself, for that is good for my soul. But heresy is separation from God. Now I have no wish to be separated from God.' At this saying they were astonished at his discernment and returned, edified.

6. It was said of Abba Agathon that he spent a long time building a cell with his disciples. At last when it was finished, they came to live there. Seeing something during the first week which seemed to him harmful, he said to his disciples, 'Get up, let us leave this place.' But they were dismayed and replied, 'If you had already decided to move, why have we taken so much trouble building the cell? People will be scandalized at us, and will say, "Look at them, moving again; what unstable people!"' He saw they were held back by timidity and so he said to them, 'If some are scandalized, others, on the contrary, will be much edified and will say, "How blessed are they who go away for God's sake, having no other care." However, let him who wants to come, come; as for me, I am going.' Then they prostrated themselves to the ground and besought him to allow them to go with him.

7. It was said of him that he often went away taking nothing but his knife for making wicker-baskets.

8. Someone asked Abba Agathon, 'Which is better, bodily asceticism or interior vigilance?' The old man replied, 'Man is like a tree, bodily asceticism is the foliage, interior vigilance the fruit. According to that which is written, "Every tree that bringeth not forth good fruit shall be cut down and cast into the fire" (Matt. 3.10) it is clear that all our care should be directed towards the fruit, that is to say, guard of the spirit; but it needs the protection and the embellishment of the foliage, which is bodily asceticism.'

9. The brethren also asked him, 'Amongst all good works, which is the virtue which requires the greatest effort?' He answered, 'For-

give me, but I think there is no labour greater than that of prayer to God. For every time a man wants to pray, his enemies, the demons, want to prevent him, for they know that it is only by turning him from prayer that they can hinder his journey. Whatever good work a man undertakes, if he perseveres in it, he will attain rest. But prayer is warfare to the last breath.'

10. Abba Agathon was wise in spirit and active in body. He provided everything he needed for himself, in manual work, food, and clothing.

11. The same Abba Agathon was walking with his disciples. One of them, finding a small green pea on the road, said to the old man, 'Father, may I take it?' The old man, looking at him with astonishment, said, 'Was it you who put it there?' 'No,' replied the brother, 'How then,' continued the old man, 'can you take up something which you did not put down?'

12. A brother came to find Abba Agathon and said to him, 'Let me live with you.' On his way he had found a piece of nitre on the road and had brought it with him. 'Where did you find that nitre?' asked the old man. The brother replied, 'I found it on the road as I was coming and I picked it up.' The old man said to him, 'If you are coming to live with me, how can you take that which you did not put down?' Then he sent him to put it back where he had found it.

13. A brother asked the old man, 'I have received a command, but there is danger of temptation in the place connected with it. Because of the command I wish to do it, but I am afraid of such danger.' The old man said to him, 'If this were Agathon's problem, he would fulfil the commandment and thus he would overcome the temptation.'

14. A meeting had been held at Scetis about some matter, and a decision was taken about it. When Agathon came in later, he said to them, 'You have not decided this matter rightly.' 'Who are you,' they retorted, 'to talk like that?' 'A son of man,' said he, 'for it is written, "If truly ye say that which is right, judge righteously, sons of men."' (Ps. 7.2)

15. It was said of Abba Agathon that for three years he lived with a stone in his mouth, until he had learnt to keep silence.

16. It was said of him and of Abba Amoun that, when they had anything to sell, they would name the price just once and silently accept what was given them in peace. Just as, when they wished to buy something, they gave the price they were asked in silence and took the object adding no further word.

17. The same Abba Agathon said, 'I have never offered *agapes;* but the fact of giving and receiving has been for me an *agape,* for I consider the good of my brother to be a sacrificial offering.'

18. Whenever his thoughts urged him to pass judgement on something which he saw, he would say to himself, 'Agathon, it is not your business to do that.' Thus his spirit was always recollected.

19. The same abba said, 'A man who is angry, even if he were to raise the dead, is not acceptable to God.'

20. At one time Abba Agathon had two disciples each leading the anchoretic life according to his own measure. One day he asked the first, 'How do you live in the cell?' He replied, 'I fast until the evening, then I eat two hard biscuits.' He said to him, 'Your way of life is good, not overburdened with too much asceticism.' Then he asked the other one, 'And you, how do you live?' He replied, 'I fast for two days, then I eat two hard biscuits.' The old man said, 'You work very hard by enduring two conflicts; it is a labour for someone to eat every day without greed; there are others who, wishing to fast for two days, are greedy afterwards; but you, after fasting for two days, are not greedy.'

21. A brother asked Abba Agathon about fornication. He answered, 'Go, cast your weakness before God and you shall find rest.'

22. Abba Agathon and another old man were ill. While they were lying in their cell, the brother who was reading Genesis to them came to the chapter where Jacob said, 'Joseph is no more, Simeon is no more, and thou dost take Benjamin away from me; thou wilt bring my grey hairs in sorrow to the grave.' (Gen. 42.36, 38)The other old man began to say, 'Are not the ten enough for you, Abba Jacob?' But Abba Agathon replied, 'Let be, old man, if God is the God of the righteous, who shall condemn Jacob?'

23. Abba Agathon said, 'If someone were very specially dear to me, but I realized that he was leading me to do something less good, I should put him from me.'

24. He also said, 'A man ought at all times to be aware of the judgements of God.'

25. One day when the brethren were conversing about charity, Abba Joseph said, 'Do we really know what charity is?' Then he told how when a brother came to see Abba Agathon, he greeted him and did not let him go until he had taken with him a small knife which he had.

26. Abba Agathon said, 'If I could meet a leper, give him my body and take his, I should be very happy.' That indeed is perfect charity.

27. It was also said of him that, coming to the town one day to sell his wares, he encountered a sick traveller lying in the public place without anyone to look after him. The old man rented a cell and lived with him there, working with his hands to pay the rent and spending the rest of his money on the sick man's needs. He stayed there four months till the sick man was restored to health. Then he returned in peace to his cell.

28. Abba Daniel said, 'Before Abba Arsenius came to live with my Fathers, they dwelt with Abba Agathon. Now Abba Agathon loved Abba Alexander because he was both ascetic and discreet. Now it happened that all the disciples were washing their rushes in the river, but Abba Alexander was washing his with discretion. The other brothers said to the old man, 'Brother Alexander is getting nowhere.' Wishing to cure them he said to him, 'Brother Alexander, wash them thoroughly because they are flax.' The brother was hurt by these words. Afterwards the old man comforted him, saying, 'Did I not know that you were working well? But I said that in front of them in order to cure them by your obedience, brother.'

29. It was said of Abba Agathon that he forced himself to fulfill all the commandments. When he sailed in a vessel he was the first to handle the oars and when the brethren came to see him he laid the table with his own hands, as soon as they had prayed, because he was full of the love of God. When he was at the point of death he remained three days with his eyes fixed, wide-open. The brethren roused him, saying, 'Abba Agathon, where are you?' He replied, 'I

am standing before the judgement seat of God.' They said, 'Are you not afraid, Father?' He replied, 'Until this moment, I have done my utmost to keep the commandments of God; but I am a man; how should I know if my deeds are acceptable to God?' The brethren said to him, 'Do you not have confidence in all that you have done according to the law of God?' The old man replied, 'I shall have no confidence until I meet God. Truly the judgement of God is not that of man.' When they wanted to question him further, he said to them, 'Of your charity, do not talk to me any more, for I no longer have time.' So he died with joy. They saw him depart like one greeting his dearest friends. He preserved the strictest vigilance in all things, saying, 'Without great vigilance a man does not advance in even a single virtue.'

30. Going to town one day to sell some small articles, Abba Agathon met a cripple on the roadside, paralysed in his legs, who asked him where he was going. Abba Agathon replied, 'To town, to sell some things.' The other said, 'Do me the favour of carrying me there.' So he carried him to the town. The cripple said to him, 'Put me down where you sell your wares.' He did so. When he had sold an article, the cripple asked, 'What did you sell it for?' and he told him the price. The other said, 'Buy me a cake,' and he bought it. When Abba Agathon had sold a second article, the sick man asked, 'How much did you sell it for?' And he told him the price of it. Then the other said, 'Buy me this,' and he bought it. When Agathon, having sold all his wares, wanted to go, he said to him, 'Are you going back?' and he replied, 'Yes.' Then said he, 'Do me the favour of carrying me back to the place where you found me.' Once more picking him up. he carried him back to that place. Then the cripple said, 'Agathon, you are filled with divine blessings, in heaven and on earth.' Raising his eyes, Agathon saw no man; it was an angel of the Lord, come to try him.

AMMONAS

Ammonas was Abba Anthony's disciple and successor on the Outer Mountain of Pispir. He probably came from Scetis. He later became a bishop. Several letters are attributed to him.

1. A brother asked Abba Ammonas, 'Give me a word,' and the old man replied, 'Go, make your thoughts like those of the evildoers who are in prison. For they are always asking when the magistrate will come, awaiting him in anxiety. Even so the monk ought to give himself at all times to accusing his own soul, saying, "Unhappy wretch that I am. How shall I stand before the judgement seat of Christ? What shall I say to him in my defence?" If you give yourself continually to this, you may be saved.'

2. It was said of Abba Ammonas that he had killed a basilisk. Going into the desert one day to draw water from the lake and seeing a basilisk, he threw himself face to the ground saying: 'Lord, either I die or he does,' and immediately, by the power of God, the basilisk burst asunder.

3. Abba Ammonas said, 'I have spent fourteen years in Scetis asking God night and day to grant me the victory over anger.'

4. One of the Fathers telling about the Cells, said there was once a hard-working old man there who wore a mat. He went to find Abba Ammonas, who, when he saw him wearing the mat, said to him, 'This is no use to you.' But the old man questioned him in the following way, 'Three thoughts occupy me, either, should I wander in the deserts, or should I go to a foreign land where no-one knows me, or should I shut myself up in a cell without opening the door to anyone, eating only every second day.' Abba Ammonas replied, 'It is not right for you to do any of these three things. Rather, sit in your cell and eat a little every day, keeping the world of the publican always in your heart, and you may be saved.'

5. Some brethren found life difficult where they were living. Wanting to leave, they came to find Abba Ammonas. He was out on the river. Seeing them walking along the bank of the river, he asked the sailors to put him ashore. Then he called the brethren, saying to them, 'I am Ammonas, to whose dwelling you are wanting to go.' Having comforted their hearts, he sent them back whence they had come, for this difficulty did not arise from sickness of soul, but simply from natural annoyance.

6. One day when Abba Ammonas went to cross the river, he found the ferry-boat ready to go and sat down in it. Then another

boat came to the place and transported the men who were there. They said to him, 'Come here, Father, and cross the river with us.' But he replied, 'I will not embark except in the public vessel.' As he had a handful of palm branches, he sat down, weaving them, and then undoing them, until the boat came alongside. Thus he made the crossing. Then the brethren made him a reverence, saying 'Why did you do that?' the old man said to them, 'So as to walk without any anxiety of spirit.' That is an example; we must walk in the way of God in peace.

7. Abba Ammonas was going to pay a visit to Abba Anthony, one day, and he lost his way. So sitting down, he fell asleep for a little while. On waking, he prayed thus to God, 'I beseech you, O Lord my God, do not let your creature perish.' Then there appeared to him as it were a man's hand in the heavens, which showed him the way, till he reached Abba Anthony's cave.

8. Abba Anthony predicted that this Abba Ammonas would make progress in the fear of God. He led him outside his cell, and showing him a stone, said to him, 'Hurt this stone, and beat it.' He did so. Then Anthony asked him, 'Has the stone said anything?' He replied, 'No.' Then Anthony said, 'You too will be able to do that,' and that is what happened. Abba Ammonas advanced to the point where his goodness was so great, he took no notice of wickedness. Thus, having become bishop, someone brought a young girl who was pregnant to him, saying, 'See what this unhappy wretch has done; give her a penance.' But he, having marked the young girl's womb with the sign of the cross, commanded that six pairs of fine linen sheets should be given her, saying, 'It is for fear that, when she comes to give birth, she may die, she or the child, and have nothing for the burial.' But her accusers resumed, 'Why did you do that? Give her a punishment.' But he said to them, 'Look, brothers, she is near to death; what am I to do?' Then he sent her away and no old man dared accuse anyone any more.

9. It was said of him that some people came to him to be judged, and Abba Ammonas feigned madness. A woman standing near him said to her neighbour, 'The old man is mad.' Abba Ammonas heard it, caller her, and said, 'How much labour have I given myself in the desert to acquire this folly and through you I have lost it today!'

10. Abba Ammonas came one day to eat in a place where there was a monk of evil repute. Now it happened that a woman came and entered the cell of the brother of evil reputation. The dwellers in that place, having learnt this, were troubled and gathered together to chase the brother from his cell. Knowing that Bishop Ammonas was in the place, they asked him to join them. When the brother in question learnt this, he hid the woman in a large cask. The crowd of monks came to the place. Now Abba Ammonas saw the position clearly but for the sake of God he kept the secret; he entered, seated himself on the cask and commanded the cell to be searched. Then when the monks had searched everywhere without finding the woman, Abba Ammonas said, 'What is this? May God forgive you!' After praying, he made everyone go out, then taking the brother by the hand he said, 'Brother, be on your guard.' With these words, he withdrew.

11. Abba Ammonas was asked, 'What is the "narrow and hard way?" ' (Matt. 7.14) He replied, 'The "narrow and hard way" is this, to control your thoughts, and to strip yourself of your own will, for the sake of God. This is also the meaning of the sentence, "Lo, we have left everything and followed you." ' (Matt. 19.27)

ACHILLES

1. Three old men, of whom one had a bad reputation, came one day to Abba Achilles. The first asked him, 'Father, make me a fishing-net.' 'I will not make you one,' he replied. Then the second said, 'Of your charity make one, so that we may have a souvenir of you in the monastery.' But he said, 'I do not have time.' Then the third one, who had a bad reputation, said, 'Make me a fishing-net, so that I may have something from your hands, Father.' Abba Achilles answered him at once, 'For you, I will make one.' Then the two other old men asked him privately, 'Why did you not want to do what we asked you, but you promised to do what he asked?' The old man gave them this answer, 'I told you I would not make one, and you were not disappointed, since you thought that I had no time. But if I had not made one for him, he would have said, "The

old man has heard about my sin, and that is why he does not want to make me anything," and so our relationship would have broken down. But now I have cheered his soul, so that he will not be overcome with grief.'

2. Abba Bitimius said, 'One day when I was going down to Scetis, someone gave me some fruit to take to the old men. So I knocked on the door of Abba Achilles' cell, to give him some. But he said to me, "Brother, from now on I do not want you to knock on my door with any sort of food and do not go to knock at any other cells either." So I withdrew to my cell, and took the fruit to the church.'

3. Abba Achilles came one day to Abba Isaiah's cell at Scetis, and found him in the act of eating something. He had mixed it with salt and water on a plate. The old man, seeing that he was hiding it behind some plaited reeds, said to him, 'Tell me, what are you eating?' He replied, 'Forgive me, Father, I was cutting palm-leaves and I went out in the heat; and I put a morsel into my mouth, with some salt, but the heat burnt my throat and the mouthful did not go down. So I was obliged to add a little water to the salt, in order to swallow it. Forgive me, Father.' The old man said, 'Come, all of you, and see Isaiah eating sauce in Scetis. If you want to eat sauce, go to Egypt.'

4. An old man who came to see Abba Achilles found him spitting blood out of his mouth. He asked him, 'What is the matter, Father?' The old man answered, 'The word of a brother grieved me, I struggled not to tell him so and I prayed God to rid me of this word. So it became like blood in my mouth and I have spat it out. Now I am in peace, having forgotten the matter.'

5. Abba Ammoes said, 'With Abba Bitimius, we went to see Abba Achilles. We heard him meditating on this saying, "Do not fear, Jacob, to go down into Egypt." (Gen. 46.3) For a long time he remained making this meditation. When we knocked, he opened the door and asked us where we came from. Being afraid to say we came from the Cells, we replied, from the mountain of Nitria. Then he said to us, "What can I do for you who come from so far away?" He asked us to come in. We noticed that he had been working the whole night and had woven a great deal and we asked him to say a word to us. He said to us, "From yesterday evening till now, I have

woven twenty measures, although I do not need it; but it is for fear God should be angry and accuse me, saying, 'Why did you not work, when you could have done so?' That is why I give myself this labour and do as much as I can." So we went away, greatly edified.'

6. Another time, a great old man came to the Thebaid to see Abba Achilles and said to him, 'Father, you are a temptation to me.' He said to him, 'Come, even you, old man, you are still tempted because of me?' In his humility, the old man replied, 'Yes, Father.' Now there was an old blind and lame man sitting close to the door. The old man said to him, 'I should like to have stayed here several days, but I cannot because of the old man.' At these words, Abba Achilles wondered at the old man's humility, and said, 'This is not fornication, but hatred of the evil demons.'

AMMOES

1. It was said of Abba Ammoes that when he went to church, he did not allow his disciple to walk beside him but only at a certain distance; and if the latter came to ask him about his thoughts, he would move away from him as soon as he had replied, saying to him, 'It is for fear that, after edifying words, irrelevant conversation should slip in, that I do not keep you with me.'

2. At first, Abba Ammoes said to Abba Isaiah, 'What do you think of me now?' He said to him, 'You are an angel, Father.' Later on he said to him, 'And now, what do you think of me?' He replied, 'You are like Satan. Even when you say a good word to me, it is like steel.'

3. It was said of Abba Ammoes that, illness having kept him in bed for many long years, he never allowed himself to think about his cell or look to see what it contained. For people brought him many things, on account of his illness. When John, his disciple, entered or went out, he would close his eyes, so as not to see what he was doing. For he knew that he was a faithful monk.

4. Abba Poemen said that a brother came to find Abba Ammoes to ask him for a word. He remained with him for seven days

without the old man answering him. Then, sending him away, the latter said to him, 'Go, watch yourself; as for me my sins have become a well of darkness between me and God.'

5. It was said of Abba Ammoes that he had fifty measures of wheat for his use and had put them out in the sun. Before they were properly dried off, he saw something in that place which seemed to him to be harmful so he said to his servants, 'Let us go away from here.' But they were grieved at this. Seeing their dismay he said to them, 'Is it because of the loaves that you are sad? Truly, I have seen monks fleeing, leaving their white-washed cells and also their parchments, and they did not close the doors, but went leaving them open.'

AMOUN OF NITRIA

Amoun, the third great founder of Egyptian monasticism, with Anthony and Pachomius. Born in c. A. D. 295 he married, then he and his wife lived as ascetics for eighteen years. In 330, he retired to Nitria and became the first monk there. Disciples joined him and he became their leader. He died c. A. D. 353.

1. Abba Amoun of Nitria came to see Abba Anthony and said to him, 'Since my rule is stricter than yours how is it that your name is better known amongst men than mine is?' Abba Anthony answered, 'It is because I love God more than you.'

2. It was said of Abba Amoun that a very small quantity of wheat every two months was sufficient for him. Now he went to find Abba Poemen and said to him, 'When I go to my neighbour's cell, or when he comes to mine for some need or other, we are afraid of entering into conversation, for fear of slipping into worldly subjects.' The old man replied, 'You are right, for young men need to be watchful.' Then Abba Amoun continued, 'But the old men, what do they do?' He replied, 'The old men who have advanced in virtue, have nothing in them that is worldly; there is nothing worldly in their mouths of which they could speak.' 'But,' Amoun replied, 'When I am obliged to speak to my neighbour, do you prefer me to speak of the Scriptures or of the sayings of the Fathers?' The old

man answered him, 'If you can't be silent, you had better talk about the sayings of the Fathers than about the Scriptures; it is not so dangerous.'

3. A brother came to Scetis to see Abba Amoun and said to him, 'My Father is sending me out on an errand but I am afraid of fornication.' The old man answered, 'Whatever the hour when the temptation comes upon you, say, "God of all virtue, by the prayers of my Father, save me from it."' So one day when a young girl closed the door upon him, he began to cry out with all his might, 'God of my father, save me,' and immediately he found himself on the road to Scetis.

ANOUB

Anoub was one of the seven brothers of Poemen whose sayings occupy a large place in the Apophthegmata. Three of the brothers, Anoub, Paësius and Poemen lived together at first in Scetis, with Poemen as their leader. After the first devastation of Scetis (407–8) they went with their brothers to Terenuthis where they decided to stay together and live the cenobitic life, with Anoub taking charge. The Devastation of Scetis marks a turning point in the history of early monasticism in Egypt; the monks dispersed, and gradually the centre shifted from Egypt to Palestine. This story of Anoub and his brothers indicates a new reason for the formation of cenobitic communities, that is, protection against invaders.

1. Abba John said of Abba Anoub and Abba Poemen and the rest of their brethren who come from the same womb and were made monks in Scetis, that when the barbarians came and laid waste that district for the first time, they left for a place called Terenuthis until they decided where to settle. They stayed in an old temple several days. Then Abba Anoub said to Abba Poemen, 'For love's sake do this: let each of us live in quietness, each one by himself, without meeting one another the whole week.' Abba Poemen replied, 'We will do as you wish.' So they did this. Now there was in the temple a statue of stone. When he woke up in the morning, Abba Anoub threw stones at the face of the statue and in the evening he said to it, 'Forgive me.' During the whole week he did this. On Saturday

they came together and Abba Poemen said to Abba Anoub, 'Abba, I have seen you during the whole week throwing stones at the face of the statue and kneeling to ask it to forgive you. Does a believer act thus?' The old man answered him, 'I did this for your sake. When you saw me throwing stones at the face of the statue, did it speak, or did it become angry?' Abba Poemen said, 'No.' 'Or again, when I bent down in penitence, was it moved, and did it say, "I will not forgive you?"' Again Abba Poemen answered 'No.' Then the old man resumed, 'Now we are seven brethren; if you wish us to live together, let us be like this statue, which is not moved whether one beats it or whether one flatters it. If you do not wish to become like this, there are four doors here in the temple, let each one go where he will.' Then the brethren prostrated themselves and said to Abba Anoub, 'We will do as you wish, Father, and we will listen to what you say to us.' Abba Poemen added, 'Let us live together to the rest of our time, working according to the word which the old man has given us.' He made one of them housekeeper and all that he brought them, they ate and none of them had the authority to say, 'Bring us something else another time,' or perhaps, 'We do not want to eat this.' Thus they passed all their time in quietness and peace.

2. Abba Anoub said, 'Since the day when the name of Christ was invoked upon me, no lie has come out of my mouth.'

ABRAHAM

1. It was said of an old man that for fifty years he had neither eaten bread nor drunk wine readily. He even said, 'I have destroyed fornication, avarice and vain-glory in myself.' Learning that he had said this, Abba Abraham came and said to him, 'Did you really say that?' He answered, 'Yes.' Then Abba Abraham said to him, 'If you were to find a woman lying on your mat when you entered your cell would you think that it is not a woman?' 'No,' he replied, 'But I should struggle against my thoughts so as not to touch her.' Then Abba Abraham said, 'Then you have not destroyed the passion, but it still lives in you although it is controlled. Again, if you are walking along and you see some gold amongst the stones and shells,

can your spirit regard them all as of equal value?' 'No,' he replied, 'But I would struggle against my thoughts, so as not to take the gold.' The old man said to him, 'See, avarice still lives in you, though it is controlled.' Abba Abraham continued, 'Suppose you learn that of two brothers one loves you while the other hates you, and speaks evil of you; if they come to see you, will you receive them both with the same love?' 'No,' he replied, 'But I should struggle against my thoughts so as to be as kind towards the one who hates me as towards the one who loves me.' Abba Abraham said to him, 'So then, the passions continue to live; it is simply that they are controlled by the saints.'

2. A brother questioned Abba Abraham, saying, 'If I find myself eating often, what will come of it?' The old man replied in this way, 'What are you saying, brother? Do you eat so much? Or perhaps you think that you have come to the threshing floor to thresh grain?'

3. Abba Abraham told of a man of Scetis who was a scribe and did not eat bread. A brother came to beg him to copy a book. The old man whose spirit was engaged in contemplation, wrote, omitting some phrases and with no punctuation. The brother, taking the book and wishing to punctuate it, noticed that words were missing. So he said to the old man, 'Abba, there are some phrases missing.' The old man said to him, 'Go, and practise first that which is written, then come back and I will write the rest.'

ARES

1. Abba Abraham went to see Abba Ares. They were sitting together when a brother came to the old man and said to him, 'Tell me what I must do to be saved.' He replied, 'Go, and for the whole of this year eat only bread and salt in the evening. Then come back here and I will talk to you again.' The monk went away and did this. When the year was over he came back to Abba Ares. Now by chance it happened that Abba Abraham was there again. Once more the old man said to the brother, 'Go, and for the whole of this year fast for two days at a time.' When the brother had gone, Abba

Abraham said to Abba Ares, 'Why do you prescribe an easy yoke to all the brethren, while you impose such a heavy burden on this brother?' The old man replied, 'How I send them away depends upon what the brethren came to seek. Now it is for the sake of God that this one comes to hear a word, for he is a hard worker and what I tell him he carries out eagerly. It is because of this that I speak the word of God to him.'

ALONIUS

1. Abba Alonius said, 'If a man does not say in his heart, in the world there is only myself and God, he will not gain peace.'

2. He also said, 'If I had not destroyed myself completely, I should not have been able to rebuild and shape myself again.'

3. He also said, 'If only a man desired it for a single day from morning till night, he would be able to come to the measure of God.'

4. One day Abba Agathon questioned Abba Alonius saying, 'How can I control my tongue so as to tell no more lies?' And Abba Alonius said to him, 'If you do not lie, you prepare many sins for yourself.' 'How is that?' said he. The old man said to him, 'Suppose two men have committed a murder before your eyes and one of them fled to your cell. The magistrate, seeking him, asks you, "Have you seen the murderer?" If you do not lie, you will deliver that man to death. It is better for you to abandon him unconditionally to God, for he knows all things.'

APPHY

1. They used to say of a bishop of Oxyrrynchus, named Abba Apphy, that when he was a monk he submitted himself to a very severe way of life. When he became a bishop he wished to practise the same austerity, even in the world, but he had not the strength to do so. Therefore he prostrated himself before God saying, 'Has your grace left me because of my episcopate?' Then he was given

this revelation, 'No, but when you were in solitude and there was
no one else it was God who was your helper. Now that you are in
the world, it is man.'

APOLLO

Apollo became a monk in Scetis after a hideous act of outrage. He is an
example, if a somewhat extreme example, of the rough Coptic monks who
formed the greater number of the monks of Egypt; the contrast between
such a man and the scholarly Evagrius or the Roman aristocrat, Arsenius,
is very marked and explains some of the problems that arose between them.

1. There was in the Cells an old man called Apollo. If someone
came to find him about doing a piece of work, he would set out
joyfully, saying, 'I am going to work with Christ today, for the
salvation of my soul, for that is the reward he gives.'

2. It was said of a certain Abba Apollo of Scetis, that he had been
a shepherd and was very uncouth. He had seen a pregnant woman
in the field one day and being urged by the devil, he had said, 'I
should like to see how the child lies in her womb.' So he ripped her
up and saw the foetus. Immediately his heart was troubled and,
filled with compunction, he went to Scetis and told the Fathers
what he had done. Now he heard them chanting, 'The years of our
age are three score years and ten, and even by reason strength
fourscore; yet their span is but toil and trouble.' (Ps. 90.10) He said
to them, 'I am forty years old and I have not made one prayer; and
now, if I live another year, I shall not cease to pray God that he may
pardon my sins.' In fact, he did not work with his hands but passed
all his time in prayer, saying, 'I, who as man have sinned, do you,
as God, forgive.' So his prayer became his activity by night and day.
A brother who lived with him heard him saying, 'I have sinned
against you, Lord; forgive me, that I may enjoy a little peace.' And
he was sure that God had forgiven him all his sins, including the
murder of the woman; but for the child's murder, he was in doubt.
Then an old man said to him, 'God has forgiven you even the death
of the child, but he leaves you in grief because that is good for your
soul.'

3. With regard to receiving the brethren, the same abba said that one should bow before the brethren who come, because it is not before them, but before God that we prostrate ourselves. 'When you see your brother,' he said, 'you see the Lord your God.' He added, 'We have learnt that from Abraham. (cf. Gen. 18) When you receive the brethren, invite them to rest awhile, for this is what we learn from Lot who invited the angels to do so.' (cf. Gen. 19.3)

ANDREW

1. Abba Andrew said, 'These three things are appropriate for a monk: exile, poverty, and endurance in silence.'

AIO

They said there was a certain old man in the Thebaid, Abba Antionus, who did many good works while he was young, but when he grew old he became sick and blind. Since he was ill, the brethren took great care of him, even putting his food in his mouth. They asked Abba Aio what would come of this solicitude. He replied, 'I tell you, if when he eats even one date he does so eagerly and willingly, God takes that away from his works; but if he receives it reluctantly and unwillingly, God will keep his works intact, since he has to do this against his will. The brethren will receive their reward.'

AMMONATHAS

1. A magistrate came one day to Pelusia to levy the poll-tax on the monks, as on the secular population. All the brothers assembled together about this proposal and went to Abba Ammonathas. Some of the Fathers thought they ought to go and see the emperor about it. Abba Ammonathas said to them, 'So much trouble is not necessary. Rather remain quietly in your cells, fast for two weeks, and I alone, with the grace of God, will deal with this matter.' So the

brothers went back to their cells. The old man stayed in the peace
of his own cell. At the end of a fortnight the brethren were dis-
satisfied with the old man, whom they had not seen stir, and they
said, 'The old man has done nothing about our business.' On the
fifteenth day, according to their agreement, the brethren assembled
again and the old man came with a letter bearing the emperor's seal.
On seeing this the brethren said to him, in great astonishment,
'When did you get that, abba?' Then the old man, said, 'Believe me,
brother, I went that night to the emperor, who wrote this letter;
then, going to Alexandria, I had it countersigned by the magistrate
and thus I returned to you.' Hearing this, the brothers were filled
with fear, and did penance before him. So their business was settled,
and the magistrate troubled them no further.

·|BETA|·

BASIL THE GREAT

Basil the Great (c. 330–79) was the brother of Gregory of Nyssa and Macrina. After an excellent education he became a monk in Syria and Egypt and settled for a time as a hermit in Neocaesarea (358). In 370 he succeeded Eusebius as Bishop of Caesarea and was the defender of Orthodoxy against the heresy of Arius. He organized monastic life in and around Caesarea, bringing structure and organization into the way of life learnt in Egypt. He put forward in two books precepts for the monastic life, called The Longer Rule *and* The Shorter Rule; *this was revised by Theodore the Studite in the early ninth century, and is a basic document for Eastern monasticism.*

1. One of the old men said, 'When Saint Basil came to the monastery one day, he said to the abbot, after the customary exhortation, "Have you a brother here who is obedient?" The other replied, "They are all your servants, master, and strive for their salvation."

But he repeated, "Have you a brother who is really obedient?" Then the abbot led a brother to him and Saint Basil used him to serve during the meal. When the meal was ended, the brother brought him some water for rinsing his hands and Saint Basil said to him, "Come here, so that I also may offer you water." The brother allowed the bishop to pour the water. Then Saint Basil said to him, "When I enter the sanctuary, come, that I may ordain you deacon." When this was done, he ordained him priest and took him with him to the bishop's palace because of his obedience.'

BESSARION

The sayings of Bessarion recorded here are given in the first person by his disciple Doulas. No. 4 shows him visiting John of Lycopolis at the time of the destruction of the pagan temples in Alexandria in 391, when the Serapion was overthrown. That person, Theophilus of Alexandria, appears to have used the simpler Coptic monks as shock troops in his conflicts with both paganism and heresy; the story of Hypatia is after all based on actual events. This story also introduces the presence of women ascetics in the desert, some of whose sayings are recorded later.

1. Abba Doulas, the disciple of Abba Bessarion said, 'One day when we were walking beside the sea I was thirsty and I said to Abba Bessarion, "Father, I am very thirsty." He said a prayer and said to me, "Drink some of the sea water." The water proved sweet when I drank some. I even poured some into a leather bottle for fear of being thirsty later on. Seeing this, the old man asked me why I was taking some. I said to him, "Forgive me, it is for fear of being thirsty later on." Then the old man said, "God is here, God is everywhere." '

2. Another time when Abba Bessarion had occasion to do so, he said a prayer and crossed the river Chrysoroas on foot and then continued his way. Filled with wonder, I asked his pardon and said, 'How did your feet feel when you were walking on the water?' He replied, 'I felt the water just to my heels, but the rest was dry.'

3. On another day, while we were going to see an old man, the sun was setting. So Abba Bessarion said this prayer, 'I pray you,

Lord, that the sun may stand still till we reach your servant,' and that is what happened.

4. On another day, when I came to his cell I found him standing at prayer with his hands raised towards heaven. For fourteen days he remained thus. Then he called me and told me to follow him. We went into the desert. Being thirsty, I said to him, 'Father, I am thirsty.' Then, taking my sheepskin, the old man went about a stone's throw away and when he had prayed, he brought it back, full of water. Then we walked on and came to a cave where, on entering we found a brother seated, engaged in plaiting a rope. He did not raise his eyes to us, nor greet us, since he did not want to enter into conversation with us. So the old man said to me, 'Let us go; no doubt the old man is not sure if he ought to speak with us.' We continued our journey towards Lycopolis, till we reached Abba John's cell. After greeting him, we prayed, then the old man sat down to speak of the vision which he had had. Abba Bessarion said it had been made known to him that the temples would be over-thrown. That is what happened: they were overthrown. On our return, we came again to the cave where we had seen the brother. The old man said to me, 'Let us go in and see him; perhaps God has told him to speak to us.' When we had entered, we found him dead. The old man said to me, 'Come, brother, let us take the body; it is for this reason God has sent us here.' When we took the body to bury it we perceived that it was a woman. Filled with astonishment, the old man said, 'See how the women triumph over Satan, while we still behave badly in the towns.' Having given thanks to God, who protects those who love him, we went away.

5. One day a man possessed with a devil came to Scetis, and they prayed over him, but the devil did not leave him, for it was obsti-nate. The priests said, 'What can we do against this devil? No one can drive him away, except Abba Bessarion, but if we call him, he will not come, even to the church. Therefore let us do this: since he comes to church early, before anyone else, let us make the possessed sleep here and when he comes, let us keep to our prayer, and say to him, "Abba, awaken the brother." ' This is what they did. When the old man came early, they kept to their prayer and said to him, 'Awaken the brother.' The old man said to him, 'Arise and

go.' Immediately the devil departed from him and from that hour he was healed.

6. Abba Bessarion said, 'For fourteen days and nights, I have stood upright in the midst of thorn-bushes, without sleeping.'

7. A brother who had sinned was turned out of the church by the priest; Abba Bessarion got up and went with him, saying, 'I, too, am a sinner.'

8. The same Abba Bessarion said, 'For fourteen years I have never lain down, but have always slept sitting or standing.'

9. The same abba said, 'When you are at peace, without having to struggle, humiliate yourself for fear of being led astray by joy which is inappropriate; we magnify ourselves and we are delivered to warfare. For often, because of our weakness, God does not allow us to be tempted, for fear we should be overcome.'

10. A brother who shared a lodging with other brothers asked Abba Bessarion, 'What should I do?' The old man replied, 'Keep silence and do not compare yourself with others.'

11. Abba Bessarion, at the point of death, said, 'The monk ought to be as the Cherubim and the Seraphim: all eye.'

12. Abba Bessarion's disciples related that his life had been like that of a bird of the air, or a fish, or an animal living on earth, passing all the time of his life without trouble or disquiet. The care of a dwelling did not trouble him, and the desire for a particular place never seemed to dominate his soul, no more than the abundance of delights, or the possession of houses or the reading of books. But he seemed entirely free from all the passions of the body, sustaining himself on the hope of good things to come, firm in the strength of his faith; he lived in patience, like a prisoner who is led everywhere, always suffering cold and nakedness, scorched by the sun. He always lived in the open air, afflicting himself on the edge of the desert like a vagabond. Often he found it good to be carried over the sea to distant and uninhabited regions. When he happened to come into pleasanter places where the brethren lived a life in common, he would sit outside at the gate, weeping and lamenting like one shipwrecked and flung back on to the earth. Then if one of the

brethren coming out found him there, sitting like one of the poor beggars living in the world, and filled with compassion approached him, asking, 'Man, why are you weeping? If you are in need of something, as far as we can we will see you receive it, only come in, share our table and rest yourself.' He would reply, 'I cannot live under a roof so long as I have not found again the riches of my house,' adding that he had lost great riches in various ways. 'I have fallen amongst pirates, I have suffered shipwreck, I have dishonoured my rank, becoming unknown, famous as I was.' The brother, moved by these words, returned, bringing a morsel of bread and giving it him, saying, 'Take this, Father; all the rest, as you say, God will restore to you; home, honour, and riches of which you speak.' But he, bewailing himself yet more, sighed deeply, adding, 'I cannot say if I shall find again those lost good things I seek, but I am still more afflicted, every day suffering the danger of death, having no respite because of my great calamities. For always I must wander, in order to finish my course.'

BENJAMIN

1. Abba Benjamin said, 'When we returned to Scetis, once the harvest was over, in payment they brought each of us a plaster vessel containing a pint of oil from Alexandria. When the time of harvest came again, the brothers brought what was left to the church. For my own part, I had not uncorked my vessel but had taken a little by piercing it with a stiletto, imagining in my heart that I had achieved something splendid. But when the brothers brought their plaster vessels as they were while mine was pierced, I was as ashamed as though I had committed fornication.'

2. Abba Benjamin, priest of the Cells, said, 'One day at Scetis we went to an old man, intending to take him a little oil but he said to us, "Look at the little vessel you brought me three years ago; it has remained there where you put it." At these words we wondered at the old man's virtue.'

3. The same abba said, 'We went to another old man who detained us for a meal and he offered us oil of horse-radish. We said

to him, "Father, give us rather a little good oil." At these words he crossed himself and said, 'I did not know there was any other kind.'

4. As he was dying, Abba Benjamin said to his sons, 'If you observe the following, you can be saved, "Be joyful at all times, pray without ceasing and give thanks for all things." '

5. He also said, 'Walk in the royal way, measuring the landmarks without meanness.'

BIARE

1. Someone questioned Abba Biare in these words, 'What shall I do to be saved?' He replied, 'Go, reduce your appetite and your manual work, dwell without care in your cell and you will be saved.'

·|GAMMA|·

GREGORY THE THEOLOGIAN

1. Abba Gregory said, 'These three things God requires of all the baptized: right faith in the heart, truth on the tongue, temperance in the body.'

2. He also said, 'The whole life of a man is but one single day for those who are working hard with longing.'

GELASIUS

Gelasius trained as an ascetic in Egypt. He became abbot of Nilopolis in the mid fifth century. He was a scholar and a great abbot, involved both in the ecclesiastical politics of his time and in the law-suits of his monastery. He was a firm supporter of Juvenal, and held to the formularies of Chalcedon. The second story here introduces the famous Saint Symeon Stylites, on his pillar outside Antioch. Symeon is shown in the important role of arbitrator, to whom secular disputes as well as religious matters were brought in his role as prophet and holy man.

1. It was said of Abba Gelasius that he had a leather Bible worth eighteen pieces of silver. In fact it contained the whole of the Old and New Testaments. He had put it in the church so that any of the brethren who wished, could read it. A strange brother came to see the old man and, seeing the Bible, wished to have it, and stole it as he was leaving. The old man did not run after him to take it from him, although he knew what he was doing. So the brother went to the city and tried to sell it, and finding a purchaser, he asked thirteen pieces of silver for it. The purchaser said to him, 'Lend it to me, first, so that I may examine it, then I will give you a price.' So he gave it to him. Taking it, the purchaser brought it to Abba Gelasius for him to examine it and told him the price which the seller had set. The old man said to him, 'Buy it, for it is beautiful, and worth the price you tell me.' This man when he returned, said something quite different to the seller, and not what the old man had said to him. 'I have shown it to Abba Gelasius,' he said, 'and he replied that it was dear, and not worth the price you said.' Hearing this, he asked, 'Didn't the old man say anything else?' 'No,' he replied. Then the seller said, 'I do not want to sell it any more.' Filled with compunction, he went to find the old man, to do penance and ask him to take his book back. But he did not wish to make good his loss. So the brother said to him, 'If you do not take it back, I shall have no peace.' The old man answered, 'If you won't have any peace, then I will take it back.' So the brother stayed there until his death, edified by the old man's way of life.

2. A cell surrounded by a plot of land had been left to Abba Gelasius by an old man, also a monk, who had his dwelling near Nilopolis. Now a peasant farmer under Batacus, who was then living at Nilopolis in Palestine, went to find Batacus, asking to receive the plot of land, because, according to the law, it ought to return to him. Batacus was a violent man and he tried to take the field from Abba Gelasius by force. But our Abba Gelasius, not wishing that a monastic cell should be ceded to a secular, would not give up the land. Batacus, noticing that Abba Gelasius' beasts of burden were carrying olives from the field that had been left to him,

turned them by force from their course and took the olives for himself; scarcely did he return the animals with their drivers, having caused them to suffer outrages. The blessed old man did not reclaim the fruit, but he did not cede possession of the land for the reason we have given above. Furious with him, Batacus, who had other matters to deal with also (for he loved lawsuits), betook himself to Constantinople, making the journey on foot. When he came near to Antioch, where Saint Symeon's fame was shining with great brilliance, he heard tell of him (he was indeed an eminent man) and, as a Christian, he desired to see the saint.

Blessed Symeon, from the top of his column, saw him as soon as he entered the monastery and asked him, 'Where do you come from and where are you going?' He replied, 'I am from Palestine and I am going to Constantinople.' He continued, 'And for what reasons?' Batacus replied, 'About many matters. I hope, thanks to the prayers of your holiness, to return and bow before your holy footprints.' Then Saint Symeon said to him, 'Wretch, you don't want to say that you are going to act against the man of God. But your way is not favourable for you and you will not see your house again. If you will follow my advice, leave these parts and hurry to him and ask his pardon, if you are still alive when you reach that place.' Immediately Batacus was seized with fever. His fellow travellers put him into a litter and he hastened, according to the word of Saint Symeon, to reach Abba Gelasius and to ask his pardon. But when he came to Beirut, he died without seeing his house again, according to the old man's prophecy. It is his son, also called Batacus, who has told this to many trustworthy men, at the same time as he gave the account of his father's death.

3. Many of his disciples used to relate the following also: One day someone had brought them a fish and when it was cooked, the cook took it to the cellarer. An urgent reason obliged him to leave the store-room. So he left the fish on the ground in a dish, asking a young disciple of Abba Gelasius to look after it for a short while until his return. The boy was seized with desire and began to eat the fish greedily. The cellarer, finding him eating it on his return, was angry with the boy who was sitting on the ground and without being careful about what he did he kicked him. Being struck on a mortal part, by demonic power the boy gave up his spirit and died.

The cellarer, overcome with fear, laid him on his own bed, covered him and went to throw himself at Abba Gelasius' feet, telling him what had happened. Gelasius advised him not to speak of it to anyone and ordered him to bring the boy, when everyone had gone to rest in the evening, to the *diaconicum,* place him before the altar and then to withdraw. Coming to the *diaconicum,* the old man continued in prayer; at the hour of the night psalmody, when the brethren assembled, the old man withdrew, followed by the little boy. No-one knew what had been done, save he and the cellarer, until his death.

4. Not only his disciples, but many of those who met him, often told this about Abba Gelasius. At the time of the ecumenical synod at Chalcedon, Theodosius who had taken the initiative in the schism of Dioscorus in Palestine, foreseeing that the bishops would return to their particular churches (for he was also present at Chalcedon, expelled from his fatherland because his fate was to stir up trouble), hastened to Abba Gelasius in his monastery. He spoke to him, opposing the synod, saying that the teaching of Nestorius had prevailed. By this means he thought to win over the holy man and bring him to his own delusion and schism. But he, because of the bearing of his interlocutor and the prudence with which God inspired him, understood the injurious nature of his words. Not only did he not join himself to this apostasy, as almost all the others did, but he sent him away covered with reproach. In fact, he made the young child whom he had raised from the dead come into their midst and he spoke thus, with great respect, 'If you want to argue about the faith, you have those close to you who will listen to you and answer you; for my part, I have not time to hear you.' These words filled Theodosius with confusion. Hurriedly he left for the holy city and there got all the monks on his side, under the pretext of fervent zeal. Then, using this as his aid, he seized possession of the throne of Jerusalem. He had prepared the position for himself by assassinations and he did many things contrary to divine law and canonical precept. Having become master and attained his goal, laying hands on many bishops to set them on the thrones of bishops who had not yet retired, he made Abba Gelasius come to him. He invited him into the sanctuary, endeavouring to win him over, even while fearing him. When Gelasius entered the sanctuary, Theodosius said to

him, 'Anathematize Juvenal.' But he remained unmoved and replied, 'I do not know any bishop of Jerusalem but Juvenal.' Theodosius, fearing others would imitate his holy zeal, ordered him to be driven out of the church, covering him with ridicule. The schismatics took him and put faggots round him, threatening to burn him. But seeing that even that did not make him give in nor frighten him and fearing a popular rising, for he was very celebrated (all this had been given him by Providence from above), they sent our martyr, who had offered himself as a holocaust to Christ, safe and sound away.

5. It was said of him that in his youth he had led a life of poverty as an anchorite. At that time in the same region there were many other men who, with him, had embraced the same life. Among them there was an old man of very great simplicity and poverty, living in a single cell to the end, although in his old age he had disciples. This old man's particular acts of asceticism had been to guard against having two tunics and till the day of his death not to think of the morrow whilst he was with his companions.

When Abba Gelasius, with the divine assistance founded his monastery, he was given many gifts and he also acquired beasts of burden and cattle, which were needed for the monastery. In the beginning he had discussed the foundation of a monastery with the divine Pachomius and had recourse to him throughout its foundation. The old man, of whom we have spoken above, seeing him engaged on this, and wishing to preserve the great love he had for him, said to him, 'Abba Gelasius, I am afraid your spirit will become enslaved by the lands and all the other possessions of the monastery.' But he replied, 'Your spirit is more enslaved by the needle with which you work than the spirit of Gelasius by these goods.'

6. It was said of Abba Gelasius that he was often assailed by the thought of going to the desert. One day he said to his disciple, 'Do me the favour, brother, of bearing with whatever I may do, and say nothing to me for the whole of this week.' Taking a reed, he began to walk in his little *atrium*. When he was tired, he sat down a little, then stood up again to walk about. When evening came, he said to himself, 'He who walks in the desert does not eat bread, but herbs; so because you are weary, eat a few vegetables.' He did so, then said to himself again, 'He who is in the desert does not lie in a bed, but in the open air; so do the same.' So he lay down and slept in the

atrium. He walked thus for three days in the monastery, eating a few chicory leaves in the evening and sleeping the whole night in the open air and he grew weary. Then, taking the thought which troubled him, he refuted it in these words, 'If you are not able to perform the works of the desert, live patiently in your cell, weeping for your sins, without wandering here and there. For the eye of God always sees the works of a man and nothing escapes him and he knows those who do good.'

GERONTIUS

1. Abba Gerontius of Petra said that many, tempted by the pleasures of the body, commit fornication, not in their body but in their spirit, and while preserving their bodily virginity, commit prostitution in their soul. 'Thus it is good, my well-beloved, to do that which is written, and for each one to guard his own heart with all possible care.' (Prov. 4. 23)

⋄| DELTA |⋄

DANIEL

*Daniel was a disciple of Arsenius. He was present at his death in A.D.
449. Daniel being left his tunic, hair-shirt and sandals said, 'And I
unworthy wear them that I may receive a blessing.'*

1. It was said concerning Abba Daniel, that when the barbarians
invaded Scetis and the Fathers fled away, the old man said, 'If God
does not care for me, why still live?' Then he passed through the
midst of the barbarians without being seen. He said to himself
therefore, 'See how God has cared for me, since I am not dead. Now
I will do that which is human and flee with the Fathers.'

2. A brother asked Abba Daniel, 'Give me a commandment and
I will keep it.' He replied, 'Never put your hand in the dish with
a woman, and never eat with her; thus you will escape a little the
demon of fornication.'

3. Abba Daniel said, 'At Babylon the daughter of an important
person was possessed by a devil. A monk for whom her father had

[51]

a great affection said to him, "No-one can heal your daughter except some anchorites whom I know; but if you ask them to do so, they will not agree because of their humility. Let us therefore do this: when they come to the market, look as though you want to buy their goods and when they come to receive the price, we will ask them to say a prayer and I believe she will be healed." When they came to the market they found a disciple of the old men setting there selling their goods and they led him away with the baskets, so that he should receive the price of them. But when the monk reached the house, the woman possessed with the devil came and slapped him. But he only turned the other cheek, according to the Lord's Command. (Matt. 5.39) The devil, tortured by this, cried out, "What violence! The commandment of Jesus drives me out." Immediately the woman was cleansed. When the old men came, they told them what had happened and they glorified God saying, "This is how the pride of the devil is brought low, through the humility of the commandment of Christ." '

4. Abba Daniel also said, 'The body prospers in the measure in which the soul is weakened, and the soul prospers in the measure in which the body is weakened.'

5. One day Abba Daniel and Abba Ammoes went on a journey together. Abba Ammoes said, 'When shall we, too, settle down, in a cell, Father?' Abba Daniel replied, 'Who shall separate us henceforth from God? God is in the cell, and, on the other hand, he is outside also.'

6. Abba Daniel said that when Abba Arsenius was at Scetis, there was a monk there who used to steal the possessions of the old men. Abba Arsenius took him into his cell in order to convert him and to give the old men some peace. He said to him, 'Everything you want I will get for you, only do not steal.' So he gave him gold, coins, clothes and everything he needed. But the brother began to steal again. So the old men, seeing that he had not stopped, drove him away saying, 'If there is a brother who commits a sin through weakness, one must bear it, but if he steals, drive him away, for it is hurtful to his soul and troubles all those who live in the neighbourhood.'

7. This is what Abba Daniel, the Pharanite, said, 'Our Father Abba Arsenius told us of an inhabitant of Scetis, of notable life and of simple faith; through his naiveté he was deceived and said, "The bread which we receive is not really the body of Christ, but a symbol." Two old men having learnt that he had uttered this saying, knowing that he was outstanding in his way of life, knew that he had not spoken through malice, but through simplicity. So they came to find him and said, "Father, we have heard a proposition contrary to the faith on the part of someone who says that the bread which we receive is not really the body of Christ, but a symbol." The old man said, "It is I who have said that." Then the old men exhorted him saying, "Do not hold this position, Father, but hold one in conformity with that which the catholic Church has given us. We believe, for our part, that the bread itself is the body of Christ and that the cup itself is his blood and this in all truth and not a symbol. But as in the beginning, God formed man in his image, taking the dust of the earth, without anyone being able to say that it is not the image of God, even though it is not seen to be so; thus it is with the bread of which he said that it is his body; and so we believe that it is really the body of Christ." The old man said to them, "As long as I have not been persuaded by the thing itself, I shall not be fully convinced." So they said, "Let us pray God about this mystery throughout the whole of this week and we believe that God will reveal it to us." The old man received this saying with joy and he prayed in these words, "Lord, you know that it is not through malice that I do not believe and so that I may not err through ignorance, reveal this mystery to me, Lord Jesus Christ." The old men returned to their cells and they also prayed God, saying, "Lord Jesus Christ, reveal this mystery to the old man, that he may believe and not lose his reward." God heard both the prayers. At the end of the week they came to church on Sunday and sat all three on the same mat, the old man in the middle. Then their eyes were opened and when the bread was placed on the holy table, there appeared as it were a little child to these three alone. And when the priest put out his hand to break the bread, behold an angel descended from heaven with a sword and poured the child's blood into the chalice. When the priest cut the bread into small pieces, the angel also cut the child in pieces. When they drew near to receive the sacred elements the old man alone received a

morsel of bloody flesh. Seeing this he was afraid and cried out, "Lord, I believe that this bread is your flesh and this chalice your blood." Immediately the flesh which he held in his hand became bread, according to the mystery and he took it, giving thanks to God. Then the old men said to him, "God knows human nature and that man cannot eat raw flesh and that is why he has changed his body into bread and his blood into wine, for those who receive it in faith." Then they gave thanks to God for the old man, because he had allowed him not to lose the reward of his labour. So all three returned with joy to their own cells.'

8. The same Abba Daniel told of another great old man who dwelt in lower Egypt, who in his simplicity, said that Melchizedek was the son of God. When blessed Cyril, Archbishop of Alexandria, was told about this he sent someone to him. Learning that the old man was a worker of miracles and that all he asked of God was revealed to him, and that it was because of his simplicity that he had given utterance to this saying, using guile the Archbishop said to him, 'Abba, I think that Melchizedek is the son of God, while a contrary thought says to me, no, that he is simply a man, high-priest of God. Since I am thus plagued, I have sent someone to you that you may pray God to reveal to you what he is.' Confident of his gift, the old man said without hesitation, 'Give me three days, I will ask God about this matter and I will tell you who he is.' So he withdrew and prayed to God about this question. Coming three days later he said to the blessed Cyril that Melchizedek was a man. The archbishop said to him, 'How to you know, Abba?' He replied, 'God has shewn me all the patriarchs in such a way that each one, from Adam to Melchizedek, passed before me. Therefore be sure that it is so.' Then the old man withdrew, having preached to himself that Melchizedek was a man. Then the blessed Cyril rejoiced greatly.

DIOSCORUS

Dioscorus was a monk in Nitria. He was one of the Four Tall Brothers who were involved in the Origenist disputes with Theophilus. Palladius says Melania met Dioscorus on her visit to Egypt in A.D. 373–4. He was made Bishop of Hermopolis ten miles from Nitria, and attended the Council of Constantinople in 394. He was later deposed and excom-

municated for supposed Origenist sympathies. He died in the early fifth century.

1. It was said of Abba Dioscorus the Nachiaste, that he ate bread of barley and lentils. Every year he made a resulution about a particular thing, saying, 'I will not meet anyone this year'; or else, 'I will not speak'; or else, 'I will not eat cooked food'; or else, 'I will not eat fruit or vegetables.' In all his work he acted thus, and when he had gained one point, he began another. Each year he did this.

2. A brother questioned Abba Poemen in this way, 'My thoughts trouble me, making me put my sins aside, and concern myself with my brother's faults.' The old man told him the following story about Abba Dioscorus, 'In his cell he wept over himself, while his disciple was sitting in another cell. When the latter came to see the old man he asked him, "Father, why are you weeping?" "I am weeping over my sins," the old man answered him. Then his disciple said, "You do not have any sins, Father." The old man replied, "Truly, my child, if I were allowed to see my sins, three or four men would not be enough to weep for them."

3. Abba Dioscorus said, 'If we wear our heavenly robe, we shall not be found naked, but if we are found not wearing this garment, what shall we do, brothers? We, even we also, shall hear the voice that says, "Cast them into outer darkness; there men will weep and gnash their teeth." (Matt 22.13) And, brothers, there will be great shame in store for us, if, after having worn this habit for so long, we are found in the hour of need not having put on the wedding garment. Oh what compunction will seize us! What darkness will fall upon us, in the presence of our fathers and our brothers, who will see us being tortured by the angels of punishment!'

DOULAS

1. Abba Doulas said, 'If the enemy induces us to give up our inner peace, we must not listen to him, for nothing is equal to this peace and the privation of food. The one and the other join together to fight the enemy. For they make interior vision keen.'

2. He also said, 'Detach yourself from the love of the multitude lest your enemy question your spirit and trouble your inner peace.'

⋄| EPSILON |⋄

EPIPHANIUS, BISHOP OF CYPRUS

Epiphanius was a Palestinian who learned his monasticism in Egypt as a disciple of Abba Hilarion. His monastery was at Besanduk near Eleutheropolis, between Jerusalem and Gaza. He was an opponent of Origenism. Saying 3 shows him upholding the traditions of Egypt against the abbot of his own monastery in Palestine with regard to prayer and psalmody. He, like Bessarion, was also concerned in the overthrow of the pagan temples in Alexandria. As a bishop, he set more store by books and reading than was usual with monks trained in Egypt.

1. The holy Bishop Epiphanius related that some crows, flying all around the temple of Serapis, in the presence of blessed Athanasius, cried without interruption, 'Caw, caw.' Then some pagans, standing in front of blessed Athanasius cried out, 'Wicked old man, tell us what these crows are crying.' He answered, 'These crows are saying, "Caw, caw", and in the Ausonion (or Latin) language, this word means "tomorrow".' He added, 'Tomorrow you shall see the glory of God.' Just afterwards, the death of the Em-

peror Julian was announced. At this news they all ran to the temple
of Serapis crying out against him and saying, 'If you did not want
him, why did you accept his gifts?'

2. The same related that there was a charioteer in Alexandria,
whose mother was called Mary. In an equestrian fight he had a fall.
Then getting up again he surpassed the men who had overthrown
him and carried off the victory. The crowd cried out, 'The son of
Mary has fallen; he has risen again and is the victor.' While these
cries were still being heard, an uproar ran through the crowd in
connection with the temple of Serapis; the great Theophilus had
gone and overthrown the statue of Serapis and made himself master
of the temple.

3. The blessed Epiphanius, Bishop of Cyprus, was told this by the
abbot of a monastery which he had in Palestine, 'By your prayers
we do not neglect our appointed round of psalmody, but we are
very careful to recite Terce, Sext and None.' Then Epiphanius
corrected them with the following comment, 'It is clear that you
do not trouble about the other hours of the day, if you cease from
prayer. The true monk should have prayer and psalmody continually in his heart.'

4. One day Saint Epiphanius sent someone to Abba Hilarion with
this request, 'Come, and let us see one another before we depart
from the body.' When he came, they rejoiced in each other's company. During their meal, they were brought a fowl; Epiphanius
took it and gave it to Hilarion. Then the old man said to him,
'Forgive me, but since I received the habit I have not eaten meat that
has been killed.' Then the bishop answered, 'Since I took the habit,
I have not allowed anyone to go to sleep with a complaint against
me and I have not gone to rest with a complaint against anyone.'
The old man replied, 'Forgive me, your way of life is better than
mine.'

5. The same old man said, 'Melchizedek, the image of Christ,
blessed Abraham, the father of the Jews; how much more does truth
itself, which is the Christ, bless and sanctify all those who believe
in it.'

6. The same old man said, 'The Canaanite woman cries out, and
she is heard; (Matt. 15) the woman with the issue of blood is silent,

and she is called blessed; (Luke 8) the pharisee speaks, and he is condemned;(Matt. 9) the publican does not open his mouth, and he is heard.' (Luke 18)

7. The same old man said, 'David the prophet prayed late at night; waking in the middle of the night, he prayed before the day; at the dawn of day he stood before the Lord; in the small hours he prayed, in the evening and at mid-day he prayed again, and this is why he said, "Seven times a day have I praised you." ' (Ps.119.164)

8. He also said, 'The acquisition of Christian books is necessary for those who can use them. For the mere sight of these books renders us less inclined to sin, and incites us to believe more firmly in righteousness.'

9. He also said, 'Reading the Scriptures is a great safeguard against sin.'

10. He also said, 'It is a great treachery to salvation to know nothing of the divine law.'

11. He also said, 'Ignorance of the Scriptures is a precipice and a deep abyss.'

12. The same abba said, 'The righteous sin through their mouths, but the ungodly sin in their whole bodies. This is why David sings; "Set, O Lord, a watch before my mouth and keep the door of my lips." (Ps. 141.3)And again, "I will take heed to my ways that I do not sin with my tongue." ' (Ps. 39.1)

13. Someone asked him, 'Why are there ten commandments in the Law and nine Beatitudes?' He replied, 'The Decalogue corresponds with the number of the plagues of Egypt, while the figure of the Beatitudes is three times the image of the Trinity.'

14. Someone else asked him, 'Is one righteous man enough to appease God?' He replied, 'Yes, for he himself has written: "Find a man who lives according to righteousness, and I will pardon the whole people." ' (Jer. 5.1)

15. The same abba said, 'God remits the debts of sinners who are penitent, for example, the sinful woman and the publican, but of the righteous man he even asks interest. This is what he says to his

apostles, "Except your righteousness exceed that of the scribes and pharisees, you will never enter the kingdom of heaven." ' (Matt. 5.20)

16. He also said, 'God sells righteousness at a very low price to those who wish to buy it: a little piece of bread, a cloak of no value, a cup of cold water, a mite.'

17. He added, 'A man who receives something from another because of his poverty or his needs has therein his reward, and because he is ashamed, when he repays it he does so in secret. But it is the opposite for the Lord God; he receives in secret, but he repays it in the presence of the angels, the archangels and the righteous.'

EPHREM

(possibly Ephrem the Syrian, the hymn writer)

1. While yet a child, Abba Ephrem had a dream and then a vision. A branch of vine came out of his tongue, grew bigger and filled everything under heaven. It was laden with beautiful fruit. All the birds of heaven came to eat of the fruit of the vine, and the more they ate, the more the fruit increased.

2. Another time, one of the saints had a vision. According to the commandment of God, a band of angels descended from heaven, holding in their hands a *kephalis* (that is to say, a piece of papyrus covered with writing), and they said to one another, 'To whom should we give this?' Some said, 'To this one,' others, 'To that one.' Then the answer came in these words, 'Truly, they are holy and righteous, but none of them is able to receive this, except Ephrem.' The old man saw that the *kephalis* was given to Ephrem and he saw as it were a fountain flowing from his lips. Then he understood that that which came from the lips of Ephrem was of the Holy Spirit.

3. Another time, when Ephrem was on the road, a prostitute tried by her flatteries, if not to lead him to shameful intercourse, at least to make him angry, for no-one had every seen him angry. He said to her, 'Follow me.' When they had reached a very crowded

place, he said to her, 'In this place, come, do what you desire.' But she, seeing the crowd, said to him, 'How can we do what we want to do in front of so great a crowd, without being ashamed?' He replied, 'If you blush before men, how much more should we blush before God, who knows what is hidden in darkness?' She was covered with shame and went away without having achieved anything.

EUCHARISTUS THE SECULAR

1. Two Fathers asked God to reveal to them how far they had advanced. A voice came which said, 'In a certain village in Egypt there is a man called Eucharistus and his wife who is called Mary. You have not yet reached their degree of virtue.' The two old men set out and went to the village. Having enquired, they found his house and his wife. They said to her, 'Where is your husband?' She replied, 'He is a shepherd and is feeding the sheep.' Then she made them come into the house. When evening came, Eucharistus returned with the sheep. Seeing the old men, he set the table and brought water to wash their feet. The old men said to him, 'We shall not eat anything until you have told us about your way of life.' Eucharistus replied with humility, 'I am a Shepherd, and this is my wife.' The old men insisted but he did not want to say more. Then they said, 'God has sent us to you.' At these words, Eucharistus was afraid and said, 'Here are these sheep; we received them from our parents, and if, by God's help we make a little profit, we divide it into three parts: one for the poor, the second for hospitality, and the third for our personal needs. Since I married my wife, we have not had intercourse with one another, for she is a virgin; we each live alone. At night we wear hair-shirts and our ordinary clothes by day. No-one has known of this till now.' At these words they were filled with admiration and went away giving glory to God.

EULOGIUS THE PRIEST

1. A certain Eulogius, a disciple of blessed John the bishop, a priest and great ascetic, used to fast two days together and often

extended his fast to the whole week, eating only bread and salt. Men thought highly of him. He went to Abba Joseph at Panephysis, in the hope of finding greater austerity with him. The old man received him joyfully and supplied him with everything he had to refresh him. Eulogius' disciples said, 'The priest only eats bread and salt.' Abba Joseph ate in silence. The visitors spent three days there without hearing them chanting or praying, for the brothers laboured in secret. They went away without having been edified. By the will of God, it became so dark that they lost their way and returned to the old man. Before knocking on the door, they heard chanting. So they waited for a suitable moment and then knocked. Those who were inside, having ended their psalmody, received them joyfully. Then, because of the heat, the disciples of Eulogius rushed to the water jar and offered it to him. Now it contained a mixture of sea-water and river-water, so that he could not drink it. Coming to himself, Eulogius threw himself at the old man's feet and, wanting to know about his manner of life, he asked him, 'Abba, what is this? You did not chant before, but only after we left. And now when I take the jug, I find salt water in it.' The old man said to him, 'The brother is distraught and has mixed sea-water with it by mistake.' But Eulogius pressed the old man, wanting to learn the truth. So the old man said, 'This little bottle of wine is for hospitality, but that water is what the brothers always drink.' Then he instructed him in discernment of thoughts and in controlling all the merely human in himself. So he became more balanced and ate whatever was brought him and learnt how to work in secret. Then he said to the old man, 'Truly, your way of life is indeed genuine.'

EUPREPIUS

1. Abba Euprepius said, 'Knowing that God is faithful and mighty, have faith in him and you will share what is his. If you are depressed, you do not believe. We all believe that he is mighty and we believe all is possible to him. As for your own affairs, behave with faith in him about them, too, for he is able to work miracles in you also.'

2. The same old man helped some thieves when they were stealing. When they had taken away what was inside his cell, Abba Euprepius saw that they had left his stick and he was sorry. So he took it and ran after them to give it to them. But the thieves did not want to take it, fearing that something would happen to them if they did. So he asked someone he met who was going the same way to give the stick to them.

3. Abba Euprepius said, 'Bodily things are compounded of matter. He who loves the world loves occasions of falling. Therefore if we happen to lose something, we must accept this with joy and gratitude, realising that we have been set free from care.'

4. A brother questioned Abba Euprepius about his life. And the old man said, 'Eat straw, wear straw, sleep on straw: that is to say, depise everything and acquire for yourself a heart of iron.'

5. A brother asked the same old man, 'How does the fear of God dwell in the soul?' The old man said, 'If a man is possessed of humility and poverty, and if he does not judge others, the fear of God will come to him.'

6. He also said, 'May fear, humility, lack of food and compunction be with you.'

7. In his early days, Abba Euprepius went to see an old man and said to him, 'Abba, give me a word so that I may be saved.' The other replied, 'If you wish to be saved, when you go to see someone, do not begin to speak before you are spoken to.' Filled with compunction at this saying, he made a prostration, saying, 'I have read many books before, but never have I received such teaching,' and he went away greatly edified.

HELLADIUS

1. It was said of Abba Helladius that he spent twenty years in the Cells, without ever raising his eyes to see the roof of the church.

2. Of the same Abba Helladius, it was said that he was accustomed to eat bread and salt, and that when Easter came, he would

say, 'The brothers eat bread and salt; as for me, I must make a little effort because of Easter. Therefore, since I eat sitting down all the other days, now that it is Easter, I will make this effort, and eat standing up.'

EVAGRIUS

Evagrius was born in Ibora in Pontus A.D. 345–6. He was ordained as a reader by Saint Basil, and deacon by Saint Gregory Nazianzen. He accompanied Saint Gregory to the Great Synod of Constantinople. In 382 he went to Jerusalem where he was nursed during a severe illness by Melania. In A.D. 383 he lived in Egypt and was for two years a monk in Nitria. He spent ten years as a disciple of Macarius of Alexandria in Cellia and was renowned both for his learning and the austerity of his life. He was the centre of the group who supported Origen, but died in 400 before the matter came to a crisis in Egypt. He was a well-educated monk and wrote about the spiritual life; his most famous works are the Praktikos *and* Chapters on Prayer.

1. Abba Evagrius said, 'Sit in your cell, collecting your thoughts. Remember the day of your death. See then what the death of your body will be; let your spirit be heavy, take pains, condemn the vanity of the world, so as to be able to live always in the peace you have in view without weakening. Remember also what happens in hell and think about the state of the souls down there, their painful silence, their most bitter groanings, their fear, their strife, their waiting. Think of their grief without end and the tears their souls shed eternally. But keep the day of resurrection and of presentation to God in remembrance also. Imagine the fearful and terrible judgement. Consider the fate kept for sinners, their shame before the face of God and the angels and archangels and all men, that is to say, the punishments, the eternal fire, worms that rest not, the darkness, gnashing of teeth, fear and supplications. Consider also the good things in store for the righteous: confidence in the face of God the Father and His Son, the angels and archangels and all the people of the saints, the kingdom of heaven, and the gifts of that realm, joy and beatitude.

'Keep in mind the remembrance of these two realities. Weep for the judgement of sinners, afflict yourself for fear lest you too feel those pains. But rejoice and be glad at the lot of the righteous. Strive to obtain those joys but be a stranger to those pains. Whether you be inside or outside your cell, be careful that the remembrance of these things never leaves you, so that, thanks to their remembrance, you may at least flee wrong and harmful thoughts.'

2. He also said, 'Restrain yourself from affection towards many people, for fear lest your spirit be distracted, so that your interior peace may not be disturbed.'

3. He also said, 'It is a great thing to pray without distraction but to chant psalms without distraction is even greater.'

4. He also said, 'Always keep your death in mind and do not forget the eternal judgement, then there will be no fault in your soul.'

5. He also said, 'Take away temptations and no-one will be saved.'

6. He also said that one of the Fathers used to say, 'Eat a little without irregularity; if charity is joined to this, it leads the monk rapidly to the threshhold of *apatheia*.'

7. One day at the Cells, there was an assembly about some matter or other and Abba Evagrius held forth. Then the priest said to him, 'Abba, we know that if you were living in your own country you would probably be a bishop and a great leader; but at present you sit here as a stranger.' He was filled with compunction, but was not at all upset and bending his head he replied, 'I have spoken once and will not answer, twice but I will proceed no further.' (Job 40.5)

EUDEMON

1. Abba Eudemon said this about Abba Paphnutius the Father of Scetis: 'I went down there while I was still young, and he would not let me stay, saying to me, "I do not allow the face of a woman to dwell in Scetis, because of the conflict with the enemy." '

◆| DZÊTA |◆

ZENO

Zeno was a famous disciple of Abba Silvanus, on Sinai. Like other monks in the early days in Egypt, he moved about a good deal in Egypt, Syria and Palestine. At the end of his life he settled near Gaza and in 451 he shut himself up and would see no-one until he died.

1. Abba Zeno, the disciple of blessed Silvanus said, 'Do not live in a famous place, do not settle close to a man with a great name, and do not lay foundations for building yourself a cell one day.'

2. It was said of Abba Zeno, that from the outset he never wished to receive anything from anyone at all. Those who brought him something came away hurt that he had not accepted anything. Others came to him, wanting to receive some token from a great old man and he had nothing to give them so they too came away hurt. The old man said, 'What shall I do, since those who bring things are hurt just as much as those who wish to receive something?

I know what seems right to me: when someone brings me something, I will accept it and I will give it to anyone who asks me for
something.' So he did that and was at peace and satisfied everyone.

3. An Egyptian brother came to see Abba Zeno in Syria, and
accused himself to the old man about his temptations. Filled with
admiration, Zeno said, 'The Egyptians hide the virtues they possess
and ceaselessly accuse themselves of faults they do not have, while
the Syrians and Greeks pretend to have virtues they do not have,
and hide the faults of which they are guilty.'

4. Some brothers came to see him and asked him, 'What does this
saying in the book of Job mean: "Heaven is not pure in his presence?" ' (Job 15.15) The old man replied, 'The brothers have passed
over their sins and inquired about heavenly things. This is the
interpretation of this saying: "God alone is pure," therefore he said,
"Heaven is not pure." '

5. It was said of Abba Zeno, that when he was living in Scetis, he
came out of his cell by night, going in the direction of the
marshes. He spent three days and three nights wandering at ran-
dom. At last, tired out, his strength failing him, he fell down as
though he were dying. Behold, a little child stood before him with
bread and a jar of water and said to him, 'Get up, and eat.' He stood
up and prayed, thinking that it was a delusion. The other said to
him, 'You have done well.' And he prayed a second, and then a third
time. The child said again, 'You have done well.' Then the old man
stood up, took some food and ate. The child said to him, 'As far as
you have walked, so far are you from your cell. So then, get up, and
follow me.' Immediately he found himself in his cell. So the old man
said to the child, 'Enter, and let us pray.' But when the old man went
inside, the other vanished.

6. Another time, the same Abba Zeno was walking in Palestine
and he was tired. He sat down near a cucumber plant to eat and he
said to himself, 'Take a cucumber and eat it. Truly it is only a little
thing.' But he answered himself, 'Thieves are taken away to punishment. Examine yourself therefore, to see if you can bear punishment.' He got up and stood in the sun for five days. When he was
quite burnt he said, 'You cannot bear punishment,' and he said to

his thoughts, 'Since you cannot bear punishment, do not steal, and do not eat.'

7. Abba Zeno said, 'If a man wants God to hear his prayer quickly, then before he prays for anything else, even his own soul, when he stands and stretches out his hands towards God, he must pray with all his heart for his enemies. Through this action God will hear everything that he asks.'

8. In a village there was said to be a man who fasted to such a degree that he was called 'the Faster'. Abba Zeno had heard of him, and he sent for him. The other came gladly. They prayed and sat down. The old man began to work in silence. Since he could not succeed in talking to him the Faster began to get bored. So he said to the old man, 'Pray for me, Abba, for I want to go.' The old man said to him. 'Why?' The other replied, 'Because my heart is as if it were on fire and I do not know what is the matter with it. For truly, when I was in the village and I fasted until the evening, nothing like this happened to me.' The old man said, 'In the village you fed yourself through your ears. But go away and from now on eat at the ninth hour and whatever you do, do it secretly.' As soon as he had begun to act on this advice, the Faster found it difficult to wait until the ninth hour. And those who knew him said, 'The Faster is possessed by the devil.' So he went to tell all this to the old man who said to him, 'This way is according to God.'

ZACHARIAS

Zacharias was the son of Abba Carion who brought him up in the desert of Scetis. The story of his youth is told under 'Carion'. Macarius and Moses consulted the boy and his wisdom was recognised also by Poemen. He seems to have died young.

1. Abba Macarius said to Abba Zacharias, 'Tell me, what is the work of a monk?' He said to him, 'How is it that you are asking me, Father?' Abba Macarius said, 'Zacharias, my child, you inspire me with confidence. It is God who urges me to ask you.' Then Zacharias said to him, 'Father, in my opinion, he is a monk who does violence to himself in everything.'

2. Going to draw water one day, Abba Moses found Abba Zacharias praying beside the well and the spirit of God rested above him.

3. One day Abba Moses said to brother Zacharias, 'Tell me what I ought to do?' At these words the latter threw himself on the ground at the old man's feet and said, 'Are you asking me, Father?' The old man said to him, 'Believe me, Zacharias, my son, I have seen the Holy Spirit descending upon you and since then I am constrained to ask you.' Then Zacharias drew his hood off his head put it under his feet and trampled on it, saying, 'The man who does not let himself be treated thus, cannot become a monk.'

4. While he was sitting one day in Scetis, Abba Zacharias had a vision. He went to tell his father, Carion, about it. The old man, who was an ascetic, did not understand this matter. He got up and beat him soundly, saying that it came from the demons. But Zacharias went on thinking about it, and he went by night to Abba Poemen, to tell the matter to him and how his heart burned within him. Then the old man, seeing that this came from God, said to him, 'Go to such and such an old man and whatever he tells you to do, do it.' Zacharias went to the old man and even before he could ask anything, he forestalled him, telling him everything that had happened and saying that this vision came from God. 'But go,' he said, 'and submit yourself to your father.'

5. Abba Poemen said that Abba Moses asked Abba Zacharias, who was at the point of death, 'What do you see?' He said, 'Is it not better to hold my peace, Father?' And he said, 'Yes, it is better to hold your peace, my child.' At the hour of his death, Abba Isidore who was sitting there looked towards heaven and said, 'Rejoice, Zacharias, my son, because the doors of the kingdom of heaven are opened to you.'

❖| ETA |❖

ISAIAH

1. Abba Isaiah said, 'Nothing is so useful to the beginner as insults. The beginner who bears insults is like a tree that is watered every day.'

2. He also said to those who were making a good beginning by putting themselves under the direction of the holy Fathers, 'As with purple dye, the first colouring is never lost.' And, 'Just as young shoots are easily trained back and bent, so it is with beginners who live in submission.'

3. He also said, 'A beginner who goes from one monastery to another is like an animal who jumps this way and that, for fear of the halter.'

4. He also said that when there was an agape and the brethren were eating in the church and talking to one another, the priest of Pelusia reprimanded them in these words, 'Brethren, be quiet. For I have seen a brother eating with you and drinking as many cups as you and his prayer is ascending to the presence of God like fire.'

5. It was said of Abba Isaiah that one day he took a branch and went to the threshing-floor to thresh and said to the owner, 'Give me some wheat.' The latter replied, 'Have you brought in the harvest, Father?' He said, 'No.' The owner said to him, 'How then can you expect to be given wheat, if you have not harvested?' Then the old man said to him, 'So then, if someone does not work, he does not receive wages?' The owner replied, 'No.' At that, the old man went away. Seeing what he had done, the brethren bowed before him, asking him to tell them why he had acted thus. The old man said to them, 'I did this as an example: whoever has not worked will not receive a reward from God.'

6. The same Abba Isaiah called one of the brethren, washed his feet, put a handful of lentils into the pot and brought them to him as soon as they had boiled. The brother said to him, 'They are not cooked, Abba.' The old man replied, 'Is it not enough simply to have seen the fire? That alone is a great consolation.'

7. He also said, 'When God wishes to take pity on a soul and it rebels, not bearing anything and doing its own will, he then allows it to suffer that which it does not want, in order that it may seek him again.'

8. He also said, 'When someone wishes to render evil for evil, he can injure his brother's soul even by a single nod of the head.'

9. The same Abba Isaiah, when someone asked him what avarice was, replied, 'Not to believe that God cares for you, to despair of the promises of God and to love boasting.'

10. He was also asked what calumny is and he replied, 'It is ignorance of the glory of God, and hatred of one's neighbour.'

11. He was also asked what anger is and he replied, "Quarrelling, lying and ignorance.'

ELIAS

1. Abba Elias said, 'For my part: I fear three things: the moment when my soul will leave my body, and when I shall appear before God, and when the sentence will be given against me.'

2. The old men said of Abba Agathon to Abba Elias, in Egypt, 'He is a good abba.' The old man answered them, 'In comparison with his own generation, he is good.' They said to him, 'And what is he in comparison with the ancients?' He gave them this answer, 'I have said to you that in comparison with his generation he is good but as to that of the ancients, in Scetis I have seen a man who, like Joshua the son of Nun could make the sun stand still in the heavens.' At these words they were astounded and gave glory to God.

3. Abba Elias, the minister, said, 'What can sin do where there is penitence? And of what use is love where there is pride?'

4. Abba Elias said, 'I saw someone who was carrying a skin of wine on his arm, and, in order to make the demons blush, for it was a fantasy, I said to the brother, "Of your charity take off your cloak." He took off his cloak, and was not found to be carrying anything. I say that so that you may not believe even that which you see or hear. Even more, observe your thoughts, and beware of what you have in your heart and your spirit, knowing that the demons put ideas into you so as to corrupt your soul by making it think of that which is not right, in order to turn your spirit from the consideration of your sins and of God.'

5. He also said, 'Men turn their minds either to their sins, or to Jesus, or to men.'

6. He also said, 'If the spirit does not sing with the body, labour is in vain. Whoever loves tribulation will obtain joy and peace later on.'

7. He also said, 'An old man was living in a temple and the demons came to say to him, "Leave this place which belongs to us," and the old man said, "No place belongs to you." Then they began to scatter his palm leaves about, one by one, and the old man went on gathering them together with perseverance. A little later the devil took his hand and pulled him to the door. When the old man reached the door, he seized the lintel with the other hand crying out, "Jesus, save me." Immediately the devil fled away. Then the old man began to weep. Then the Lord said to him, "Why are you weeping?" and the old man said, "Because the devils have dared to seize a man and treat him like this." The Lord said to him, "You had been careless. As soon as you turned to me again, you see I was

beside you." I say this, because it is necessary to take great pains, and anyone who does not do so, cannot come to his God. For he himself was crucified for our sake.'

8. A brother who followed the life of stillness in the monastery of the cave of Abba Saba came to Abba Elias and said to him, 'Abba, give me a way of life.' The old man said to the brother, 'In the days of our predecessors they took great care about these three virtues: poverty, obedience and fasting. But among monks nowadays avarice, self-confidence and great greed have taken charge. Choose whichever you want most.'

HERACLIDES

1. A brother who was attacked by the devil unburdened himself to Abba Heraclides. He told him the following in order to comfort him: 'An old man had a disciple who for many years had obeyed him in everything. Now one day when he was attacked by the devil, he made a prostration before the old man, saying, "Let me become a monk on my own." The old man replied, "Survey the district and we will build a cell for you." So they found a place a mile away. They went there and built the cell. The old man said to the brother, "What I tell you to do, do it. Each time you are afflicted, eat, drink, sleep; only do not come out of your cell until Saturday; then come to see me." The brother spent two days according to these orders, but the third day, a prey to *accidie,* he said to himself, "Why did the old man arrange that for me?" Standing up, he sang many psalms, and after sunset he ate, then went to lie down on his mat to sleep. But he saw an Ethiopian lying there who gnashed his teeth at him. Driven by great fear, he ran to the old man, knocked on his door and said, "Abba, have pity on me, open the door." The old man, seeing he had not obeyed his instructions did not open it till morning, very early; then he opened it, and found him outside imploring him to help him. Then, full of pity, he made him come inside. The other said, "Father, I need you; on my bed I saw a black Ethiopian, as I was going to sleep." The old man replied, "You suffered that because you did not keep to my instructions." Then, according to his capacity, he taught him the discipline of the solitary life, and in a short time he became a good monk.'

·| THETA |·

THEODORE OF PHERME

Theodore was trained as a monk in Scetis, probably by Macarius the Great. He was an educated man, and was ordained deacon, though he refused through humility to exercise this office. After the first devastation of Scetis he went to Pherme, which Palladius describes as 'a mountain in Egypt . . . which borders on the great desert of Scetis'.

1. Abba Theodore of Pherme had acquired three good books. He came to Abba Macarius and said to him, 'I have three excellent books from which I derive profit; the brethren also make use of them and derive profit from them. Tell me what I ought to do: keep them for my use and that of the brethren, or sell them and give the money to the poor?' The old man answered him in this way, 'Your actions are good; but it is best of all to posses nothing.' Hearing that, he went and sold his books and gave the money for them to the poor.

[73]

2. A brother lived in the Cells and in his solitude he was troubled. He went to tell Abba Theodore of Pherme about it. The old man said to him, 'Go, be more humble in your aspirations, place yourself under obedience and live with others.' Later, he came back to the old man and said, 'I do not find any peace with others.' The old man said to him, 'If you are not at peace either alone or with others, why have you become a monk? Is it not to suffer trials? Tell me how many years you have worn the habit?' He replied, 'For eight years.' Then the old man said to him, 'I have worn the habit seventy years and on no day have I found peace. Do you expect to obtain peace in eight years?' At these words the brother went away strengthened.

3. A brother came to Abba Theodore and spent three days begging him to say a word to him without getting any reply. So he went away grieved. Then the old man's disciple said to him, 'Abba, why did you not say a word to him? See, he has gone away grieved.' The old man said to him, 'I did not speak to him, for he is a trafficker who seeks to glorify himself through the words of others.'

4. He also said, 'If you are friendly with someone who happens to fall into the temptation of fornication, offer him your hand, if you can, and deliver him from it. But if he falls into heresy and you cannot persuade him to turn from it, separate yourself quickly from him, in case, if you delay, you too may be dragged down with him into the pit.

5. It was said of Abba Theodore of Pherme that the three things he held to be fundamental were: poverty, asceticism, flight from men.

6. One day Abba Theodore was entertaining himself with the brethren. While they were eating, they drank their cups with respect, but in silence, without even saying 'pardon'. So Abba Theodore said, 'The monks have lost their manners and do not say, "pardon."'

7. A brother questioned him saying, 'Abba, would you approve of my not eating bread for several days?' The old man said to him, 'You do well, and I have done the same.' The brother said, 'I mean to take my chick-peas to the bakery, and have them made into flour.' The old man replied, 'If you are going to the bakery, why not make the flour into bread? What need is there to go out twice?'

8. One of the old men came to Abba Theodore and said to him, 'Look how such and such a brother has returned to the world.' The old man said to him, 'Does that surprise you? No, rather be astonished when you hear that someone has been able to escape the jaws of the enemy.'

9. A brother came to Abba Theodore and began to converse with him about things which he had never yet put into practice. So the old man said to him, 'You have not yet found a ship nor put your cargo aboard it and before you have sailed, you have already arrived at the city. Do the work first; then you will have the speed you are making now.'

10. The same abba came one day to see Abba John, a eunuch from birth, and during their conversation he said to him, "When I was at Scetis, the works of the soul were our work, and we considered manual work to be subordinate; now the work of the soul has become subordinate and what was secondary is the chief work.'

11. A brother questioned him saying, 'What is the work of the soul which we now consider to be subordinate, and what is that which was subordinate and which we now consider to be our chief work?' The old man said, 'Everything you do as a commandment of God is the work of the soul; but to work and to gather goods together for a personal motive ought to be held as subordinate.' Then the brother said, 'Explain this matter to me.' So the old man said, 'Suppose you hear it said that I am ill and you ought to visit me; you say to yourself, "Shall I leave my work and go now? I had better finish my work and then go." Then another idea comes along and perhaps you never go; or again, another brother says to you, "Lend me a hand, brother"; and you say, "Shall I leave my own work and go and work with him? If you do not go, you are disregarding the commandment of God which is the work of the soul, and doing the work of your hands which is subordinate.'

12. Abba Theodore of Pherme said, 'The man who remains standing when he repents, has not kept the commandment.'

13. He also said, 'There is no other virtue than that of not being scornful.'

14. He also said, 'The man who has learnt the sweetness of the cell flees from his neighbour but not as though he despised him.'

15. He also said, 'If I do not cut myself off from these feelings of compassion, they will not let me be a monk.'

16. He also said, 'In these days many take their rest before God gives it them.'

17. He also said, 'Do not sleep in a place where there is a woman.'

18. A brother said to Abba Theodore, 'I wish to fulfil the commandments.' The old man told him that Abba Theonas had said to him, 'I want to fill my spirit with God.' Taking some flour to the bakery, he had made loaves which he gave to the poor who asked him for them; others asked for more, and he gave them the baskets, then the cloak he was wearing, and he came back to his cell with his loins girded with his cape. Afterwards he took himself to task telling himself that he had still not fulfilled the commandment of God.'

19. Once when Abba Joseph was ill, he sent someone to say to Abba Theodore, 'Come here, that I may see you before I leave the body.' It was the middle of the week and he did not go, but sent to say to him, 'If you wait until Saturday, I shall come; but if you depart, we shall see one another in the world to come.'

20. A brother said to Abba Theodore, 'Speak a word to me, for I am perishing,' and sorrowfully he said to him. 'I am myself in danger, so what can I say to you?'

21. A brother came to see Abba Theodore to learn weaving from him. He took a rope with him. The old man said to him, 'Go, and come back early tomorrow.' Getting up, the old man steeped the rope and prepared what was necessary, saying, 'Work in such and such a way,' and he left him. Then he went back to his cell and sat down. When the time came he gave the brother something to eat and sent him away. The brother returned in the small hours and the old man said to him, 'Pick up your rope and take it away, for you have come to cast me into temptation and trouble.' So he did not let him come in any more.

22. Abba Theodore's disciple said, 'Someone came today to sell some onions and he filled a basin with them for me. The old man said, 'Fill one with wheat and give it to him.' There were two heaps of wheat, one of good wheat, the other of unsorted wheat. I filled him a basin of the unsorted wheat. Then the old man looked at me with anger and sorrow, and from fear, I fell down on the ground and broke the basin. When I made a prostration before him the old man said, 'Get up, it is not your fault but mine, because of what I said to you.' Then he went and filled his lap with good wheat and gave it to the tradesman with the onions.

23. One day Abba Theodore went to draw water with a brother. The brother going ahead, saw a dragon in the lake. The old man said to him, 'Go, and walk on his head.' But he was afraid and did not go. So the old man went. The beast saw him and fled away into the desert, as if it was ashamed.

24. Abba Theodore was asked, 'If there was a sudden catastrophe, would you be frightened, abba?' The old man replied, 'Even if the heavens and the earth were to collide, Theodore would not be frightened.' He had prayed God to take away fear from him and it was because of this that he was questioned.

25. It was said about him that, though he was made a deacon at Scetis, he refused to exercise the office and fled to many places from it. Each time the old men brought him back to Scetis, saying, 'Do not leave your deaconate.' Abba Theodore said to them, 'Let me pray God that he may tell me for certain whether I ought to take my part in the liturgy.' Then he prayed God in this manner, 'If it is your will that I should stand in this place, make me certain of it.' Then appeared to him a column of fire, reaching from earth to heaven, and a voice said to him, 'If you can become like this pillar, go, be a deacon.' On hearing this he decided never to accept the office. When he went to church the brethren bowed before him saying, 'If you do not wish to be deacon, at least hold the chalice.' But he refused, saying, 'If you do not leave me alone, I shall leave this place.' So they left him in peace.

26. It was said of him, that when Scetis was laid waste, he went to live in Pherme. When he grew old he was ill. So he was brought food. Whatever the first one brought him, he gave to the second,

and so on; what he received from the first, he offered to the next. When the time to eat came, he ate what the one who came then brought him.

27. It was said of Abba Theodore that when he settled down at Scetis, a demon came to him wanting to enter his cell, but he bound him to the outside of his cell. Once more another demon tried to enter, and he bound him too. A third demon came as well, and finding the other two bound, said to them, 'Why are you standing outside like this?' They said to him, 'He is sitting inside, and will not let us enter.' So the demon tried to enter by force. The old man bound him too. Fearing the prayers of the old man, they begged him, saying, 'Let us go,' and the old man said to them, 'Go away.' Then they went off covered with confusion.

28. One of the Fathers told this about Abba Theodore of Pherme: 'One evening I came to him and found him wearing a torn habit, his chest bare and his cowl hanging in front of it. Now it happened that a great man came to see him. When he had knocked, the old man went to open the door, and having met him, sat down at the door to talk with him. Then I took one side of his cape and covered his shoulders with it. But the old man put out his hand and snatched it off. When the great man had gone, I said to him, 'Abba, why did you do that? This man came to be edified, perhaps he will be shocked.' Then the old man said to me, 'What do you mean, abba? Are we still the slaves of men? We did what was necessary, the rest is superfluous. He who wishes to be edified, let him be edified; he who wishes to be shocked, let him be shocked; as for me, I meet people as they find me.' Then he said to his disciple, 'If someone comes to see me, do not say anything out of human respect, but if I am eating, say to him, "He is eating"; and if I am sleeping, say to him, "He is sleeping."'

29. Three thieves came to him one day and while the first two held him, the third took away his property. When he had taken the books, he wanted to take the habit as well. So he said to them, 'Leave that.' But they did not agree. So, fighting with his hands he pushed them both away. Seeing this, they were very frightened. Then the old man said to them, 'Do not fear; divide these things into four parts: take three and leave me one.' So they did this and in his part he got the habit which he used for the *synaxis*.

THEODORE OF ENATON

Theodore of Enaton was a companion of Abba Or and a disciple of Abba
Amoun. He went to Enaton in 308, a monastery nine miles west of
Alexandria. By the end of the fourth century it was the leading monastery
in Egypt under its vigorous abbot, Longinus. Theodore was still alive in
364.

1. Abba Theodore of Enaton said, 'When I was young, I lived in
the desert. One day I went to the bakery to make two loaves, and
there I found a brother also wanting to make bread, but there was
no-one to help him. So I put mine on one side, to lend him a hand.
When the work was done, another brother came, and again I lent
him a hand in cooking his food. Then a third came, and I did the
same; and similarly one after the other, I baked for each of those
who came. I made six batches. Later I made my own two loaves,
since no-one else came.'

2. It was said of Abba Theodore and Abba Lucius of Enaton that
they spent fifty years mocking their temptations by saying, 'After
this winter, we will leave here.' When the summer came, they said,
'After this summer, we will go away from here.' They passed all
their lives in this way, these Fathers whose memory we should
always preserve.

3. Abba Theodore of Enaton said, 'If God reproaches us for
carelessness in our prayers and infidelities in our psalmody, we
cannot be saved.'

THEODORE OF SCETIS

1. Abba Theodore of Scetis said, 'A thought comes to me which
troubles me and does not leave me free; but not being able to lead
me to act, it simply stops me progressing in virtue; but a vigilant
man would cut it off and get up to pray.'

THEODORE OF ELEUTHEROPOLIS

1. Abba Abraham of Iberia asked Abba Theodore of Eleutheropolis, 'Father, which is right? Ought I to seek glory for myself,

or ignominy?' The old man said, 'As far as I am concerned, I prefer to seek glory rather than ignominy. If I do something good, and praise myself for it, I can condemn my thoughts by saying to myself that I do not deserve the praise; but ignominy comes from evil deeds. How then can I appease my conscience if men have been shocked because of me? It is better, therefore, to do good and praise oneself for it.' Abba Abraham said, 'Father, you have spoken well.'

2. Abba Theodore said, 'Privation of food mortifies the body of the monk.' Another old man said, 'Vigils mortify it still more.'

3. Abba Theodore also said, 'If you are temperate, do not judge the fornicator, for you would then transgress the law just as much. And he who said, "Do not commit formication," also said, "Do not judge." '*

THEONAS

1. Abba Theonas said, 'When we turn our spirit from the contemplation of God, we become the slaves of carnal passions.'

THEOPHILUS THE ARCHBISHOP

Theophilus, Archbishop of Alexandria, was much opposed to Origenism and expelled those who held with Origen's teaching from Nitria and Cells. His quarrel with the Four Tall Brethren was particularly fierce. He was however reconciled with the monks before his death in A.D. 412. The ambiguity of his relationship with the monks is mirrored in these sayings attributed to him.

1. One day blessed Theophilus the archbishop came to the mountain of Nitria and the abba of the mountain came to meet him. The archbishop said to him, 'Father, in this way of life which you follow, what do you find to be best?' The old man said to him, 'The act of accusing myself, and of constantly reproaching myself to

*3 is from J.-C. Guy's text (p. 22).

myself.' Abba Theophilus said to him, 'There is no other way but this.'

2. The same Abba Theophilus, the archbishop, came to Scetis one day. The brethren who were assembled said to Abba Pambo, 'Say something to the archbishop, so that he may be edified.' The old man said to them, 'If he is not edified by my silence, he will not be edified by my speech.'

3. Theophilus the archbishop summoned some Fathers to go to Alexandria one day, to pray and to destroy the heathen temples there. As they were eating with him, they were brought some veal for food and they ate it without realising what it was. The bishop, taking a piece of meat, offered it to the old man beside him, saying, 'Here is a nice piece of meat, abba, eat it.' But he replied, 'Till this moment, we believed we were eating vegetables, but if it is meat, we do not eat it.' None of them tasted any more of the meat which was brought.

4. The same Abba Theophilus said, 'What fear, what trembling, what uneasiness will there be for us when our soul is separated from the body. Then indeed the force and strength of the adverse powers come against us, the rulers of darkness, those who command the world of evil, the principalities, the powers, the spirits of evil. They accuse our souls as in a lawsuit, bringing before it all the sins it has committed, whether deliberately or through ignorance, from its youth until the time when it has been taken away. So they stand accusing it of all it has done. Furthermore, what anxiety do you suppose the soul will have at that hour, until sentence is pronounced and it gains its liberty. That is its hour of affliction, until it sees what will happen to it. On the other hand, the divine powers stand on the opposite side, and they present the good deeds of the soul. Consider the fear and trembling of the soul standing between them until in judgement it receives the sentence of the righteous judge. If it is judged worthy, the demons will receive their punishment, and it will be carried away by the angels. Then thereafter you will be without disquiet, or rather you will live according to that which is written: "Even as the habitation of those who rejoice is in you." (Ps. 87.7) Then will the Scripture be fulfilled: "Sorrow and sighing shall flee away." (Isaiah 35.10)

'Then your liberated soul will go on to that joy and ineffable glory in which it will be established. But if it is found to have lived carelessly, it will hear that terrible voice: "Take away the ungodly, that he may not see the glory of the Lord." (cf. Isaiah 26.10) Then the day of anger, the day of affliction, the day of darkness and shadow seizes upon it. Abandoned to outer darkness and condemned to everlasting fire it will be punished through the ages without end. Where then is the vanity of the world? Where is vain-glory? Where is carnal life? Where is enjoyment? Where is imagination? Where is ease? Where is boasting? Riches? Nobility? Father, mother, brother? Who could take the soul out of its pains when it is burning in the fire, and remove it from bitter torments?

'Since this is so, in what manner ought we not to give ourselves to holy and devout works? What love ought we to acquire? What manner of life? What virtues? What speed? What diligence? What prayer? What prudence? Scripture says: "In this waiting, let us make every effort to be found blameless and without reproach in peace." (cf. I Cor. 1.7–8) In this way, we shall be worthy to hear it said: "Come, O blessed of my Father, inherit the kingdom prepared for you from the foundation of the world." (Matt. 25.34) Amen.'

5. The same Abba Theophilus, the archbishop, at the point of death, said, 'You are blessed, Abba Arsenius, because you have always had this hour in mind.'

THEODORA

Theodora was one of the great women ascetics of the desert. Palladius mentions a Theodora 'the wife of the tribune who reached such a depth of poverty that she became a recipient of alms and finally died in the monastery of Hesychas near the sea'. She consulted Archbishop Theophilus and appears as a woman consulted by many monks about monastic life.

1. Amma Theodora asked Archbishop Theophilus about some words of the apostle saying, 'What does this mean, "Knowing how to profit by circumstances"?' (Col. 4, 5) He said to her, 'This saying

shows us how to profit at all times. For example, is it a time of excess for you? By humility and patience buy up the time of excess, and draw profit from it. Is it the time of shame? Buy it up by means of resignation and win it. So everything that goes against us can, if we wish, become profitable to us.'

2. Amma Theodora said, 'Let us strive to enter by the narrow gate. Just as the trees, if they have not stood before the winter's storms cannot bear fruit, so it is with us; this present age is a storm and it is only through many trials and temptations that we can obtain an inheritance in the kingdom of heaven.'

3. She also said, 'It is good to live in peace, for the wise man practises perpetual prayer. It is truly a great thing for a virgin or a monk to live in peace, especially for the younger ones. However, you should realize that as soon as you intend to live in peace, at once evil comes and weighs down your soul through *accidie*, faintheartedness, and evil thoughts. It also attacks your body through sickness, debility, weakening of the knees, and all the members. It dissipates the strength of soul and body, so that one believes one is ill and no longer able to pray. But if we are vigilant, all these temptations fall away. There was, in fact a monk who was seized by cold and fever every time he began to pray, and he suffered from headaches, too. In this condition, he said to himself, "I am ill, and near to death; so now I will get up before I die and pray." By reasoning in this way, he did violence to himself and prayed. When he had finished, the fever abated also. So, by reasoning in this way, the brother resisted, and prayed and was able to conquer his thoughts.'

4. The same Amma Theodora said, 'A devout man happened to be insulted by someone, and he said to him, "I could say as much to you, but the commandment of God keeps my mouth shut."' Again she said this, 'A Christian discussing the body with a Manichean expressed himself in these words, "Give the body discipline and you will see that the body is for him who made it."'

5. The same amma said that a teacher ought to be a stranger to the desire for domination, vain-glory, and pride; one should not be able to fool him by flattery, nor blind him by gifts, nor conquer him by the stomach, nor dominate him by anger; but he should be

patient, gentle and humble as far as possible; he must be tested and without partisanship, full of concern, and a lover of souls.

6. She also said that neither asceticism, nor vigils nor any kind of suffering are able to save, only true humility can do that. There was an anchorite who was able to banish the demons; and he asked them, 'What makes you go away? Is it fasting?' They replied, 'We do not eat or drink.' 'Is it vigils?' They replied, 'We do not sleep.' 'Is it separation from the world?' 'We live in the deserts.' 'What power sends you away then?' They said, 'Nothing can overcome us, but only humility.' 'Do you see how humility is victorious over the demons?'

7. Amma Theodora also said, 'There was a monk, who, because of the great number of his temptations said, "I will go away from here." As he was putting on his sandals, he saw another man who was also putting on his sandals and this other monk said to him, "Is it on my account that you are going away? Because I go before you wherever you are going." '

8. The same amma was asked about the conversations one hears; 'If one is habitually listening to secular speech, how can one yet live for God alone, as you suggest?' She said, 'Just as when you are sitting at table and there are many courses, you take some but without pleasure, so when secular conversations come your way, have your heart turned towards God, and thanks to this disposition, you will hear them without pleasure, and they will not do you any harm.'

9. Another monk suffered bodily irritation and was infested with vermin. Now originally he had been rich. So the demons said to him, 'How can you bear to live like this, covered with vermin?' But this monk, because of the greatness of his soul, was victorious over them.

10. Another of the old men questioned Amma Theodora saying, 'At the resurrection of the dead, how shall we rise?' She said, 'As pledge, example, and as prototype we have him who died for us and is risen, Christ our God.'*

---

*8–10 are additions from J.-C. Guy's text (p. 23).

⋄| IOTA |⋄

JOHN THE DWARF

John the Dwarf, son of poor parents in Tese, was born about 339. The second story here clearly belongs to his youth at home before he became a monk, while he was living with his family. At the age of eighteen he went to Scetis and was trained by Abba Ammoes for twelve years. One of the most vivid characters in the desert, he attracted many disciples and in order to preserve his own solitude he dug himself a cave underground. He was ordained priest, and the number of his sayings, recorded and preserved, points to his importance among his disciples. After 407 he went to Suez and the Mountain of Anthony.

1. It was said of Abba John the Dwarf that he withdrew and lived in the desert at Scetis with an old man of Thebes. His abba, taking a piece of dry wood, planted it and said to him, 'Water it every day with a bottle of water, until it bears fruit.' Now the water was so far away that he had to leave in the evening and return the following morning. At the end of three years the wood came to life

[85]

and bore fruit. Then the old man took some of the fruit and carried it to the church saying to the brethren, 'Take and eat the fruit of obedience.'

2. It was said of Abba John the Dwarf, that one day he said to his elder brother, 'I should like to be free of all care, like the angels, who do not work, but ceaselessly offer worship to God.' So he took off his cloak and went away into the desert. After a week he came back to his brother. When he knocked on the door, he heard his brother say, before he opened it 'Who are you?' He said, 'I am John, your brother.' But he replied, 'John has become an angel, and henceforth he is no longer among men.' Then the other begged him saying, 'It is I.' However, his brother did not let him in, but left him there in distress until morning. Then, opening the door, he said to him, 'You are a man and you must once again work in order to eat.' Then John made a prostration before him, saying, 'Forgive me.'

3. Abba John the Dwarf said, 'If a king wanted to take possession of his enemy's city, he would begin by cutting off the water and the food and so his enemies, dying of hunger, would submit to him. It is the same with the passions of the flesh: if a man goes about fasting and hungry the enemies of his soul grow weak.'

4. He also said, 'He who gorges himself and talks with a boy has already in his thought committed fornication with him.'

5. He also said, 'Going up the road again towards Scetis with some ropes, I saw the camel driver talking and he made me angry; so, leaving my goods, I took to flight.'

6. On another occasion in summertime, he heard a brother talking angrily to his neighbour, saying, 'Ah! you too?' So leaving the harvest, he took to flight.

7. Some old men were entertaining themselves at Scetis by having a meal together; amongst them was Abba John. A venerable priest got up to offer drink, but nobody accepted any from him, except John the Dwarf. They were surprised and said to him, 'How is it that you, the youngest, dared to let yourself be served by the priest?' Then he said to them, 'When I get up to offer drink, I am glad when everyone accepts it, since I am receiving my reward; that is the reason, then, that I accepted it, so that he also might gain his

reward and not be grieved by seeing that no-one would accept anything from him.' When they heard this, they were all filled with wonder and edification at his discretion.

8. One day when he was sitting in front of the church, the brethren were consulting him about their thoughts. One of the old men who saw it became a prey to jealousy and said to him, 'John, your vessel is full of poison.' Abba John said to him, 'That is very true, abba; and you have said that when you only see the outside, but if you were able to see the inside, too, what would you say then?'

9. The brethren used to tell how the brethren were sitting one day at an *agape* and one brother at table began to laugh. When he saw that, Abba John began to weep, saying, 'What does this brother have in his heart, that he should laugh, when he ought to weep, because he is eating at an *agape*?'

10. Some brethren came one day to test him to see whether he would let his thoughts get dissipated and speak of the things of this world. They said to him, 'We give thanks to God that this year there has been much rain and the palm trees have been able to drink, and their shoots have grown, and the brethren have found manual work.' Abba John said to them, 'So it is when the Holy Spirit descends into the hearts of men; they are renewed and they put forth leaves in the fear of God.'

11. It was said of him that one day he was weaving rope for two baskets, but he made it into one without noticing, until it had reached the wall, because his spirit was occupied in contemplation.

12. Abba John said, 'I am like a man sitting under a great tree, who sees wild beasts and snakes coming against him in great numbers. When he cannot withstand them any longer, he runs to climb the tree and is saved. It is just the same with me; I sit in my cell and I am aware of evil thoughts coming against me, and when I have no more strength against them, I take refuge in God by prayer and I am saved from the enemy.'

13. Abba Poemen said of Abba John the Dwarf that he had prayed God to take his passions away from him so that he might become free from care. He went and told an old man this: 'I find myself in peace, without an enemy,' he said. The old man said to

him, 'Go, beseech God to stir up warfare so that you may regain the affliction and humility that you used to have, for it is by warfare that the soul makes progress.' So he besought God and when warfare came, he no longer prayed that it might be taken away, but said, 'Lord, give me strength for the fight.'

14. Abba John said, 'Here is what one of the old men in ecstasy said: "Three monks were standing at the edge of the sea, and a voice came to them from the other side saying, 'Take wings of fire and come here to me.' The first two did so and reached the other shore, but the third remained, crying and weeping exceedingly. But later wings were given to him also, not of fire, but weak and without strength, so that with great difficulty he reached the other shore, sometimes under water, sometimes above it. So it is with the present generation; if they are given wings they are not of fire, but wings that are weak and without power." '

15. A brother questioned Abba John saying, 'How is it that my soul, bruised with wounds, does not blush to speak against my neighbour?' The old man told him a parable relating to slander, 'There was a poor man who had a wife. He saw another very beautiful woman and he took her. They were both quite naked. A feast was being held somewhere near and both women begged him to take them with him. Taking both of them, he put them into a barrel and put them aboard a ship and so they reached the place. When it became hot, the people lay down to rest. One of the women looked out of the barrel and seeing no-one, went to a pile of rubbish and joining old rags together, made herself a girdle and then walked about confidently. The other, sitting inside the barrel, naked, said, "Look at that courtesan who is not ashamed to walk about naked." Grieved at this, her husband said to her, "This is truly wonderful! She at least hides her nakedness, but, as for you, you are completely naked; are you not ashamed to say that?" So it is when one speaks against one's neighbour.'

16. The old man also said this to a certain brother about the soul which wishes to be converted, 'There was in a city a courtesan who had many lovers. One of the governors approached her, saying, "Promise me you will be good, and I will marry you." She promised this and he took her and brought her to his house. Her lovers,

seeking her again, said to one another, "That lord has taken her with him to his house, so if we go to his house and he learns of it, he will condemn us. But let us go to the back, and whistle to her. Then, when she recognizes the sound of the whistle she will come down to us; as for us, we shall be unassailable." When she heard the whistle, the woman stopped her ears and withdrew to the inner chamber and shut the doors.' The old man said that this courtesan is our soul, that her lovers are the passions and other men; that the lord is Christ; that the inner chamber is the eternal dwelling; those who whistle are the evil demons, but the soul always takes refuge in the Lord.

17. One day when Abba John was going up to Scetis with some other brothers, their guide lost his way for it was night-time. So the brothers said to Abba John, 'What shall we do, abba, in order not to die wandering about, for the brother has lost the way?' The old man said to them, 'If we speak to him, he will be filled with grief and shame. But look here, I will pretend to be ill and say I cannot walk any more; then we can stay here till the dawn.' This he did. The others said, 'We will not go on either, but we will stay with you.' They sat there until the dawn, and in this way they did not upset the brother.

18. There was an old man at Scetis, very austere of body, but not very clear in his thoughts. He went to see Abba John to ask him about forgetfulness. Having received a word from him, he returned to his cell and forgot what Abba John had said to him. He went off again to ask him and having heard the same word from him he returned with it. As he got near his cell, he forgot it again. This he did many times; he went there, but while he was returning he was overcome by forgetfulness. Later, meeting the old man he said to him, 'Do you know, abba, that I have forgotten again what you said to me? But I did not want to overburden you, so I did not come back.' Abba John said to him, 'Go and light a lamp.' He lit it. He said to him, 'Bring some more lamps, and light them from the first.' He did so. Then Abba John said to the old man, 'Has that lamp suffered any loss from the fact that other lamps have been lit from it?' He said, 'No.' The old man continued, 'So it is with John; even if the whole of Scetis came to see me, they would not separate me from the love of Christ. Consequently, whenever you want to, come

to me without hesitation.' So, thanks to the endurance of these two men, God took forgetfulness away from the old man. Such was the work of the monks of Scetis; they inspire fervour in those who are in the conflict and do violence to themselves to win others to do good.

19. A brother questioned Abba John, saying, 'What ought I to do? A brother often comes to fetch me for work, and since I am ill and weak, I get tired out working; what should I do, in order to keep the commandment?' The old man answered him saying, 'Caleb said to Joshua, the son of Nun: "I was forty years old when Moses, the servant of the Lord, sent me with you into the desert in this land; and now I am eighty-five years of age; as then, so now I can still take part in the battle and withdraw from it." (cf. Jos. 14.7–11) In the same way you, too, if you are strong enough to go out and to come in, go to work; but if you cannot do it, sit down in your cell and weep for your sins and when they find you filled with compunction, they will not compel you to go out.'

20. Abba John said, 'Who sold Joseph?' A brother replied saying, 'It was his brethren.' The old man said to him, 'No, it was his humility which sold him, because he could have said, "I am their brother" and have objected, but, because he kept silence, he sold himself by his humility. It is also his humility which set him up as chief in Egypt.'

21. Abba John said, 'We have put the light burden on one side, that is to say, self-accusation, and we have loaded ourselves with a heavy one, that is to say, self-justification.'

22. He also said, 'Humility and the fear of God are above all virtues.'

23. The same abba was sitting in church one day and he gave a sigh, unaware that there was someone behind him. When he noticed it he lay prostrate before him, saying, 'Forgive me, abba, for I have not yet made a beginning.'

24. The same abba said to his disciple, 'Let us honour one only, and everyone will honour us; for if we despise one, that is God, everyone will despise us, and we will be lost.'

25. It was said of Abba John that when he went to church at Scetis, he heard some brethren arguing, so he returned to his cell. He went round it three times and then went in. Some brethren who had seen him, wondered why he had done this, and they went to ask him. He said to them, 'My ears were full of that argument, so I circled round in order to purify them, and thus I entered my cell with my mind at rest.'

26. One day a brother came to Abba John's cell. It was late and he was in a hurry to leave. While they were speaking of the virtues, dawn came without their noticing it. Abba John came out with him to see him off, and they went on talking until the sixth hour. Then he made him go in again and after they had eaten, he sent him away.

27. Abba John gave this advice, 'Watching means to sit in the cell and be always mindful of God. This is what is meant by, "I was on the watch and God came to me." ' (Matt. 25, 36)

28. He also said, 'Who is as strong as the lion? And yet, because of his greed he falls into the net, and all his strength is brought low.'

29. He also said that the Fathers of Scetis ate bread and salt and said, 'We do not regard bread and salt as indispensable.' So they were strong for the work of God.

30. One day a brother came to Abba John to take away some baskets. He came out and said to him, 'What do you want, brother?' He said, 'Baskets, abba.' Going inside to bring them to him, he forgot them, and sat down to weave. Again the brother knocked. When Abba John came out, the brother said, 'Bring me the baskets, abba.' The old man went in once more and sat down to weave. Once more the brother knocked and, coming out, Abba John said, 'What do you want, brother?' He replied, 'The baskets, abba.' Then, taking him by the hand, Abba John led him inside, saying, 'If you want the baskets, take them and go away, because really, I have no time for such things.'

31. A camel-driver came one day to pick up some goods and take them elsewhere. Going inside to bring him what he had woven, Abba John forgot about it because his spirit was fixed in God. So once more the camel-driver disturbed him by knocking on the door and once more Abba John went in and forgot. The camel-driver

knocked a third time and Abba John went in saying, 'Weaving—camel; weaving—camel.' He said this so that he would not forget again.

32. The same abba was very fervent. Now someone who came to see him praised his work, and he remained silent, for he was weaving a rope. Once again the visitor began to speak and once again he kept silence. The third time he said to the visitor, 'Since you came here, you have driven away God from me.'

33. An old man came to Abba John's cell and found him asleep, with an angel standing above him, fanning him. Seeing this, he withdrew. When Abba John got up, he said to his disciple, 'Did anyone come in while I was asleep?' He said, 'Yes, an old man.' Then Abba John knew that this old man was his equal, and that he had seen the angel.

34. Abba John said, 'I think it best that a man should have a little bit of all the virtues. Therefore, get up early every day and acquire the beginning of every virtue and every commandment of God. Use great patience, with fear and long-suffering, in the love of God, with all the fervour of your soul and body. Exercise great humility, bear with interior distress; be vigilant and pray often with reverence and groaning, with purity of speech and control of your eyes. When you are despised do not get angry; be at peace, and do not render evil for evil. Do not pay attention to the faults of others, and do not try to compare yourself with others, knowing you are less than every created thing. Renounce everything material and that which is of the flesh. Live by the cross, in warfare, in poverty of spirit, in voluntary spiritual asceticism, in fasting, penitence and tears, in discernment, in purity of soul, taking hold of that which is good. Do your work in peace. Persevere in keeping vigil, in hunger and thirst, in cold and nakedness, and in sufferings. Shut yourself in a tomb as though you were already dead, so that at all times you will think death is near.'

35. It was said of the same Abba John that when he returned from the harvest or when he had been with some of the old men, he gave himself to prayer, meditation and psalmody until his thoughts were re-established in their previous order.

36. One of the Fathers said of him, 'Who is this John, who by his humility has all Scetis hanging from his little finger?'

37. One of the Fathers asked Abba John the Dwarf, 'What is a monk?' He said, 'He is toil. The monk toils at all he does. That is what a monk is.'

38. Abba John the Dwarf said, 'There was a spiritual old man who lived a secluded life. He was held in high estimation in the city and enjoyed a great reputation. He was told that a certain old man, at the point of death, was calling for him, to embrace him before he fell asleep. He thought to himself, if I go by day, men will run after me, giving me great honour, and I shall not be at peace in all that. So I will go in the evening in the darkness and I shall escape everyone's notice. But lo, two angels were sent by God with lamps to give him light. Then the whole city came out to see his glory. The more he wished to flee from the glory, the more he was glorified. In this was accomplished that which is written: "He who humbles himself will be exalted."' (Luke 14.11)

39. Abba John the Dwarf said, 'A house is not built by beginning at the top and working down. You must begin with the foundations in order to reach the top.' They said to him, 'What does this saying mean?' He said, 'The foundation is our neighbour, whom we must win, and that is the place to begin. For all the commandments of Christ depend on this one.'

40. What follows was said about Abba John. The parents of a young girl died, and she was left an orphan; she was called Paësia. She decided to make her house a hospice, for the use of the Fathers of Scetis. So for a long time she gave hospitality and served the Fathers. But in the course of time, her resources were exhausted and she began to be in want.

Some wicked men came to see her and turned her aside from her aim. She began to live an evil life, to the point of becoming a prostitute. The Fathers, learning this, were deeply grieved, and calling Abba John the Dwarf said to him, 'We have learnt that this sister is living an evil life. While she could, she gave us charity, so now it is our turn to offer her charity and to go to her assistance. Go to see her then, and according to the wisdom which God has given you, put things right for her.' So Abba John went to her, and said to the old door-keeper, 'Tell your mistress I am here.' But she sent him away saying, 'From the beginning you have eaten her goods, and see how poor she is now.' Abba John said to her, 'Tell her, I have something which will be very helpful to her.' The door-keeper's children, mocking him, said to him, 'What have you to give her, that makes you want to meet her?' He replied, 'How do you know what I am going to give her?' The old woman went up and spoke to her mistress about him. Paësia said to her, 'These monks are always going about in the region of the Red Sea and finding pearls.' Then she got ready and said to the door-keeper, 'Please bring him to me.' As he was coming up, she prepared for him and lay down on the bed. Abba John entered and sat down beside her. Looking into her eyes, he said to her, 'What have you got against Jesus that you behave like this?' When she heard this she became completely rigid. Then Abba John bent his head and began to weep copiously. She asked him, 'Abba, why are you crying?' He raised his head, then lowered it again, weeping, and said to her, 'I see Satan playing in your face, how should I not weep?' Hearing this, she said to him, 'Abba, is it possible to repent?' He replied 'Yes.' She said, 'Take me wherever you wish.' 'Let us go,' he said and she got up to go with him. Abba John noticed that she did not make any arrangements with regard to her house; he said nothing, but he was surprised. When they reached the desert, the evening drew on. He, making a little pillow with the sand, and marking it with the sign of the cross, said to her, 'Sleep here.' Then, a little further on, he did the same for himself, said his prayers, and lay down. Waking in the middle of the night, he saw a shining path reaching from heaven to her, and he saw the angels of God bearing away her soul. So he got up and went to touch her feet. When he saw that she was dead he threw himself face downwards on the ground, praying to God. He heard this: 'One single hour of repentance has brought her more than the penitence of many who persevere without showing such fervour in repentance.'

41. The old man said that there were three philosophers who were friends. The first died and left his son to the care of one of the others. When he grew up he had intercourse with the wife of his guardian, who found them out and turned the boy out of doors. Although the young man came and asked his guardian to forgive

him he would not receive him, but said, 'Go and work for three
years as a ferryman and I will forgive you.' After three years the
young man came to him again, and this time he said, 'You still have
not done penance; go and work for three more years, and give away
all you earn, bearing all insults.' So he did this, and then his guardian
said to him, 'Now go to Athens and learn philosophy.' There was
an old man who sat at the philosophers' gate and he used to insult
everyone who entered it. When he insulted this young man, the boy
began to laugh, and the old man said, 'Why are you laughing, when
I have insulted you?' He told him, 'Would you not expect me to
laugh? For three years I have paid to be insulted and now I am
insulted free of charge. That is why I laughed.' Abba John said,
'The gate of the Lord is like that, and we Fathers go through many
insults in order to enter joyfully into the city of God.'

42. Abba John said to his brother, 'Even if we are entirely despised in the eyes of men, let us rejoice that we are honoured in the
sight of God.'

43. Abba Poemen said that Abba John said that the saints are like
a group of trees, each bearing different fruit, but watered from the
same source. The practices of one saint differ from those of another,
but it is the same Spirit that works in all of them.

44. Abba John said, 'If a man has in his soul the tools of God, he
will be able to stay in his cell, even if he has none of the tools of
this world. If a man has the tools of this world, but lacks those of
God, he can still use those tools to stay in the cell. But if a man has
neither the tools of God nor of this world, it is absolutely impossible
for him to stay in his cell.'

45. The old man also said, 'You know that the first blow the devil
gave to Job was through his possessions; and he saw that he had not
grieved him nor separated him from God. With the second blow,
he touched his flesh, but the brave athlete did not sin by any word
that came out of his mouth in that either. In fact, he had within his
heart that which is of God, and he drew on that source unceasingly.'

46. One day Abba John was sitting down in Scetis, and the
brethren came to him to ask him about their thoughts. One of the
elders said, 'John, you are like a courtesan who shows her beauty

to increase the number of her lovers.' Abba John kissed him and said, 'You are quite right, Father.' One of his disciples said to him, 'Do you not mind that in your heart?' But he said, 'No, I am the same inside as I am outside.'

47. They said that when he was given his wages for all the work he had done in the harvest, he took it to Scetis, saying, 'My widows and my orphans are in Scetis.'*

JOHN THE CENOBITE

1. A brother lived in a cenobium and he was a very vigorous ascetic. Some brothers who had heard about him in Scetis, came to see him. They entered the place where he was working. He greeted them, and turning round, went back to his work. When they saw what he was doing, the brethren said to him, 'John, who clothed you in the habit? Who made you a monk? Have you not been taught to take the sheepskin from the brothers and to say to them, let us pray; or perhaps, sit down.' He said to them, 'John, the sinner, has no time to attend to that.'

ISIDORE THE PRIEST

Isidore the Priest was a monk of Scetis and early companion of Macarius. He is mentioned by Cassian as one of the heads of the four communities in Scetis.

1. It was said of Abba Isidore, priest of Scetis, that when anyone had a brother who was sick, or careless or irritable, and wanted to send him away, he said, 'Bring him here to me.' Then he took charge of him and by his long-suffering he cured him.

2. A brother asked him, 'Why are the demons so frightened of you?' The old man said to him, 'Because I have practised asceticism

---

*41–7 are additions from J.-C. Guy's text (pp. 23–4).

since the day I became a monk, and not allowed anger to reach my lips.'

3. He also said that for forty years he had been tempted to sin in thought but that he had never consented either to covetousness or to anger.

4. He also said, 'When I was younger and remained in my cell I set no limit to prayer; the night was for me as much the time of prayer as the day.'

5. Abba Poemen used to say this about Abba Isidore: every night he plaited a bundle of palms, and the brethren pleaded with him saying, 'Rest a little, for you are getting old.' But he said to them, 'Even if Isidore were burned, and his ashes thrown to the winds, I would not allow myself any relaxation because the Son of God came here for our sake.'

6. The same abba said concerning Abba Isidore that his thoughts said to him, 'You are a great man.' He said to them, 'Am I to be compared with Abba Anthony; am I become like Abba Pambo, or like the other Fathers who pleased God?' When he said this he was at peace. When the demons who are at war with men tried to make him afraid, suggesting that, after all this, he would still go to hell, he replied, 'Even if I am sent there, I shall find you beneath me.'

7. Abba Isidore said, 'One day I went to the market place to sell some small goods; when I saw anger approaching me, I left the things and fled.'

8. Abba Isidore went one day to see Abba Theophilus, archbishop of Alexandria and when he returned to Scetis the brethren asked him, 'What is going on in the city?' But he said to them, 'Truly, brothers, I did not see the face of anyone there, except that of the archbishop.' Hearing this they were very anxious and said to him, 'Has there been a disaster there, then, abba?' He said, 'Not at all, but the thought of looking at anyone did not get the better of me.' At these words they were filled with admiration, and strengthened in their intention of guarding the eyes from all distraction.

9. The same Abba Isidore said, 'It is the wisdom of the saints to recognize the will of God. Indeed, in obeying the truth, man sur-

passes everything else, for he is the image and likeness of God. Of all evil suggestions, the most terrible is that of following one's own heart, that is to say, one's own thought, and not the law of God. A man who does this will be afflicted later on, because he has not recognized the mystery, and he has not found the way of the saints in order to work in it. For now is the time to labour for the Lord, for salvation is found in the day of affliction: for it is written: "By your endurance you will gain your lives." ' (Luke 21.19)

10. Abba Poemen also said about Abba Isidore that wherever he addressed the brothers in church he said only one thing, 'Forgive your brother, so that you also may be forgiven.'*

ISIDORE OF PELUSIA

1. Abba Isidore of Pelusia said, 'To live without speaking is better than to speak without living. For the former who lives rightly does good even by his silence but the latter does no good even when he speaks. When words and life correspond to one another they are together the whole of philosophy.'

2. The same abba said, 'Prize the virtues and do not be the slave of glory; for the former are immortal, while the latter soon fades.'

3. He also said, 'Many desire virtue, but fear to go forward in the way that leads to it, while others consider that virtue does not even exist. So it is necessary to persuade the former to give up their sloth, and teach the others what virtue really is.'

4. He also said, 'Vice takes men away from God and separates them from one another. So we must turn from it quickly and pursue virtue, which leads to God and unites us with another. Now the definition of virtue and of philosophy is: simplicity with prudence.'

5. He also said, 'The heights of humility are great and so are the depths of boasting; I advise you to attend to the first and not to fall into the second.'

*10 is an addition from J.-C. Guy's text (pp. 24–5).

6. He also said, 'The desire for possessions is dangerous and terrible, knowing no satiety; it drives the soul which it controls to the heights of evil. Therefore let us drive it away vigorously from the beginning. For once it has become master it cannot be overcome.'

ISAAC, PRIEST OF THE CELLS

Isaac of the Cells was an anchorite in Nitria. He was a disciple of Abba Cronius whom he succeeded as priest and superior in Nitria in 395. He was exiled by Archbishop Theophilus as an Origenist with the Four Tall Brothers.

Saying 5 introduces the theme of homosexual temptations which is noticeably absent from the first generation in Scetis; it appears as part of the decline in monastic standards after the devastations. There is in these sayings a nostalgia for the virtues and austerities of the early days which mark them as belonging to the third generation.

1. One day they came to make Abba Isaac a priest. Hearing this, he ran away to Egypt. He went into a field and hid himself in the midst of the hay. So the clergy went after him in pursuit. Reaching the same field, they stopped there to rest a little, for it was night. They unharnessed the ass to let it graze. The ass went close to the old man, so, when dawn came and they looked for her, they found Abba Isaac too, which filled them with astonishment. They wanted to bind him, but he did not allow it, saying, 'I will not run away again. For it is the will of God, and wherever I flee, I find that.'

2. Abba Isaac said, 'When I was younger, I lived with Abba Cronius. He would never tell me to do any work, although he was old and tremulous; but he himself got up and offered food to me and to everyone. Then I lived with Abba Theodore of Pherme and he did not tell me to do anything either, but he himself set the table and said to me, "Brother, if you want to, come and eat." I replied, "I have come to you to help you, why do you never tell me to do anything?" But the old man gave me no reply whatever. So I went to tell the old men. They came and said to him, "Abba, the brother has come to your holiness in order to help you. Why do you never

tell him to do anything?" The old man said to them, "Am I a cenobite, that I should give him orders? As far as I am concerned, I do not tell him anything, but if he wishes he can do what he sees me doing." From that moment I took the initiative and did what the old man was about to do. As for him, what he did, he did in silence; so he taught me to work in silence.'

3. Abba Isaac and Abba Abraham lived together. When he came home one day, Abba Abraham found Abba Isaac in tears. He asked him, 'Why are you weeping?' The old man replied, 'Why should we not weep? For where have we to go? Our Fathers are dead. Manual work is not enough to pay for the cost of the journey by boat for us to go and visit the old men, and so henceforth we are orphans; that is why I am weeping.'

4. Abba Isaac said, 'I knew a brother who wanted to eat an ear of wheat while he was harvesting in a field. He said to the foreman of the field, "Will you allow me to eat an ear of wheat?" The latter was astonished at these words and said to him, "Father, this field belongs to you, why are you asking me this?" See how conscientious the brother was.'

5. He also said to the brethren, 'Do not bring young boys here. Four churches in Scetis are deserted because of boys.'

6. It was said of Abba Isaac that he ate the ashes from the incense offering with his bread.

7. Abba Isaac said to the brethren, 'Our Fathers and Abba Pambo wore old garments woven from palm fronds and mended all over; now you are foppishly dressed. Go away from here; leave this place.' When they prepared to go harvesting he said to them, 'I am not giving you any more directions because you would not keep them.'

8. One of the Fathers related how, in the time of Abba Isaac, a brother came into the church of the Cells one day, wearing a little hood. The old man turned him out saying, 'This place is for monks; you are a secular and you may not live here.'

9. Abba Isaac said, 'I have never allowed a thought against my brother who has grieved me to enter my cell; I have seen to it that no brother should return to his cell with a thought against me.'

10. Abba Isaac had a serious illness which lasted for a long time. The brother made him a little broth out of flour into which he put some fruit. The old man did not want to taste it so the brother tempted him saying, 'Take a little, Father, because you are ill.' But the old man said to him, 'Truly, brother, I should like this illness to last for thirty years.'

11. Concerning Abba Isaac it was said that when he was at the point of death the old men gathered round him saying, 'What shall we do without you?' He said to them, 'See how I have walked before you; if you want to follow me and keep the commandments of God, God will send you his grace and will protect this place; but if you do not keep his commandments, you cannot remain in this place. We ourselves, when our Fathers were on the point of dying, were full of grief, but, keeping the Lord's commandments and their admonitions, we have held fast as though they were still with us. Do the same in your turn, and you will be saved.'

12. Abba Isaac said that Abba Pambo used to say, 'The monk's garment should be such that he could throw it out of his cell for three days and no-one would take it.'

JOSEPH OF PANEPHYSIS

Abba Joseph lived as a solitary in Panephysis with his disciples; Abba Lot and Abba Poemen consulted him. The group appears to have been of some importance; Cassian stayed there for some time and Conferences XI–XVII *and* XIX–XXIV *are situated there.*

1. Some Fathers went to Panephysis to see Abba Joseph and ask him what kind of reception they should give to the brethren to whom they gave lodging, whether they ought to mix with them and speak freely with them. Before they asked him, the old man said to his disciple, 'Consider what I am going to do today, and remain still.' Then the old man put two mats, one on his right and one on his left and said, 'Sit down.' Then he went inside his cell and put on beggar's garments. Then he came out again and walked in between them. After this, he went back to put on his own clothes again; coming out once more, he sat down between them. They were surprised at

the things he did. So he said to them: 'Have you considered what I have done?' They replied that they had. 'Was I changed by those contemptible garments?' They said 'No.' Then he said to them: 'I remained the same, then, in both sets of clothes, the former did not change me and the latter have not done me harm. This is how we ought to behave when we receive visiting brethren, according to the holy Gospel which says, "Render to Caesar the things which are Caesar's and to God the things which are God's." (Matt. 22.21) So when brothers come, let us receive them and speak freely with them. On the other hand, when we are alone we ought to weep, in order that we may persevere.' At these words the visitors were filled with astonishment because he had answered what they had in their hearts even before they had asked him and they gave glory to God.

2. Abba Poemen said to Abba Joseph, 'Tell me how to become a monk.' He said, 'If you want to find rest here below, and hereafter, in all circumstances say, Who am I? and do not judge anyone.'

3. The same abba asked Abba Joseph another question saying, 'What should I do when the passions attack me? Should I resist them, or let them enter?' The old man said to him, 'Let them enter and fight against them.' So he returned to Scetis where he remained. Now someone from Thebes came to Scetis and said to the brethren, 'I asked Abba Joseph if I ought to resist the passions when they approach, or let them enter and he replied I ought not to allow them the smallest entry but cut them off immediately.' When Abba Poemen learned that Abba Joseph had spoken to the brother from Thebes in this way, he got up and went to see him at Panephysis and said, 'Abba, I consulted you about my thoughts and you have said one thing to me, and another to the Theban.' The old man said to him, 'Do you not know that I love you?' He said, 'Yes.' 'And did you not say to me: speak to me as you speak to yourself?' 'That is right.' Then the old man said, 'Truly, if the passions enter you and you fight them you become stronger. I spoke to you as to myself. But there are others who cannot profit in this way if the passions approach them, and so they must cut them off immediately.'

4. A brother asked Abba Joseph, saying, 'What should I do, for I do not have the strength to bear evil, nor to work for charity's sake?' The old man said to him, 'If you cannot do any of these

things, at least guard your conscience from all evil with regard to your neighbour and you will be saved.'

5. One of the brethren related this, 'One day I went to lower Heracliopolis to see Abba Joseph. Now in the monastery there was a very good mulberry tree. At early dawn he said to me, 'Go and eat.' But as it was Friday I did not go, because of the fast; so I asked him, 'For God's sake, explain this to me. Here you are saying to me, go and eat but I did not go, because of the fast. I blushed for shame thinking of your command. I asked myself what was the old man's intention in saying that and I wondered if I ought to have done it, since he told me to.' The old man said, 'At the beginning the Fathers do not speak to the brothers as they ought to do, but rather in an ambiguous manner, and if they see that they do what is right, then they no longer speak like that, but tell them the truth when they know they are obedient in all things.'

6. Abba Joseph said to Abba Lot, 'You cannot be a monk unless you become like a consuming fire.'

7. Abba Lot went to see Abba Joseph and said to him, 'Abba, as far as I can I say my little office, I fast a little, I pray and meditate, I live in peace and as far as I can, I purify my thoughts. What else can I do?' Then the old man stood up and stretched his hands towards heaven. His fingers became like ten lamps of fire and he said to him, 'If you will, you can become all flame.'

8. A brother asked Abba Joseph this, 'I want to leave the monastery, and live as a solitary.' The old man said to him, 'Go wherever you find your soul is most at peace, and stay there, without blame.' The brother said to him, 'But I am at peace both in the monastery and in the solitary life; will you tell me what to do?' The Old man said to him, 'If you are at peace both in the monastery and in the solitary life, put these two thoughts as it were in the balance and wherever you see your thoughts will profit most and make progress, that is what you should do.'

9. One of the old men joined one of his companions and went with him to visit Abba Joseph. He said to him, 'Tell your disciple to saddle the ass.' The other replied, 'Call him, and he will do whatever you want.' 'What is his name?' 'I do not know.' 'How long

has he been with you, and you do not know his name?' He replied, 'For two years.' The other said, 'If in two years you have not learnt your disciple's name, do I need to know it for a single day?'

10. Some brothers happened one day to meet at Abba Joseph's cell. While they were sitting there, questioning him, he became cheerful and, filled with happiness he said to them, 'I am a king today, for I reign over the passions.'

11. It was said of Abba Joseph of Panephysis that when he was at the point of death, while some old men were seated round him, he looked towards the window and saw the devil sitting close to it. Then calling his disciple he said to him, 'Bring my stick, for there is one there who thinks I am getting old and have no more strength against him.' As he gripped his stick the old men saw that the devil fled through the window like a dog, and disappeared from sight.

JAMES

1. Abba James said, 'It is better to receive hospitality than to offer it.'

2. He warned anyone who receives praise to think of his sins and realize that he does not deserve what has been said of him.

3. He also said, 'Just as a lamp lights up a dark room, so the fear of God, when it penetrates the heart of a man illuminates him, teaching him all the virtues and commandments of God.'

4. He also said, 'We do not need words only, for, at the present time, there are many words among men, but we need works, for this is what is required, not words which do not bear fruit.'

HIERAX

1. A brother questioned Abba Hierax saying, 'Give me a word. How can I be saved?' The old man said to him, 'Sit in your cell, and if you are hungry, eat, if you are thirsty, drink; only do not speak evil of anyone, and you will be saved.'

2. He also said, 'I have never uttered, or wished to hear, a worldly remark.'

JOHN THE EUNUCH

1. In his youth Abba John the Eunuch questioned an old man, 'How have you been able to carry out the work of God in peace? For we cannot do it, not even with labour.' The old man said, 'We were able to do it, because we considered the work of God to be primary, and bodily needs to be subsidiary; but you hold bodily necessities to be primary and the work of God to be secondary; that is why you labour, and that is why the Saviour said to the disciples, "Seek first his kingdom and his righteousness, and all these things shall be yours as well." ' (Matt. 6.33)

2. Abba John said, 'Our Father, Abba Anthony, said he had never put his own personal advantage before the good of a brother.'

3. Abba John the Cilician, hegumen of Rhaithou, said to the brethren, 'My sons, in the same way that we have fled from the world, let us equally flee from the desires of the flesh.'

4. He also said, 'Let us imitate our Fathers: they lived in this place with much austerity and peace.'

5. He also said, 'My sons, let us not make this place dirty, since our Fathers cleansed it from the demons.'

6. And he said, 'This is a place for asceticism, not for worldly business.'

JOHN OF THE CELLS

1. Abba John of the Cells told us this story: 'There was in Egypt a very rich and beautiful courtesan, to whom noble and powerful people came. Now one day she happened to be near the church and she wanted to go in. The sub-deacon, who was standing at the doors, would not allow her to enter saying, "You are not worthy to enter the house of God, for you are impure." The bishop heard the noise of their argument and came out. Then the courtesan said to him, "He will not let me enter the church." So the Bishop said to her,

"You are not allowed to enter it, for you are not pure." She was filled with compunction and said to him, "Henceforth I will not commit fornication any more." The bishop said to her, "If you bring your wealth here, I shall know that you will not commit fornication any more." She brought her wealth and the bishop burnt it all in the fire. Then she went into the church, weeping and saying, "If this has happened to me below, what would I not have suffered above?" So she was converted and became a vessel of election.'

JOHN OF THE THEBAID

1. Abba John of the Thebaid said, 'First of all the monk must gain humility; for it is the first commandment of the Lord who said: "Blessed are the poor in spirit, for theirs is the kingdom of heaven." ' (Matt. 5.3)

ISIDORE THE PRIEST

1. It was said of Abba Isidore the Priest that one day a brother came to invite him to a meal. But the old man refused to go, saying, 'Adam was deceived by food and had to live outside Paradise.' The brother said to him, 'Are you so afraid to leave your cell?' The other responded, 'My child, I am afraid because the devil, like a roaring lion, seeketh whom he may devour.' (1 Peter 5.8) He often said, 'When someone gives himself a drink, he will not escape being attacked by thoughts. Lot, indeed, being constrained by his daughters, got drunk with wine, and through the effect of drunkenness, the devil easily brought him to a shameful act of fornication.'

2. Abba Isidore said, 'If you truly desire the kingdom of heaven, despise riches and respond to divine favours.'

3. He also said, 'It is impossible for you to live according to God if you love pleasures and money.'

4. He also said, 'If you fast regularly, do not be inflated with pride, but if you think highly of yourself because of it, then you

had better eat meat. It is better for a man to eat meat than to be inflated with pride and to glorify himself.'

5. He also said, 'Disciples must love as their fathers those who are truly their masters and fear them as their leaders; they should not lose their fear because of love, nor because of fear should love be obscured.'

6. He also said, 'If you desire salvation, do everything that leads you to it.'

7. It was said of Abba Isidore that when a brother went to see him, he would escape to the furthest corner of his cell. The brethren said to him, 'Abba, what are you doing?' He said, 'Even the wild animals, when they flee to their lairs, are saved.' He said this for the edification of the brethren.

JOHN THE PERSIAN

1. A demoniac boy came one day to be healed, and some brothers from an Egyptian monastery arrived. As one old man was coming out to meet them he saw a brother sinning with the boy, but he did not accuse him; he said, 'If God who has made them sees them and does not burn them, who am I to blame them?'

2. One of the Fathers related of Abba John the Persian that his great charity had brought him to a profound innocence. He dwelt in Arabia of Egypt. One day he borrowed some money from a brother and bought some flax for his work. Then a brother came and asked him, 'Abba, give me a little flax so that I can make myself a cloak.' He gave him some readily. Similarly, another brother came and asked him, 'Give me a little flax, so that I can make some cloth.' So he gave him some too. Others came and asked him for things and he simply gave them cheerfully. Later, the owner of the money came to reclaim it. The old man said to him, 'I will go and get it for you.' Because he could not return it to him, he went to Abba James, who was a deacon, to ask him to give him some money so that he could return it to the brother. On the way he found a coin

on the ground but he did not touch it. He said a prayer and returned to his cell. But the brother came once more pestering him about the money, and the old man said to him, 'I am very worried about it.' Once again he went, found the coin on the ground where it was lying and once again he said a prayer and returned to his cell. But the brother came back to pester him as before. The old man said to him, 'This time I will certainly bring it to you.' Once again he got up and went to the place where the coin lay on the ground. He said a prayer and went to tell Abba James, 'Abba, as I was coming here, I found this coin on the road. Please make it known in the neighbourhood, in case someone has lost it; and if its owner is found, give it him.' So the old man went and asked about it for three days, but no one who had lost a piece of money came. Then the old man said to Abba James, 'Then if no-one has lost it, give it to this brother, for I owe it him. As I was coming to ask you for alms in order to give him his due, I found it.' The old man was astonished that, having a debt and finding that piece, he had not picked it up at once and given it to him. It was equally to his credit that when someone came to borrow something from Abba John, he did not give it him himself, but said to the brother, 'Go and help yourself to whatever you need,' and when someone brought anything back to him, he would say, 'Put it back where it belongs.' If the borrower did not return the thing he did not say anything to him.

3. It was said of Abba John the Persian that when some evildoers came to him, he took a basin and wanted to wash their feet. But they were filled with confusion, and began to do penance.

4. Someone said to Abba John the Persian, 'We have borne great afflictions for the sake of the kingdom of heaven. Shall we inherit it?' The old man said, 'As for me, I am confident I shall obtain the inheritance of Jerusalem on high, which is written in the heavens. Why should I not be confident? I have been hospitable like Abraham, meek like Moses, holy like Aaron, patient like Job, humble like David, a hermit like John, filled with compunction like Jeremiah, a master like Paul, full of faith like Peter, wise like Solomon. Like the thief, I trust that he who of his natural goodness has given me all that, will also grant me the kingdom.'

JOHN THE THEBAN

1. It was said of young John the Theban, a disciple of Abba Ammoes, that he spent twelve years serving the old man when he was ill. He stayed sitting with him on his mat. But the old man did not pay much attention to him, so much so that though he worked very hard for him, never did he say to him, 'Salvation be yours.' But when he was at the point of death and the old men surrounded him, he took his hand and said to him, 'Salvation be yours, salvation be yours, salvation be yours.' Then he entrusted him to the old men saying, 'He is an angel, not a man.'

JOHN, DISCIPLE OF ABBA PAUL

1. It was said of Abba John, the disciple of Abba Paul, that his obedience was very great. Now there were some tombs thereabouts where a hyena lived. The old man saw some dung in the place, and told John to go and fetch it. He said, 'And what shall I do about the hyena, abba?' The old man said to him jokingly, 'If she sets upon you, tie her up and bring her here.' So in the evening, the brother went there. And lo, the hyena fell upon him. According to the old man's instruction, he rushed to catch her. But the hyena ran away. He pursued her saying, 'My abba says I am to tie you up.' He seized her and bound her. Now the old man was uneasy and sat waiting for him. When he returned, he brought the hyena on a rope. When the old man saw this he was filled with wonder, but he wanted to humiliate him, so he struck him, and said, 'Fool, why have you brought a silly dog here?' Then the old man set her free at once and let her go.

ISAAC THE THEBAN

1. One day Abba Isaac went to a monastery. He saw a brother committing a sin and he condemned him. When he returned to the desert, an angel of the Lord came and stood in front of the door of

his cell, and said, 'I will not let you enter.' But he persisted saying, 'What is the matter?' and the angel replied, 'God has sent me to ask you where you want to throw the guilty brother whom you have condemned.' Immediately he repented and said, 'I have sinned, forgive me.' Then the angel said, 'Get up, God has forgiven you. But from now on, be careful not to judge someone before God has done so.'

2. It was said of Abba Apollo that he had a disciple, named Isaac, perfectly trained in all good works and he had the gift of ceaseless prayer at the time of the eucharist. When he came to church, he did not allow anyone to join him. He used to say that all things are good in their proper time, 'for there is a time for everything.' As soon as the *synaxis* was concluded, he fled as though pursued by fire and hurried back to his cell. Now at the conclusion of the *synaxis* a piece of bread and a cup of wine was often given to the brethren, but he did not accept it. Not that he wanted to refuse the *agape* of the brethren, but because he wished to preserve the ceaseless prayer of the service. Now it happened that he fell ill. When they heard of it, the brethren came to visit him. Sitting beside him they asked him, 'Abba Isaac, why do you flee from the brethren at the end of the service?' He said to them, 'I am not fleeing from the brethren, but from the wicked ruse of the demons. When someone is holding a lighted lamp, if he lingers in the open air, the lamp goes out because of the wind. We are the same, if, when we are illuminated by the holy eucharist, we linger outside our cell; our spirit is darkened.' Such was the way of life of the holy Abba Isaac.

JOSEPH OF THEBES

1. Abba Joseph the Theban said, 'Three works are approved in the eyes of the Lord; when a man is ill and temptations fall upon him, if he welcomes them with gratitude; secondly, when someone carries out all his works purely in the presence of God, having no regard for anything human; in the third place, when someone remains in submission to a spiritual father in complete renunciation of his own will. This last will gain a lofty crown indeed. As for me, I have chosen illness.'

HILARION

1. From Palestine, Abba Hilarion went to the mountain to Abba Anthony. Abba Anthony said to him, 'You are welcome, torch which awakens the day.' Abba Hilarion said, 'Peace to you, pillar of light, giving light to the world.'

ISCHYRION

1. The holy Fathers were making predictions about the last generation. They said, 'What have we ourselves done?' One of them, the great Abba Ischyrion replied, 'We ourselves have fulfilled the commandments of God.' The others replied, 'And those who come after us, what will they do?' He said, 'They will struggle to achieve half our works.' They said, 'And to those who come after them, what will happen?' He said, 'The men of that generation will not accomplish any works at all and temptation will come upon them; and those who will be approved in that day will be greater than either us or our fathers.'

✦| CAPPA |✦

CASSIAN

As a young man Cassian (360–435) joined a monastery in Bethlehem; he left there with a friend, Germanus, to study monasticism in Egypt and Syria. The material he collected during that time later formed the basis of his two books, the Institutes *and the* Conferences: *the* Institutes *describes monastic life as he had seen it in Egypt and Syria, and deals with the eight chief hindrances to perfection; in the* Conferences, *Cassian gives long expositions of various spiritual topics, set out in the form of conversations between himself and the leaders of early monasticism whom he had met in Egypt. In 415 he founded two monasteries near Marseilles; he died in 435.*

Cassian's writings are the work of a sophisticated writer reflecting on his experiences and interpreting them in the light of other influences. But the basic material he used was the tradition of desert teaching and his works filtered these early ideals for the use of the West. The Rule of S. Benedict *recommends the* Institutes *and* Conferences *'and the Lives of the Fathers, as also the Rule of our holy father Basil' (Rule ch 73) as 'tools of virtue for good-living and obedient monks', thus ensuring that the tradition passed on by Cassian would become one of the most potent and formative influences in western monasticism.*

1. Abba Cassian related the following: 'The holy Germanus and I went to Egypt, to visit an old man. Because he offered us hospitality we asked him, "Why do you not keep the rule of fasting, when you receive visiting brothers, as we have received it in Palestine?" He replied, "Fasting is always to hand but you I cannot have with me always. Furthermore, fasting is certainly a useful and necessary thing, but it depends on our choice while the law of God lays it upon us to do the works of charity. Thus receiving Christ in you, I ought to serve you will all diligence, but when I have taken leave of you, I can resume the rule of fasting again. For 'Can the wedding guests fast while the bridegroom is with them, but when the bridegroom is taken from them, then they will fast in that day.' " ' (Mark 2. 19–20)

2. The same abba said, 'There was an old man who was served by a holy virgin and men said he was not pure. The old man heard what was said. When he was on the point of dying he said to the Fathers, "When I am dead, plant my stick in the grave; if it grows and bears fruit, know that I am pure from all contact with her; but if it does not grow, know that I have sinned with her." So they planted the stick and on the third day it budded and bore fruit, and they all gave glory to God.'

3. He also said, 'We went to see another old man who made us eat. Then when we had had enough, he pressed us to take some more food. When I said to him I could not take any more, he replied, "This is the sixth time I have set the table for the brothers who come, and inviting each of them, have eaten with him, and I am still hungry. But though you have eaten only once of this food, you are already satisfied, to the extent that you cannot eat any more." '

4. The same Father related this: 'Abba John, abbot of a great monastery, went to Abba Paësius who had been living for forty years very far off in the desert. As he was very fond of him and could therefore speak freely with him, he said to him, "What good

have you done by living here in retreat for so long, and not being easily disturbed by anyone?" He replied, "Since I lived in solitude the sun has never seen me eating." Abba John said to him, "As for me, it has never seen me angry." '

5. The brothers surrounded the same Abba John who was at the point of death and ready to depart eagerly and joyously to God. They asked him to leave them a concise and salutary saying as their inheritance, which would enable them to become perfect in Christ. Groaning he said to them, 'I have never done my own will, nor taught anything which I had not previously carried out.'

6. He related with regard to another old man living in the desert, that he had asked God to grant him never to become sleepy during a spiritual conference, but, if someone uttered slanderous or useless words, to be able to go to sleep at once, so that his ears should never be touched by that poison. This old man also said that the devil, enemy of all spiritual instruction, works hard to provoke useless words. He used the following example, 'Once when I was talking to some brothers on a helpful topic, they were overcome by sleep so deep, that they could not even move their eyelids any longer. Then, wishing to show them the power of the devil, I introduced a trivial subject of conversation. Immediately, they woke up, full of joy. Then I said to them with many sighs, "Until now, we were discussing heavenly things and your eyes were heavy with sleep, but when I embarked on a useless discourse, you all woke up with alacrity. Therefore, brothers, I implore you to recognize the power of the evil demon; pay attention to yourselves, and guard yourselves from the desire to sleep when you are doing or listening to something spiritual." '

7. He also said, 'There was a distinguished official who had renounced everything and distributed his goods to the poor. He kept a little bit for his personal use because he did not want to accept the humiliation that comes from total renunciation, nor did he sincerely want to submit to the rule of the monastery. Saint Basil said to him, "You have lost your senatorial rank without becoming a monk." '

8. He also said, 'There was a monk living in a cave in the desert. His relations according to the flesh let him know, "Your father is very ill, at the point of death: come and receive his inheritance." He

replied to them, "I died to the world before he did and the dead do not inherit from the living." '

CRONIUS

Cronius, born c. A.D. 285, first lived in a monastery, but left it to join Anthony the Great in Egypt, where he acted as Anthony's Greek inter-preter. Later, he settled as an anchorite in Nitria, was ordained priest, and had many disciples, one of whom was Isaac of the Cells. He died about A.D. 386.

1. A brother said to Abba Cronius, 'Speak a work to me.' He said to him, 'When Elisha came to the Shunamite, he did not find her busy with anyone else. So she conceived and bore a child through the coming of Elisha.' (2 Kings 4) The brother said to him, 'What does this mean?' The old man said, 'If the soul is vigilant and with-draws from all distraction and abandons its own will, then the spirit of God invades it and it can conceive because it is free to do so.'

2. A brother asked Abba Cronius, 'What should I do to correct the forgetfulness which enslaves my spirit, and prevents me from perceiving anything until I am led into sin?' The old man said, 'When the strange people took possession of the ark because of the evil manner of life of the sons of Israel, they drew it until they brought it into the house of Dagon, their God and then he fell to the ground.' (1 Sam. 5) The brother said, 'What is the meaning of that?' The old man said, 'If the demons attempt to capture a man's spirit through his own impetus, they draw him in this manner until they lead him to an invisible passion. Then, at that point if the spirit returns and seeks after God and if it remembers the eternal judge-ment, immediately the passion falls away and disappears. It is writ-ten, "In returning and rest you shall be saved." ' (Isaiah 30.15)

3. A brother asked Abba Cronius, how can a man become hum-ble. The old man said to him, 'Through the fear of God.' The brother said, 'And by what work does he come to the fear of God?' The old man said, 'In my opinion, he should withdraw from all business and give himself to bodily affliction and with all his might remember that he will leave his body at the judgement of God.'

4. Abba Cronius said, 'If Moses had not led his sheep to Mount Sinai, he would not have seen the fire in the bush.' The brother questioned the old man, 'What does the bush symbolize?' He said to him, 'The bush signifies bodily action. For it is written: "The kingdom of heaven is like unto treasure hid in a field." ' (Matt. 13 .44) The brother said to the old man, 'So, man does not advance towards any reward without bodily affliction?' The old man said to him, 'Truly it is written: "Looking to Jesus, the Pioneer of and perfector of our faith who for the joy which was set before him, endured the cross." (Heb. 12.2) David also said: "I will not give sleep to mine eyes, nor slumber to my eyelids," until I find a place for the Lord.' (Ps. 132.4)

5. Abba Cronius said that Abba Joseph of Pelusia told him the following story, 'When I was living in Sinai, there was a brother who was good, ascetic and handsome. He came to church for the *synaxis* dressed in a little old *mafort* darned all over. Once when I saw him coming to the *synaxis* I said to him, "Brother, do you not see the brothers, looking like angels for the *synaxis* in church? How can you always come here in that garb?" He said to me, "Forgive me, abba, but I have nothing else." So I took him in to my cell and gave him a tunic and whatever else he needed. After that he wore them like the other brethren and was like an angel to look at. Now once it was necessary for the Fathers to send ten brethren to the emperor about something or other and he was chosen as one of the group to go. When he heard this, he made a prostration before his Father saying, "In the Lord's name, excuse me, for I am the slave of a great man down there and if he recognizes me, he will deprive me of my habit and force me to serve him again." The brothers were convinced and left him behind. But later, they learned from someone who had known him well when he was in the world that he had been head of the administration and that he had spoken as he did as a ruse, so that no-one should know this or bother him about it. So great, amongst the Fathers, was their concern to flee from glory and the peace of this world!'

CARION

Carion was a married man, an Egyptian, with a wife and two children. He left his family in order to become a monk in Scetis. During a famine, his wife sent the boy, Zacharias, to his father and he was brought up in the desert. The presence of the boy caused some comment but he proved to be a monk of zeal and discernment and even of greater spiritual understanding than his father.

1. Abba Carion said, 'I have laboured much harder than my son Zacharias and yet I have not attained to his measure in humility and silence.'

2. There was a monk in Scetis called Abba Carion. He had two children which he left with his wife when he withdrew from the world. Later, there was a famine in Egypt, and his wife came to Scetis, destitute of everything, bringing the two little children (one was a boy, called Zacharias, the other was a girl). She waited in the marsh land, at a distance from the old man. (For there was a marsh beside Scetis, and they had built churches and wells there.) Now it was the custom in Scetis, that when a woman came to talk with a brother or with someone else whom she had to see, that they should sit far away from one another while they talked. So the woman said to Abba Carion, 'You have become a monk and now there is a famine; who is going to feed your children?' Abba Carion said to her, 'Send them to me.' The woman said to the children, 'Go to your father.' When they got close to their father, the little girl ran back to her mother but the boy stayed with his father. Then the old man said to his wife, 'That is good. Take the little girl and depart; I will look after the boy.' So he was brought up in Scetis and everyone knew that he was his son. As he grew older, they murmured in the fraternity about him. Hearing of it, Abba Carion said to his son, 'Zacharias, get up; we will go away from here, because the Fathers are murmuring.' The young man said to him, 'Abba, everyone here knows that I am your son, but if we go somewhere else, we can no longer say that I am your son.' But the old man said to him, 'Rise, let us go away from here.' So they went to the Thebaid. There they were given a cell and stayed there several days. But down there the same murmuring recurred about the child. Then his father said to him, 'Zacharias, get up, we will go to Scetis.' A few days after their arrival in Scetis once again they murmured about him. Then young Zacharias went to the lake which was full of nitre, undressed, went down to it and jumped in, up to the nose. He remained there many hours, as long as he could, until his body was changed and he

became like a leper. He came out, and put on his clothes again and went back to his father who scarcely recognized him. When he went to communion as usual, Abba Isidore, the priest of Scetis, had a revelation of what he had done. When he saw him, he was filled with wonder. Then he said to him, 'Last Sunday the boy Zacharias came and communicated like a man; now he has become like an angel.'*

3. Abba Carion said, 'A monk who lives with a boy, falls, if he is not stable; but even if he is stable and does not fall, he still does not make progress.'

COPRES

1. Abba Poemen said of Abba Copres that he was so holy that when he was ill and in bed, he still gave thanks and restrained his own will.

2. Abba Copres said, 'Blessed is he who bears affliction with thankfulness.'

3. One day, the inhabitants of Scetis assembled together to discuss Melchizedek and they forgot to invite Abba Copres. Later on they called him and asked him about this matter. Tapping his mouth three times, he said 'Alas for you, Copres! For that which God commanded you to do, you have put aside, and you are wanting to learn something which you have not been required to know about.' When they heard these words, the brothers fled to their cells.

CYRUS

1. Abba Cyrus of Alexandria was asked about the temptation of fornication, and he replied, 'If you do not think about it, you have no hope, for if you are not thinking about it, you are doing it. I mean, he who does not fight against the sin and resist it in his spirit will commit the sin physically. It is very true that he who is for-

*Additional material from J.-C. Guy.

nicating in fact is not worried with thinking about it.' The old man questioned the brother, saying, 'Do you not usually talk to women?' The brother said, 'No; my thoughts are about old and new representations of them: it is their remembrance which overcomes me.' The old man said to him, 'Do not fear the dead, but flee from the living, and before all things persist in prayer.'

✦| LAMBDA |✦

LUCIUS

Lucius, a companion of Longinus from Cilicia, was a monk in Syria and later abbot of Enaton. The heretics called Euchites were also known as Messalians, 'those who pray'. This was a pietistic sect originating in Mesopotamia in the mid fourth century and spreading to Asia Minor, Egypt and Syria. It was condemned at the Council of Ephesus (431). The contrast between them in their dualism and over-spiritualized approach to prayer and the orthodoxy and common sense of the monks is made clear in this story.

1. Some of the monks who are called Euchites went to Enaton to see Abba Lucius. The old man asked them, 'What is your manual work?' They said, 'We do not touch manual work but as the Apostle says, we pray without ceasing.' The old man asked them if they did not eat and they replied they did. So he said to them, 'When you are eating, who prays for you then?' Again he asked them if they did not sleep and they replied they did. And he said to them, 'When

you are asleep, who prays for you then?' They could not find any answer to give him. He said to them, 'Forgive me, but you do not act as you speak. I will show you how, while doing my manual work, I pray without interruption. I sit down with God, soaking my reeds and plaiting my ropes, and I say, "God, have mercy on me; according to your great goodness and according to the multitude of your mercies, save me from my sins." ' So he asked them if this were not prayer and they replied it was. Then he said to them, 'So when I have spent the whole day working and praying, making thirteen pieces of money more or less, I put two pieces of money outside the door and I pay for my food with the rest of the money. He who takes the two pieces of money prays for me when I am eating and when I am sleeping; so, by the grace of God, I fulfil the precept to pray without ceasing.'

LOT

Lot was a simple Coptic monk, a disciple of Joseph of Panephysis and a friend of Arsenius. He lived as a solitary at Arsinoe near Abba Anthony. Like the majority of the Copts he was opposed to the teaching of Origen.

1. One of the old men came to Abba Lot's dwelling, near to the little marsh of Arsinoe and he asked for a cell, which Abba Lot gave him. Now the old man was ill and Abba Lot took care of him. When anyone came to see Abba Lot, he made him visit the sick old man also. But the sick man began to quote the words of Origen to the visitors. This made Abba Lot anxious and he said to himself, 'The Fathers must not think that we are like that too.' However, he was afraid to drive him away because of the commandment. So Abba Lot got up and went to Abba Arsenius and told him about the old man. Abba Arsenius said to him, 'Do not drive him away, but say to him: look, eat that which comes from God and drink as much as you like, only do not make such remarks any more. If he wants to, he will correct himself. If he does not want to change his ways, he will ask to leave this place of his own accord. Thus his departure will not come from you.' Abba Lot went away and did this. When the old man heard these word he did not want to change, but he

began to ask him, 'For the Lord's sake, send me away from here, for I can no longer bear the desert.' So he got up and left, accompanied to the door by charity.

2. It was related of a brother who had committed a fault that when he went to Abba Lot, he was troubled and hesitated, going in and coming out, unable to sit down. Abba Lot said to him, 'What is the matter, brother?' He said, 'I have committed a great fault and I cannot acknowledge it to the Fathers.' The old man said to him, 'Confess it to me, and I will carry it.' Then he said to him, 'I have fallen into fornication, and in order to do it, I have sacrificed to idols.' The old man said to him, 'Have confidence; repentance is possible. Go, sit in your cave, eat only once in two days and I will carry half of your fault with you.' After three weeks, the old man had the certainty that God had accepted the brother's repentance. Then the latter remained in submission to the old man until his death.

LONGINUS

Longinus, a friend and disciple of Lucius and later a famous abbot of the monastery of Enaton, led the monks in opposition to the Council of Chalcedon. Enaton was a leading monastery in Egypt; the Monophysite patriarchs took up residence there in the sixth century; it was sacked by the Persians in 617.

1. One day Abba Longinus questioned Abba Lucius about three thoughts saying first, 'I want to go into exile.' The old man said to him, 'If you cannot control your tongue, you will not be an exile anywhere. Therefore control your tongue here, and you will be an exile.' Next he said to him, 'I wish to fast.' The old man replied, 'Isaiah said, "If you bend your neck like a rope or a bulrush that is not the fast I will accept; but rather, control your evil thoughts."' (cf. Isaiah 58) He said to him the third time, 'I wish to flee from men.' The old man replied, 'If you have not first of all lived rightly with men, you will not be able to live rightly in solitude.'

2. Abba Longinus said, 'If ever you are ill, say to your body, "Be ill and die; if you ask me for food outside the agreed time, I will not bring you even your daily food any more."'

3. A woman had an illness they call cancer of the breast; she had heard of Abba Longinus and wanted to meet him. Now he lived at the ninth milestone from Alexandria. As the woman was looking for him, the blessed man happened to be collecting wood beside the sea. When she met him, she said to him, 'Abba, where does Abba Longinus, the servant of God live?' not knowing that it was he. He said, 'Why are you looking for that old imposter? Do not go to see him, for he is a deceiver. What is the matter with you?' The woman showed him where she was suffering. He made the sign of the cross over the sore and sent her away saying, 'Go, and God will heal you, for Longinus cannot help you at all.' The woman went away confident in this saying, and she was healed on the spot. Later, telling others what had happened and mentioning the distinctive marks of the old man, she learned that it was Abba Longinus himself.

4. Another time, they brought him one possessed by a demon. He said to those who were escorting him: 'I can do nothing for you; but go instead to Abba Zeno.' So Abba Zeno began to put pressure onto the demon to cast it out. The demon began to cry out: 'Perhaps, Abba Zeno, you think I am going away because of you; look, down there Abba Longinus is praying, and challenging me and it is for fear of his prayers that I go away, for to you I would not even have given an answer.'

5. Abba Longinus said to Abba Acacius: 'A woman knows she has conceived when she no longer loses any blood. So it is with the soul, she knows she has conceived the Holy Spirit when the passions stop coming out of her. But as long as one is held back in the passions, how can one dare to believe one is sinless? Give blood and receive the Spirit.'

•| MU |•

MACARIUS THE GREAT

Macarius the Great (the Egyptian), born c. A.D. 300, was a former camel-driver, who traded in nitre. He was one of the pioneers of Scetis. He was ordained priest and lived as an anchorite in a village until he was falsely blamed for the pregnancy of a girl there; when he was cleared, he went to Scetis. Like many of the early monks, he travelled about and was not fixed in any one place, as these stories show. Cassian said of him, 'He was the first who found a way to inhabit the desert of Scetis.' He was much influenced by Anthony the Great and visited him at least twice. He died in A.D. 390.

1. Abba Macarius said this about himself: 'When I was young and was living in a cell in Egypt, they took me to make me a cleric in the village. Because I did not wish to receive this dignity, I fled to another place. Then a devout layman joined me; he sold my manual work for me and served me. Now it happened that a virgin in the village, under the weight of temptation, committed sin. When

she became pregnant, they asked her who was to blame. She said, "The anchorite." Then they came to seize me, led me to the village and hung pots black with soot and various other things round my neck and led me through the village in all directions, beating me and saying, "This monk has defiled our virgin, catch him, catch him," and they beat me almost to death. Then one of the old men came and said, "What are you doing, how long will you go on beating this strange monk?" The man who served me was walking behind me, full of shame, for they covered him with insults too, saying, "Look at this anchorite, for whom you stood surety; what has he done?" The girl's parents said, "Do not let him go till he has given a pledge that he will keep her." I spoke to my servant and he vouched for me. Going to my cell, I gave him all the baskets I had, saying, "Sell them, and give my wife something to eat." Then I said to myself, "Macarius, you have found yourself a wife; you must work a little more in order to keep her." So I worked night and day and sent my work to her. But when the time came for the wretch to give birth, she remained in labour many days without bringing forth, and they said to her, "What is the matter?" She said, "I know what it is, it is because I slandered the anchorite, and accused him unjustly; it is not he who is to blame, but such and such a young man." Then the man who served me came to me full of joy saying, "The virgin could not give birth until she had said 'The anchorite had nothing to do with it, but I have lied about him.' The whole village wants to come here solemnly and do penance before you." But when I heard this, for fear people would disturb me, I got up and fled here to Scetis. That is the original reason why I came here.'

2. One day Macarius the Egyptian went from Scetis to the mountain of Nitria for the offering of Abba Pambo. The old men said to him, 'Father, say a word to the brethren.' He said, 'I have not yet become a monk myself, but I have seen monks. One day when I was sitting in my cell, my thoughts were troubling me, suggesting that I should go to the desert and see what I could see there. I remained for five years, fighting against this thought, saying, perhaps it comes from the demons. But since the thought persisted, I left for the desert. There I found a sheet of water and an island in the midst, and the animals of the desert came to drink there. In the midst of these animals I saw two naked men, and my body trembled,

for I believed they were spirits. Seeing me shaking, they said to me, "Do not be afraid, for we are men." Then I said to them, "Where do you come from, and how did you come to this desert?" They said, "We come from a monastery and having agreed together, we came here forty years ago. One of us is an Egyptian and the other a Libyan." They questioned me and asked me, "How is the world? Is the water rising in due time? Is the world enjoying prosperity?" I replied it was, then I asked them, "How can I become a monk?" They said to me, "If you do not give up all that is in the world, you cannot become a monk." I said to them, "But I am weak, and I cannot do as you do." So they said to me: "If you cannot become like us, sit in your cell and weep for your sins." I asked them, "When the winter comes are you not frozen? And when the heat comes do not your bodies burn?" They said, "It is God who has made this way of life for us. We do not freeze in winter, and the summer does us no harm." That is why I said that I have not yet become a monk, but I have seen monks.'

3. When Abba Macarius dwelt in the great desert, he was the only one living as an anchorite, but lower down there was another desert where several brothers dwelt. The old man was surveying the road when he saw Satan drawing near in the likeness of a man and he passed by his dwelling. He seemed to be wearing some kind of cotton garment, full of holes, and a small flask hung at each hole. The old man said to him, 'Where are you off to?' He said, 'I am going to stir up the memories of the brethren.' The old man said, 'And what is the purpose of these small flasks?' He replied, 'I am taking food for the brethren to taste.' The old man said, 'All those kinds?' He replied, 'Yes, for if a brother does not like one sort of food, I offer him another, and if he does not like the second any better, I offer him a third; and of all these varieties he will like one at least.' With these words he departed. The old man remained watching the road until he saw him coming back again. When the old man saw him, he said to him: 'Good health to you.' The other replied: 'How can I be in good health?' The old man asked him what he meant, and he replied, 'Because they all opposed me, and no one received me.' The old man said, 'Ah, you did not find any friends down there?' He replied, 'Yes, I have a monk who is a friend down there. He at least obeys me and when he sees me he changes like the wind.'

The old man asked him the name of this monk. 'Theopemtus,' he replied. With these words he went away. Then Abba Macarius got up and went to the desert below his own. When they heard of it the brothers took branches of palm to go to meet him. Each one got ready, thinking that it was to him the old man was coming down. But he enquired which was the one on the mountain called Theopemptus, and when he had found out he went to his cell. Theopemptus received him with joy. When he was alone with him the old man asked him, 'How are you getting on?' Theopemptus replied, 'Thanks to your prayers, all goes well.' The old man asked: 'Do not your thoughts war against you?' He replied: 'Up to now, it is all right,' for he was afraid to admit anything. The old man said to him, 'See how many years I have lived as an ascetic, and am praised by all, and though I am old, the spirit of fornication troubles me.' Theopemptus said, 'Believe me, abba, it is the same with me.' The old man went on admitting that other thoughts still warred against him, until he had brought him to admit them about himself. Then he said, 'How do you fast?' He replied, 'Till the ninth hour.' 'Practise fasting a little later; meditate on the Gospel and the other Scriptures, and if an alien thought arises within you, never look at it but always look upwards, and the Lord will come at once to your help.' When he had given the brother this rule, the old man then returned to his solitude. He was watching the road once more when he saw the devil, to whom he said, 'Where are you going this time?' He replied, 'To arouse the memories of the brothers,' and he went away. When he came back the saint asked him, 'How are the brothers?' He replied that it had gone badly. The old man asked him why. He replied, 'They are all obdurate, and the worst is the one friend I had who used to obey me. I do not know what has changed him, but not only does he not obey me any more, but he has become the most obdurate of them all. So I have promised myself not to go down there again at least not for a long time from now.' When he had said this, he went away leaving the old man, and the saint returned to his cell.

4. One day Abba Macarius the Great came to Abba Anthony's dwelling on the mountain. When he knocked on the door, Anthony came out to him and said to him, 'Who are you?' He replied, 'I am Macarius.' Then Anthony went inside and shut the door leaving

him there. Later, seeing his patience, he opened the door and received Macarius with joy, saying to him, 'I have wanted to see you for a long time, having heard about you.' He rendered him all the duties of hospitality and made him rest for he was very tired. When evening came, Abba Anthony soaked some palm-leaves for himself, and Abba Macarius said to him, 'Allow me to soak some for myself.' He replied: 'Do so.' Having made a large bundle, he soaked them. Then sitting down in the evening they spoke of the salvation of the soul, while they plaited the leaves. The rope which Macarius was making hung down through the window in the cave. Going in early, blessed Anthony saw the length of Abba Macarius' rope and said, 'Great power comes out of these hands.'

5. Concerning the devastation of Scetis, Abba Macarius said to the brethern, 'When you see a cell built close to the marsh, know that the devastation of Scetis is near; when you see trees, know that it is at the doors; and when you see young children, take up your sheep-skins, and go away.'

6. Again, wishing to comfort the brethren, he said, 'A mother came here with her little child, possessed with a devil, who said to his mother, "Get up, woman, let us go away from here." She replied, "I cannot walk any further," and the little child said to her, "I will carry you myself." I wondered at the devil's tricks and how eager he was to make them flee.'

7. Abba Sisoes said, 'When I was at Scetis with Macarius, we went up, seven of us, to bring in the harvest. Now a widow cried out behind us and would not stop weeping. So the old man called the owner of the field and said to him, "What is the matter with the woman that she goes on weeping?" "It is because her husband received a deposit in trust from someone and he died suddenly without saying where he had hidden it, and the owner of the deposit wants to take her and her children and make slaves of them." The old man said to him, "Tell her to come to us, when we take our mid-day rest." The woman came, and the old man said to her, "Why are you weeping all the time like this?" She replied, "My husband who had received a deposit on trust from someone, has died and he did not say when he died, where he had put it." The old man said to her, "Come, show me where you have buried him." Taking the

brethren with him, he went with her. When they had come to the place, the old man said to her, "Go away to your house." While the brethren prayed, the old man asked the dead man, "So and so, where have you put the deposit?" The corpse replied, "It is hidden in the house, at the foot of the bed." The old man said, "Rest again, until the day of resurrection." When they saw this, the brethren were filled with fear and threw themselves at his feet. But the old man said to them, "It is not for my sake that this has happened, for I am nothing, but it is because of the widow and the orphans that God has performed this miracle. This is what is remarkable, that God wants the soul to be without sin and grants it all it asks." He went to tell the widow where the deposit was. Taking it, she returned it to its owner and thus freed her children. All who heard this story gave glory to God.'

8. Abba Peter said this about the holy Macarius: 'One day he came to the cell of an anchorite who happened to be ill, and he asked him if he would take something to eat, though his cell was stripped bare. When the other replied, "Some sherbet," that courageous man did not hesitate, but went as far as Alexandria to fetch some for the sick man. The astonishing thing is that no-one knew about it.'

9. He also said that when Abba Macarius received all the brethren in simplicity, some of them asked him why he mixed with them like this. He replied, 'For twelve years I served the Lord, so that he might grant me this gift, and do you all advise me to give it up?'

10. They said about Abba Macarius that when he visited the brethren he laid this rule upon himself, 'If there is wine, drink some for the brethren's sake, but for each cup of wine, spend a day without drinking water.' So the brothers would offer him some refreshment, and the old man would accept it joyfully to mortify himself; but when his disciple got to know about it he said to the brethren, 'In the name of God, do not offer him any more, or he will go and kill himself in his cell.' When they heard that, the brethren did not offer him wine any more.

11. When Abba Macarius was returning from the marsh to his cell one day carrying some palm-leaves, he met the devil on the road with a scythe. The latter struck at him as much as he pleased, but in vain, and he said to him, 'What is your power, Macarius, that

makes me powerless against you? All that you do, I do, too; you fast, so do I; you keep vigil, and I do not sleep at all; in one thing only do you beat me.' Abba Macarius asked what that was. He said, 'Your humility. Because of that I can do nothing against you.'

12. Some Fathers questioned Abba Macarius the Egyptian, 'Why is it that whether you eat, or whether you fast, your body is always emaciated?' The old man said to them, 'The little bit of wood that is used to poke the vinebranches when they are burning ends by being entirely burnt up by the fire; in the same way, man purifies his soul in the fear of God, and the fear of God burns up his body.'

13. One day Abba Macarius went up from Scetis to Terenuthis and went into the temple to sleep. Now there were some old coffins of the pagans there. Taking one, he put it under his head as a pillow. The devils, seeing his audacity, were filled with jealousy and to make him afraid they called out, as though addressing a woman, 'So and so, come to bath with us.' Another devil replied from beneath him, as though among the dead, 'I have a stranger on top of me, and I cannot come.' But the old man was not afraid. On the contrary, he knocked on the coffin with assurance, saying, 'Awake, and go into the darkness, if you can.' Hearing this, the devils began to cry out with all their might, 'You have overcome us.' Filled with confusion, they fled.

14. It was said of Abba Macarius the Egyptian that one day when he was going up from Scetis with a load of baskets, he sat down, overcome with weariness and began to say to himself, 'My God, you know very well that I cannot go any further,' and immediately he found himself at the river.

15. A man of Egypt had a paralytic son. He brought him to the cell of Abba Macarius, and put him down at the door weeping and went a good distance away. The old man stooped down and saw the child, and said to him, 'Who brought you here?' He replied, 'My father threw me down here and went away.' Then the old man said to him, 'Get up, and go back to him.' The child was cured on the spot; he got up and rejoined his father and they returned to their own home.

16. Abba Macarius the Great said to the brothers at Scetis, when he dismissed the assembly, 'Flee, my brothers.' One of the old men asked him, 'Where could we flee to beyond this desert?' He put his finger on his lips and said, 'Flee that,' and he went into his cell, shut the door and sat down.

17. The same Abba Macarius said, 'If you reprove someone, you yourself get carried away by anger and you are satisfying your own passion; do not lose yourself, therefore, in order to save another.'

18. The same Abba Macarius while he was in Egypt discovered a man who owned a beast of burden engaged in plundering Macarius' goods. So he came up to the thief as if he was a stranger and he helped him to load the animal. He saw him off in great peace of soul, saying, 'We have brought nothing into this world, and we cannot take anything out of the world.' (1 Tim. 6.7) 'The Lord gave and the Lord has taken away; blessed be the name of the Lord.' (Job 1.21)

19. Abba Macarius was asked, 'How should one pray?' The old man said, 'There is no need at all to make long discourses; it is enough to stretch out one's hands and say, "Lord, as you will, and as you know, have mercy." And if the conflict grows fiercer say, "Lord, help!" He knows very well what we need and he shews us his mercy.'

20. Abba Macarius said, 'If slander has become to you the same as praise, poverty as riches, deprivation as abundance, you will not die. Indeed it is impossible for anyone who firmly believes, who labours with devotion, to fall into the impurity of the passions and be led astray by the demons.'

21. It was said that two brothers at Scetis had fallen into sin and that Abba Macarius of Alexandria had excommunicated them. Some brethren came and told Abba Macarius the Great of Egypt about it. He said, 'It is not the brothers who are excommunicated; it is Macarius (for he loved him).' Hearing that he had been excommunicated by the old man, Abba Macarius fled to the marsh. Then Abba Macarius the Great went out and found him eaten up by mosquitoes. He said to him, 'So you have excommunicated some brothers; and yet they live apart in the village. I myself have excom-

municated you and like a pretty young girl to the utmost privacy of her chamber, you have fled here. I have summoned the two brothers, and have learnt from them what happened, and I have told them nothing has happened. Examine yourself, then, my brother, and see if you have not been the sport of the demons, for you have lacked perception in this matter. But repent of your fault.' Then the other asked him, 'Please give me a penance.' Faced with his humility, the old man said, 'Go, fast for three weeks, eating only once a week.' For it was his usual custom to fast for the whole week.

22. Abba Moses said to Abba Macarius at Scetis, 'I should like to live in quiet prayer and the brethren do not let me.' Abba Macarius said to him, 'I see that you are a sensitive man and incapable of sending a brother away. Well, if you want to live in peace, go to the interior desert, to Petra, and there you will be at peace.' And so he found peace.

23. A brother came to see Abba Macarius the Egyptian, and said to him, 'Abba, give me a word, that I may be saved.' So the old man said, 'Go to the cemetery and abuse the dead.' The brother went there, abused them and threw stones at them; then he returned and told the old man about it. The latter said to him, 'Didn't they say anything to you?' He replied, 'No.' The old man said, 'Go back tomorrow and praise them.' So the brother went away and praised them, calling them, 'Apostles, saints and righteous men.' He returned to the old man and said to him, 'I have complimented them.' And the old man said to him, 'Did they not answer you?' The brother said no. The old man said to him, 'You know how you insulted them and they did not reply, and how you praised them and they did not speak; so you too if you wish to be saved must do the same and become a dead man. Like the dead, take no account of either the scorn of men or their praises, and you can be saved.'

24. One day when Abba Macarius was going down to Egypt with some brethren, he heard a boy saying to his mother, 'Mother, there is a rich man who likes me, but I detest him; and on the other hand, there is a poor man who hates me, and I love him.' Hearing these words, Abba Macarius marvelled. So the brethren said to him: 'What is this saying, abba, that makes you marvel?' The old man said to them, 'Truly, our Lord is rich and loves us, and we do not listen

to him; while our enemy the devil is poor and hates us, but we love his impurity.'

25. Abba Poemen asked him weeping, 'Give me a word that I may be saved.' But the old man replied, 'What you are looking for has disappeared now from among monks.'

26. One day Abba Macarius went to see Abba Anthony. He spoke to him and then returned to Scetis. The Fathers came to meet him, and as they were speaking, the old man said to them, 'I said to Abba Anthony that we do not have an offering in our district.' But the Fathers began to speak of other things without asking him to tell them the old man's reply and he himself did not tell them. One of the Fathers said about this that when the Fathers see that the brethren fail to question them about something that would be useful, they ought to begin talking about it themselves; but if they are not urged on by the brethren, they should not say anymore about it, so that they shall not be found to have spoken without being asked, and to have said unnecessary words.

27. Abba Isaiah questioned Abba Macarius saying, 'Give me a word.' The old man said to him, 'Flee from men,' Abba Isaiah said to him, 'What does it mean to flee from men?' The old man said, 'It means to sit in your cell and weep for your sins.'

28. Abba Paphnutius, the disciple of Abba Macarius, said, 'I asked my Father to say a word to me and he replied, "Do no evil to anyone, and do not judge anyone. Observe this and you will be saved."'

29. Abba Macarius said, 'Do not sleep in the cell of a brother who has a bad reputation.'

30. The brethren came one day to Abba Macarius at Scetis and they found nothing in this cell except stagnant water. So they said to him, 'Abba, come up to the village, and we will get some clean water for you.' The old man said to them, 'Brothers, do you know so-and-so's bakery in the village?' and they said that they did. The old man said to them, 'I know it, too. Do you know so-and-so's field, where the river runs?' They said, 'Yes.' The old man said to them, 'I know it too. So when I want to, I can go there myself, without your help.'

31. They said of Abba Macarius that if a brother came to see him with fear, like someone coming to see a great and holy old man, he did not say anything to him. But if one of the brethren said to him, as though to humiliate him, 'Abba, when you were a camel-driver, and stole nitre and sold it again, did not the keepers beat you?' If someone talked to him like that he would talk to them with joy about whatever they asked him.

32. They said of Abba Macarius the Great that he became, as it is written, a god upon earth, because, just as God protects the world, so Abba Macarius would cover the faults which he saw, as though he did not see them; and those which he heard, as though he did not hear them.

33. Abba Bitimius related that Abba Macarius said this: 'When I was living at Scetis, two young strangers came down there. One had a beard, the other was beginning to grow one. They came towards me saying: "Where is Abba Macarius' cell?" I said to them: "What do you want with him?" They replied, "We have heard tell of him and of Scetis and we have come to see him." I said to them, "I am he." Then they bowed low to me and said, "We want to live here." Seeing that they were delicate and had been brought up in comfort, I said to them, "You cannot live here." The elder said, "If we cannot live here, we will go somewhere else." Then I said to myself, "Why chase them away and be a stumbling block to them? Suffering will make them go away of their own accord." So I said to them, "Come and make yourselves a cell, if you can." They said, "Show us a place, and we will make one." The old man gave them an axe, a basket full of bread and salt, and showed them a lump of rock, saying, "Cut out some stones here, and bring wood from the marsh, make a roof, and live here." He added, "I thought they would choose to go away, because of the hardship. But they asked me what work they should do here." I replied, "Rope-making." And I took some leaves from the marsh and showed them the rudiments of weaving and how to handle the reeds. I said to them, "Make some baskets, give them to the keepers, and they will bring you bread." Then I went away. But they, with patience, did all that I had told them and for three years they did not come to see me. Now I wrestled with my thoughts, thinking, "What is their way of life? Why do they not come to ask me about their thoughts? Those who

live far off come to see me, but those who live quite close do not come. They do not go to anyone else either; they only go to church, in silence, to receive the oblation." I prayed to God, fasting the whole week, that he would show me their way of life. At the end of the week, I got up and went to visit them, to see how they were. When I knocked, they opened the door and greeted me in silence. Having prayed, I sat down. The elder made a sign to the younger to go out and he sat plaiting the rope, without saying anything. At the ninth hour, he knocked, and the younger one returned and made a little soup and set the table at a sign of his elder brother. He put three small loaves on it and stood in silence. As for me, I said, "Rise, and let us eat." We got up to eat and he brought a small water-bottle and we drank. When the evening came, they said to me, "Are you going away?" I replied, "No, I will sleep here." They spread a mat for me on one side, another for themselves in the opposite corner. They took off their girdles and cowls, and lay down together on the mat. When they were settled, I prayed God that he would show me their way of life. Then the roof opened and it became as light as day, but they did not see the light. When they thought I was asleep, the elder tapped the younger on the side and they got up, put on their girdles again and stretched their hands towards heaven. I could see them, but they could not see me. I saw the demons coming like flies upon the younger one, some sitting on his mouth and others on his eyes. I saw the angel of the Lord circling round about him with a fiery sword, chasing the demons far from him. But they could not come near the elder one. When early dawn came, they lay down and I made as though I had just woken up and they did the same. The elder simply said to me "Shall we recite the twelve psalms?" and I said to him, "Yes." The younger one chanted five psalms in groups of six verses and an alleluia and at each verse a tongue of flame came out of his mouth and ascended to heaven. Likewise with the elder, when he opened his mouth to chant it was like a column of fire which came forth and ascended up to heaven; in my turn, I recited a little by heart. As I went out, I said, "Pray for me." But they bowed without saying a word. So I learned that the first was a perfect man, but the enemy was still fighting against the younger. A few days later the elder brother fell asleep and three days afterwards, his younger brother died too.' When the Fathers came to see Abba Macarius, he used to take them to their cell, and say, 'Come and see the place of martyrdom of the young strangers.'

34. One day the old men of the mountain sent a delegation to Scetis to Abba Macarius with these words, 'Deign to visit us so that we may see you before you go to the Lord, otherwise all the people will be grieved.' So he came to the mountain and all the people gathered round him. The old men asked him to say a word to the brothers. When he heard this, he said, 'Let us weep, brothers, and let tears gush out of our eyes, before we go to that place where our tears shall burn our bodies.' They all wept, falling with their faces on the ground and saying, 'Father, pray for us.'

35. Another time a demon approached Abba Macarius with a knife and wanted to cut his foot. But, because of his humility he could not do so, and he said to him, 'All that you have, we have also; you are distinguished from us only by humility; by that you get the better of us.'

36. Abba Macarius said, 'If we keep remembering the wrongs which men have done us, we destroy the power of the remembrance of God. But if we remind ourselves of the evil deeds of the demons, we shall be invulnerable.'

37. Abba Paphnutius, the disciple of Abba Macarius, repeated this saying of the old man, 'When I was small with other children, I used to eat bilberries and they used to go and steal the little figs. As they were running away, they dropped one of the figs, and I picked it up and ate it. Every time I remember this, I sit down and weep.'

38. Abba Macarius said, 'Walking in the desert one day, I found the skull of a dead man, lying on the ground. As I was moving it with my stick, the skull spoke to me. I said to it, "Who are you?" The skull replied, "I was high priest of the idols and of the pagans who dwelt in this place; but you are Macarius, the Spirit-bearer. Whenever you take pity on those who are in torments, and pray for them, they feel a little respite." The old man said to him, "What is this alleviation, and what is this torment?" He said to him, "As far as the sky is removed from the earth, so great is the fire beneath us; we are ourselves standing in the midst of the fire, from the feet up

to the head. It is not possible to see anyone face to face, but the face of one is fixed to the back of another. Yet when you pray for us, each of us can see the other's face a little. Such is our respite." The old man in tears said, "Alas the day when that man was born!" He said to the skull, "Are there any punishments which are more painful than this?" The skull said to him, "There is a more grievous punishment down below us." The old man said, "Who are the people down there?" The skull said to him: "We have received a little mercy since we did not know God, but those who know God and denied Him are down below us." Then, picking up the skull, the old man buried it.'

39. They said of Abba Macarius the Egyptian that one day he went up from Scetis to the mountain of Nitria. As he approached the place he told his disciple to go on ahead. When the latter had gone on ahead, he met a priest of the pagans. The brother shouted after him saying, 'Oh, oh, devil, where are you off to?' The priest turned back and beat him and left him half dead. Then picking up his stick, he fled. When he had gone a little further, Abba Macarius met him running and said to him, 'Greetings! Greetings, you weary man!' Quite astonished, the other came up to him and said, 'What good do you see in me, that you greet me in this way?' The old man said to him, 'I have seen you wearing yourself out without knowing that you are wearing yourself out in vain.' The other said to him, 'I have been touched by your greeting and I realize that you are on God's side. But another wicked monk who met me insulted me and I have given him blows enough for him to die of them.' The old man realized that he was referring to his disciple. Then the priest fell at his feet and said, 'I will not let you go till you have made me a monk.' When they came to the place where the brother was, they put him onto their shoulders and carried him to the church in the mountain. When the people saw the priest with Macarius they were astonished and they made him a monk. Through him many pagans became Christians. So Abba Macarius said, 'One evil word makes even the good evil, while one good word makes even the evil good.'

40. They said of Abba Macarius that a thief went into his cell when he was away. Marcarius came back to his cell and found the thief loading his things onto a camel. So Macarius went into the cell, picked up his things and helped him load them onto the camel.

When the loading was finished, the thief began to beat the camel to make it get up but in vain. Seeing that it did not get up, Abba Macarius went inside his cell, found a small hoe there, picked it up and put it onto the camel saying, 'Brother, the camel wants to have this.' Then the old man kicked it, saying, 'Get up.' At once the camel got up and went forward a little, because of his command. Then it lay down again and refused to get up until it was completely unloaded; and then it set off.

41. Abba Aio questioned Abba Macarius, and said: 'Give me a word.' Abba Macarius said to him: 'Flee from men, stay in your cell, weep for your sins, do not take pleasure in the conversation of men, and you will be saved.'

MOSES

Moses, called the Robber or the Negro, was a released slave who lived as a robber in Nitria; late in life he became a monk and was trained by Isidore the Priest. He was ordained priest and became one of the great fathers of Scetis. On the advice of Macarius he retired to Petra; he was martyred with seven others by barbarian invaders.

1. It happened that Abba Moses was struggling with the temptation of fornication. Unable to stay any longer in the cell, he went and told Abba Isidore. The old man exhorted him to return to his cell. But he refused, saying, 'Abba, I cannot.' Then Abba Isidore took Moses out onto the terrace and said to him, 'Look towards the west.' He looked and saw hordes of demons flying about and making a noise before launching an attack. Then Abba Isidore said to him, 'Look towards the east.' He turned and saw an innumerable multitude of holy angels shining with glory. Abba Isidore said, 'See, these are sent by the Lord to the saints to bring them help, while those in the west fight against them. Those who are with us are more in number than they are.' Then Abba Moses, gave thanks to God, plucked up courage and returned to his cell.

2. A brother at Scetis committed a fault. A council was called to which Abba Moses was invited, but he refused to go to it. Then the priest sent someone to say to him, 'Come, for everyone is waiting

for you.' So he got up and went. He took a leaking jug, filled it with water and carried it with him. The others came out to meet him and said to him, 'What is this, Father?' The old man said to them, 'My sins run out behind me, and I do not see them, and today I am coming to judge the errors of another.' When they heard that they said no more to the brother but forgave him.

3. Another day when a council was being held in Scetis, the Fathers treated Moses with contempt in order to test him, saying, 'Why does this black man come among us?' When he heard this he kept silence. When the council was dismissed, they said to him, 'Abba, did that not grieve you at all?' He said to them, 'I was grieved, but I kept silence.'

4. It was said of Abba Moses that he was ordained and the ephod was placed upon him. The archbishop said to him, 'See, Abba Moses, now you are entirely white.' The old man said to him, 'It is true of the outside, lord and father, but what about Him who sees the inside?' Wishing to test him the archbishop said to the priests, 'When Abba Moses comes into the sanctuary, drive him out, and go with him to hear what he says.' So the old man came in and they covered him with abuse, and drove him out, saying, 'Outside, black man!' Going out, he said to himself, 'They have acted rightly concerning you, for your skin is as black as ashes. You are not a man, so why should you be allowed to meet men?'

5. Once the order was given at Scetis, 'Fast this week.' Now it happened that some brothers came from Egypt to visit Abba Moses and he cooked something for them. Seeing some smoke, the neighbours said to the ministers, 'Look, Moses has broken the commandment and has cooked something in his cell.' The ministers said, 'When he comes, we will speak to him ourselves.' When the Saturday came, since they knew Abba Moses' remarkable way of life, the ministers said to him in front of everyone, 'O Abba Moses, you did not keep the commandment of men, but it was so that you might keep the commandment of God.'

6. A brother came to Scetis to visit Abba Moses and asked him for a word. The old man said to him, 'Go, sit in your cell, and your cell will teach you everything.'

7. Abba Moses said, 'The man who flees and lives in solitude is like a bunch of grapes ripened by the sun, but he who remains amongst men is like an unripe grape.'

8. The magistrate heard about Abba Moses one day and he went to Scetis to see him. They told the old man. He got up and fled to the marsh. Some people met him and said to him, 'Old man, tell us where the cell of Abba Moses is.' He said to them, 'What do you want with him? He is a fool.' So the magistrate went back to the church and said to the ministers, 'I heard people talk about Abba Moses and I went to see him, but there was an old man going into Egypt who crossed our path and we asked him where Abba Moses' cell is, and he said to us, "What do you want with him? He is a fool."' When they heard this, the clergy were offended and said, 'What kind of an old man was it who spoke like that about the holy man to you?' He said, 'An old man wearing old clothes, a big black man.' They said, 'It was Abba Moses himself and it was in order not to meet you that he said that.' The magistrate went away greatly edified.

9. At Scetis Abba Moses used to say, 'If we keep the commandments of our Fathers, I will answer for it on God's behalf that the barbarians will not come here. But if we do not keep the commandments of God, this place will be devastated.'

10. One day, when the brethren were sitting beside him, he said to them, 'Look, the barbarians are coming to Scetis today; get up and flee.' They said to him, 'Abba, won't you flee too?' He said to them, 'As for me, I have been waiting for this day for many years, that the word of the Lord Christ may be fulfilled which says, "All who take the sword will perish by the sword."' (Matt. 26.52) They said to him, 'We will not flee either, but we will die with you.' He said to them: 'That is nothing to do with me; let everyone decide for himself whether he stops or not.' Now there were seven brothers there and he said to them, 'Look, the barbarians are drawing near to the door.' They they came in and slew them. But one fled and hid under the cover of a pile of rope and he saw seven crowns decending and crowning them.

11. A brother questioned Abba Moses saying, 'I see something in front of me and I am not able to grasp it.' The old man said to him,

'If you do not become dead like those who are in the tomb, you will not be able to grasp it.'

12. Abba Poemen said that a brother asked Abba Moses how someone could consider himself as dead towards his neighbour. The old man said to him, 'If a man does not think in his heart that he is already three days dead and in the tomb, he cannot attain this saying.'

13. It was said of Abba Moses at Scetis that when he had arranged to go to Petra, he grew tired in the course of the journey and said to himself, 'How can I find the water I need there?' Then a voice said to him, 'Go, and do not be anxious about anything.' So he went. Some Fathers came to see him and he had only a small bottle of water. He used it all up in cooking lentils for them. The old man was worried, so he went in and came out of his cell, and he prayed to God, and a cloud of rain came to Petra and filled all the cisterns. After this, the visitors said to the old man, 'Tell us why you went in and out.' The old man said to them, 'I was arguing with God, saying, "You brought me here and now I have no water for your servants." This is why I was going in and out; I was going on at God till he sent us some water.'

Seven instructions which Abba Moses sent to Abba Poemen. He who puts them into practice will escape all punishment and will live in peace, whether he dwells in the desert or in the midst of brethren.

1. The monk must die to his neighbour and never judge him at all, in any way whatever.

2. The monk must die to everything before leaving the body, in order not to harm anyone.

3. If the monk does not think in his heart that he is a sinner, God will not hear him. The brother said, 'What does that mean, to think in his heart that he is a sinner?' Then the old man said, 'When someone is occupied with his own faults, he does not see those of his neighbour.'

4. If a man's deeds are not in harmony with his prayer, he labours in vain. The brother said, 'What is this harmony between practice

and prayer?' The old man said, 'We should no longer do those things against which we pray. For when a man gives up his own will, then God is reconciled with him and accepts his prayers.' The brother asked, 'In all the affliction which the monk gives himself, what helps him?' The old man said, 'It is written, "God is our refuge and strength, a very present help in trouble." ' (Ps.46.1)

5. The old man was asked, 'What is the good of the fasts and watchings which a man imposes on himself?' and he replied, 'They make the soul humble. For it is written, "Consider my affliction and my trouble, and forgive all my sins." (Ps.25.18) So if the soul gives itself all this hardship, God will have mercy on it.'

6. The old man was asked, 'What should a man do in all the temptations and evil thoughts that come upon him?' The old man said to him, 'He should weep and implore the goodness of God to come to his aid, and he will obtain peace if he prays with discernment. For it is written, "With the Lord on my side I do not fear. What can man do to me?" ' (Ps. 118.6)

7. A brother asked the old man, 'Here is a man who beats his servant because of a fault he has committed; what will the servant say?' The old man said, 'If the servant is good, he should say, "Forgive me, I have sinned." ' The brother said to him, 'Nothing else?' The old man said, 'No, for from the moment he takes upon himself responsibility for the affair and says, "I have sinned," immediately the Lord will have mercy on him. The aim in all these things is not to judge one's neighbour. For truly, when the hand of the Lord caused all the first-born in the land of Egypt to die, no house was without its dead.' The brother said, 'What does that mean?' The old man said, 'If we are on the watch to see our own faults, we shall not see those of our neighbour. It is folly for a man who has a dead person in his house to leave him there and go to weep over his neighbour's dead. To die to one's neighbour is this: To bear your own faults and not to pay attention to anyone else wondering whether they are good or bad. Do no harm to anyone, do not think anything bad in your heart towards anyone, do not scorn the man who does evil, do not put confidence in him who does wrong to his neighbour, do not rejoice with him who injures his neighbour. This

is what dying to one's neighbour means Do not rail against anyone, but rather say, "God knows each one." Do not agree with him who slanders, do not rejoice at his slander and do not hate him who slanders his neighbour. This is what it means not to judge. Do not have hostile feelings towards anyone and do not let dislike dominate your heart; do not hate him who hates his neighbour. This is what peace is: Encourage yourself with this thought, "Affliction lasts but a short time, while peace is for ever, by the grace of God the Word. Amen." '

MATOES

1. Abba Matoes said, 'I prefer a light and steady activity, to one that is painful at the beginning but is soon broken off.'

2. He also said, 'The nearer a man draws to God, the more he sees himself a sinner. It was when Isaiah the prophet saw God, that he declared himself "a man of unclean lips." ' (Is. 6.5)

3. He also said, 'When I was young, I would say to myself: perhaps one day I shall do something good; but now that I am old, I see that there is nothing good about me.'

4. He also said, 'Satan does not know by what passion the soul can be overcome. He sows, but without knowing if he will reap, sometimes thoughts of fornication, sometimes thoughts of slander, and similarly for the other passions. He supplies nourishment to the passion which he sees the soul is slipping towards.'

5. A brother went to Abba Matoes and said to him, 'How is it that the monks of Scetis did more than the Scriptures required in loving their enemies more than themselves?' Abba Matoes said to him, 'As for me I have not yet managed to love those who love me as I love myself.'

6. A brother questioned Abba Matoes, 'What ought I to do when a brother comes to see me and it is a fast day, or in the morning? This worries me.' The old man said to him, 'If you don't fuss about it and simply eat with the brother, that is all right, but if you are not expecting anyone and you eat, that is your own will.'

7. Abba James said that he went to Abba Matoes' cell and when he left he said to him, 'I want to go to the Cells.' He said to me: 'Greet Abba John for me.' So going to Abba John's cell I said to him, 'Abba Matoes greets you.' The old man said to me, 'Abba Matoes is an Israelite indeed in whom there is no guile.' A year later I returned to Abba Matoes and gave him Abba John's greeting. The old man said: 'I am not worthy of what the old man said, but know this: whenever you hear an old man praising his neighbour more than himself, it is because he has reached a great stature: for this is perfection to praise one's neighbour more than oneself.'

8. Abba Matoes said, 'A brother came to me and said, "Slander is worse than fornication." I said to him, "That is a hard saying." He said to me, "What do you mean?" I said to him, "Slander is bad, but it is soon healed, for he who slanders often repents, saying that he has spoken unkindly; but fornication is physical death." '

9. One day Abba Matoes went to Rhaithou, in the region of Magdolos. A brother went with him, and the bishop seized the old man and made him a priest. While they were eating together the bishop said, 'Forgive me, abba; I know you did not want it but it was in order that I might be blessed by you that I dared to do it.' The old man said humbly to him, 'I did not wish it, to be sure; but what really troubles me is that I must be separated from the brother who is with me and I am not able to keep on saying the prayers quite alone.' The bishop said to him, 'If you know that he is worthy, I will ordain him too.' Abba Matoes said, 'I do not know if he is worthy of it; I know only one thing, that he is better than I.' So the bishop ordained him also. Both of them died without having approached the sanctuary to make the offering. The old man used to say, 'I have confidence in God that I shall not suffer great condemnation through the laying on of hands since I do not make the offering. For the laying on of hands is for those who are without reproach.'

10. Abba Matoes said that three old men went to Abba Paphnutius, he who is called Cephalus, to ask a word of him. The old man said to them, 'What do you want me to say to you? A spiritual word, or a bodily word?' They said, 'A spiritual word.' The old man said to them, 'Go, and choose trials rather than quietness, dishonour rather than glory, and to give rather than to receive.'

11. A brother questioned Abba Matoes saying, 'Give me a word.' He said to him, 'Go, and pray God to put compunction in your heart, and give you humility; be aware of your faults; do not judge others but put yourself below everyone; do not be friendly with a boy nor with an heretical friend; put freedom of speech far from you; control your tongue and your belly; drink only a small quantity of wine, and if someone speaks about some topic, do not argue with him but if he is right, say, "Yes"; if he is wrong, say, "You know what you are saying," and do not argue with him about what he has said. That is humility.'

12. A brother said to Abba Matoes, 'Give me a word.' He said to him, 'Restrain the spirit of controversy in yourself in everything, and weep, have compunction, for the time is drawing near.'

13. A brother questioned Abba Matoes saying, 'What am I to do? My tongue makes me suffer, and every time I go among men, I cannot control it, but I condemn them in all the good they are doing and reproach them with it. What am I to do?' The old man replied, 'If you cannot contain yourself, flee into solitude. For this is a sickness. He who dwells with brethren must not be square, but round, so as to turn himself towards all.' He went on, 'It is not through virtue that I live in solitude, but through weakness; those who live in the midst of men are the strong ones.'

MARK, DISCIPLE OF ABBA SILVANUS

1. It was said of Abba Silvanus that at Scetis he had a disciple called Mark, whose obedience was great. He was a scribe. The old man loved him because of his obedience. He had eleven other disciples who were hurt because he loved him more than them. When they knew this, the elders were sorry about it and they came one day to him to reproach him about it. Taking them with him, he went to knock at each cell, saying, 'Brother so and so, come here; I need you,' but none of them came immediately. Coming to Mark's cell, he knocked and said, 'Mark.' Hearing the old man's voice, he jumped up immediately and the old man sent him off to serve and said to the elders, 'Fathers, where are the other brothers?' Then he

went into Mark's cell and picked up his book and noticed that he had begun to write the letter 'omega', but when he had heard the old man, he had not finished writing it. Then the elders said, 'Truly, abba, he whom you love, we love too and God loves him.'

2. They said this of Abba Silvanus that, as he was walking to Scetis one day with the old men, and wishing to demonstrate his disciple Mark's obedience, and show the reason for his affection for him, he said to him, seeing a small wild boar, 'Boy, do you see that little buffalo?' He said to him, 'Yes, abba.' 'And do you see his horns, how attractive they are?' He said to him, 'Yes, abba.' The old men were astonished at his reply and edified by his obedience.

3. Abba Mark's mother came down to see him one day with great pomp. The old man went out to meet her. She said to him, 'Abba, tell my son to come out so that I may see him.' So the old man went back and said to him, 'Go out, and let your mother see you.' He was wearing ragged garments and coming from the kitchen, so he was very dirty. He went out under obedience and closed his eyes and said to them: 'Greetings, greetings, greetings!' but he did not see them at all. His mother did not recognize him. So she sent a message to the old man again, 'Abba, send me my son, so that I may see him.' He said to Mark, 'Did I not tell you to go out, so your mother would see you?' Mark said to him, 'As you said, abba, I went out; but please, do not tell me a second time to go out, because I don't want to disobey you.' The old man went out and said to the mother, 'Your son was he who came to meet you, saying, "Greetings!" ' Then he comforted her and sent her away.

4. On another occasion Mark decided to leave Scetis and go to Mount Sinai and live there. His mother sent his abba a message, begging him with tears to send her son out to see her. So the old man made him go. But as he was putting on his sheepskin to go and preparing to take leave of the old man, he suddenly burst into tears and did not go out after all.

5. It was said of Abba Silvanus that when he wished to go away to Syria, his disciple Mark said to him. 'Father, I do not want to leave this place, nor to let you go away, abba. Stay here for three days.' And on the third day Mark died.

MILESIUS

1. While travelling through a certain region, Abba Milesius saw a monk whom someone had seized under the pretext that he had committed a murder. The old man went and questioned the brothers. Learning that he had been wrongly accused, he said to those who were holding him, 'Where is the man who has been killed?' They showed him to him. Telling them all to pray, he went up to the dead man. While he was stretching his hands towards heaven, the dead man stood up. He said to him in front of everyone, 'Tell us who killed you.' The man said, 'As I was going into the church, I gave some money to the priest. He stood up and killed me; then he took me and threw me into the abba's monastery. Therefore I beseech you to take the money and give it to my children.' Then the old man said to him, 'Go, and rest until the Lord comes and awakens you.'

2. Another time, when he was living with two disciples on the borders of Persia, two of the king's sons, brothers by blood, went to hunt according to their custom. They spread nets around a wide area; at least forty miles, so as to be able to hunt and shoot everything that was found inside the nets. Now the old man happened to be there with his two disciples. Seeing him, all hairy and like a wild man, they were struck with amazement and said to him, 'Tell us if you are a man or a spirit?' He said to them, 'I am a sinful man, and I have come away to weep for my sins, and I adore Jesus the Christ, the Son of the Living God.' They said to him, 'There is no god save the sun, the fire, and the water' (which they worshipped). 'Therefore, come and make a sacrifice in their honour.' He said to them, 'They are creatures and you are wrong. But I implore you to be converted and to acknowledge the true God, the Creator of all these things.' They said to him, 'You say that the man who was condemned and crucified is the true God?' The old man said, 'He who has crucified sin and killed death, is He whom I say is the true God.' But they tortured him and the brothers, to compel them to offer sacrifice. After many torments they beheaded the two brothers, but they tortured the old man for many days. Finally they used a different procedure, and placing him between them, they shot

arrows at him, one in front and the other behind. But he said to them, 'Since you have agreed about shedding innocent blood, at the same time, tomorrow, at the same hour, your mother will no longer have you as sons, and will be deprived of your love and by your own arrows you will shed each other's blood.' They scorned his words and went to hunt the next day. A hart ran close to them. They spurred their horses and galloped after it. They threw their javelins at it, and they pierced each other's hearts, as the old man had said when he warned them. An so they died.

MOTIUS

1. A brother questioned Abba Motius, saying, 'If I go to dwell somewhere, how do you want me to live?' The old man said to him, 'If you live somewhere, do not seek to be known for anything special; do not say, for example, I do not go to the *synaxis*; or perhaps, I do not eat at the *agape*. For these things make an empty reputation and later you will be troubled because of this. For men rush there where they find these practices.' The brother said to him, 'What shall I do, then?' The old man said, 'Wherever you live, follow the same manner of life as everyone else and if you see devout men, whom you trust doing something, do the same and you will be at peace. For this is humility: to see yourself to be the same as the rest. When men see you do not go beyond the limits, they will consider you to be the same as everyone else and no-one will trouble you.'

2. Concerning Abba Motius, his disciple, Abba Isaac, told this (both of them became bishops): 'This old man was the first to build a monastery at Heracliopolis and when he left he went to another place and did the same there. But through the power of the devil, there was a brother who opposed him and grieved him. The old man got up and withdrew to his own village; he built a monastery there and lived as a recluse. After some time the old men came from the place he had left, bringing with them the brother who had distressed him, to ask him to take him into his hermitage. When they drew near to the place where Abba Sores was, they left their sheep-

skins with this abba together with the brother in question. When they knocked, Motius put up the ladder, looked out, recognized them and said, 'Where are your sheepskins?' They said, 'Down there, with the brother.' As soon as he heard the name of the brother who had distressed him, in his joy the old man took a hatchet, battered down the door and came running out to where the brother was. He went to him first of all and made a prostration to him, and embraced him. He took him into his cell. For three days he entertained them all and relaxed with them, which he was not accustomed to do; then he got up and went home with them. Later, he became a bishop. In fact he was a wonder-worker, and Blessed Cyril made his disciple, Abba Isaac, a bishop also.'

MEGETHIUS

1. They said of Abba Megethius, that if he left his cell and it occurred to him to leave the place where he was living he would go without returning to his cell. He owned nothing in this world, except a knife with which he cut reeds and every day he made three small baskets, which was all he needed for his food.

2. They said of Abba Megethius that he was very humble, for he was brought up by the Egyptians and in contact with many old men, including Abba Sisoes and Abba Poemen. He lived on the river bank at Sinai. It happened, as he himself related, that one of the holy men visited him and said to him, 'Brother, what is your way of life in this desert?' He said, 'Every second day, I eat one loaf only.' The old man said to him, 'I advise you to eat half the loaf every day.' This he did and he found rest.

3. Some of the Fathers questioned Abba Megethius, saying, 'If some cooked food remains over for the next day, do you recommend the brethren to eat it?' The old man said to them, 'If this food is bad, it is not right to compel the brethren to eat it, in case it makes them ill, but it should be thrown away. But if it is still good and is thrown away through extravagance in order to prepare more that is wrong.'

4. He also said, 'Orginally, when we met together we spoke of edifying things, encouraging one another and we were "like the angels"; we ascended up to the heavens. But now when we come together, we only drag one another down by gossiping, and so we go down to hell.'

MIUS

1. Abba Mius of Belos said, 'Obedience responds to obedience. When someone obeys God, God obeys his request.'

2. Concerning an old man who was at Scetis he said that he had been a slave and he had become a true reader of hearts. Every year he went to Alexandria, taking his wages to his masters. They went to meet him with great respect, but the old man put water into a basin and brought it to wash his masters' feet. They said to him, 'No, Father, do not overwhelm us.' But he said to them, 'I acknowledge that I am your slave and I acknowledge that you have left me free to serve God; I wash your feet, and you accept my wages, which are here.' They argued, not wishing to receive them, so he said to them, 'If you refuse to accept them, I shall remain here and serve you.' Since they revered him, they allowed him to do what he wanted; then they saw him off, giving him many provisions and money so that he could give alms for them. For this reason he became famous and beloved in Scetis.

3. A soldier asked Abba Mius if God accepted repentance. After the old man had taught him many things he said, 'Tell me, my dear, if your cloak is torn, do you throw it away?' He replied, 'No , I mend it and use it again.' The old man said to him, 'If you are so careful about your cloak, will not God be equally careful about his creature?'

MARK THE EGYPTIAN

1. It was said of Abba Mark the Egyptian that he lived for thirty years without going out of his cell. The priest used to take holy communion to him. But the devil, seeing the remarkable endurance

of this man, decided to tempt him, by making him blame the priest. He brought it about that a demoniac went to the old man, under the pretext of asking for prayers. Before anything was said, the possessed man cried out to the old man, 'Your priest smells of sin, do not let him come near you any more.' But Mark, filled with the spirit of God, said to him, 'My son, everyone rids himself of impurity, but you bring it. It is written: "Judge not for that you be not judged." (Matt. 7.1) However, even if he is a sinner, the Lord will save him, for it is written: "Pray for one another that you may be healed." ' (James 5.16) When he had said this and when he had prayed, he drove the devil out of the man and sent him away healed. When the priest came, according to his custom, the old man received him with joy. Seeing the absence of malice in the old man, the good God showed him a marvel. When the priest prepared himself to stand before the holy table, this is what the old man related, 'I saw the angel of the Lord descend from heaven and place his hand on the priest's head and he became like a pillar of fire. I was filled with wonder at this sight, and I heard a voice saying to me, "Man, why are you astonished at this? In truth, if an earthly king does not allow his nobles to stand in his presence in soiled garments, but only arrayed in glory, how much more will the divine power purify the servants of the holy mysteries who stand before the heavenly glory?" ' And the noble athlete of Christ, Mark the Egyptian, became great and was judged worthy of this grace because he had not judged the priest.

MACARIUS OF ALEXANDRIA

Macarius of Alexandria, born c. A. D. 296, was a tradesman, a seller of sweetmeats. He went to visit Pachomius at least once during Lent. He was a hermit and priest in the Cells, famous for extreme asceticism; one of his disciples was Paphnutius. He died about A. D. 393.

1. Abba Macarius of Alexandria went one day with some brethren to cut reeds. The first day the brethren said to him, 'Come and eat with us, Father.' So he went to eat with them. The next day they invited him again to eat. But he would not consent saying, 'My

children, you need to eat because you are carnal, but I do not want food now.'

2. Abba Macarius went one day to Abba Pachomius of Tabennisi. Pachomius asked him, 'When brothers do not submit to the rule, is it right to correct them?' Abba Macarius said to him, 'Correct and judge justly those who are subject to you, but judge no-one else. For truly it is written: "Is it not those inside the church whom you are to judge? God judges those outside." ' (1 Cor. 5.12–13)

3. For four months Abba Macarius visited a brother every day, and he did not once find him distracted from prayer. Filled with wonder he said, 'He is an angel on earth.'

⋄| NU |⋄

NILUS

1. Abba Nilus said, 'Everything you do in revenge against a brother who has harmed you will come back to your mind at the time of prayer.'

2. He also said, 'Prayer is the seed of gentleness and the absence of anger.'

3. He also said, 'Prayer is a remedy against grief and depression.'

4. He also said, 'Go, sell all that belongs to you and give it to the poor and taking up the cross, deny yourself; in this way you will be able to pray without distraction.'

5. He also said, 'Whatever you have endured out of love of wisdom will bear fruit for you at the time of prayer.'

6. He also said, 'If you want to pray properly, do not let yourself be upset or you will run in vain.'

7. He also said, 'Do not be always wanting everything to turn out as you think it should, but rather as God pleases, then you will be undisturbed and thankful in your prayer.'

8. He also said, 'Happy is the monk who thinks he is the outcast of all.'

9. He also said, 'The monk who loves interior peace will remain invulnerable to the shafts of the enemy, but he who mixes with crowds constantly receives blows.'

10. He also said, 'The servant who neglects his master's work should expect a beating.'

NISTERUS

1. Abba Nisterus the Great was walking in the desert with a brother. They saw a dragon and they ran away. The brother said to him, 'Were you frightened too, Father?' The old man said to him, 'I am not afraid, my child, but it is better for me to flee, so as not to have to flee from the spirit of vain-glory.'

2. A brother questioned an old man saying, 'What good work should I do so that I may live?' The old man said, 'God knows what is good. I have heard it said that one of the Fathers asked Abba Nisterus the Great, the friend of Abba Anthony, and said to him, "What good work is there that I could do?" He said to him, "Are not all actions equal? Scripture says that Abraham was hospitable and God was with him. David was humble, and God was with him. Elias loved interior peace and God was with him. So, do whatever you see your soul desires according to God and guard your heart." '

3. Abba Joseph said to Abba Nisterus, 'What should I do about my tongue, for I cannot control it?' The old man said to him, 'When you speak, do you find peace?' He replied 'No.' The old man said, 'If you do not find peace, why do you speak? Be silent and when a conversation takes place, it is better to listen than to speak.'

4. A brother saw Abba Nisterus wearing two tunics and he questioned him saying, 'If a poor man came to ask you for a tunic,

which would you give him?' He replied, 'The better one.' 'And if someone else asked you for one, what would you give him?' The old man said, 'Half of the other one.' The brother said, 'And if someone else asked for one, what would you give him?' He said, 'I should cut the rest, give him half, and gird myself with whatever was left.' So the brother said, 'And if someone came and asked you for that, what would you do?' The old man said, 'I would give him the rest and go and sit down somewhere, until God sent me something to cover myself with, for I would not ask anyone for anything.'

5. Abba Nisterus said that a monk ought to ask himself every night and every morning, 'What have we done that is as God wills and what have we left undone of that which he does not will?' 'He must do this throughout his whole life. This is how Abba Arsenius used to live. Every day strive to come before God without sin. Pray to God in his presence, for he really is present. Do not impose rules on yourself; do not judge anyone. Swearing, making false oaths, lying, getting angry, insulting people laughing, all that is alien to monks, and he who is esteemed or exalted above that which he deserves suffers great harm.'

6. They said of Abba Nisterus when he lived at Rhaithou that for three weeks of the year he would weave baskets, making six each week.*

NISTERUS THE CENOBITE

1. Abba Poemen said of Abba Nisterus that he was like the serpent of brass which Moses made for the healing of the people: he possessed all virtue and without speaking, he healed everyone.

2. Abba Poemen asked Abba Nisterus how he had managed to gain this virtue: whenever a troublesome matter came up in the monastery, he did not say anything and he never intervened. He answered, 'Forgive me, abba, but when I came for the first time to the monastery, I said to myself, "You and the donkey are the same. The donkey is beaten but he does not speak, and when ill-treated he does not reply; now you must do the same, as psalmist says, 'I

*6 is an addition from J.-C. Guy's text (p. 27).

was like a beast towards thee; nevertheless, I am continually with
thee.' " ' (Ps. 73. 22–23)

NICON

1. A brother asked one of the Fathers saying: 'How does the
devil present temptations to the saints?' The old man said to him,
'There was one of the Fathers, named Nicon, who lived on Mount
Sinai. And someone went into a Pharanite's tent and finding his
daughter alone, sinned with her. Then he said to her, "Say it was
the anchorite, Abba Nicon, who did this." So when her father came
and heard about it, he took his sword and went to confront the old
man. When he knocked on the door, the old man came out. But
when he drew his sword, intending to kill him, his hand withered.
Then the Pharanite went and spoke to his priests, and they sent for
the old man. When he came out, they inflicted many blows on him
and wanted to drive him away, but he begged them, saying, "For
God's sake, let me stay here that I may do penance." So they kept
him apart for three years and ordered that no-one should see him.
He spent three years coming each Sunday to do penance and to beg
everyone saying, "Pray for me." Later, the man who had committed
the sin and thrown the temptation onto the anchorite was possessed
with the devil, and he admitted in church: "It was I who committed
the sin and said the servant of God should be falsely denounced."
Then the whole congregation went to do penance before the old
man, saying, "Forgive us, abba." He said to them, "As to forgiveness,
be forgiven; but as for staying here I shall not remain here any
longer with you, for no-one here had enough discernment to show
compassion towards me." With that, he left that place.' The old man
said, 'You see how the devil presents temptations to the saints.'

NETRAS

1. It was related of Abba Netras, the disciple of Abba Silvanus,
that when he dwelt in his cell on Mount Sinai, he treated himself
prudently, with regard to the needs of his body; but when he
became bishop of Pharan, he curbed himself with great austerities.

His disciple said to him, 'Abba, when we were in the desert, you did not practice such asceticism.' The old man said to him, 'There in the desert, I had interior peace and poverty and I wished to manage my body so as not to be ill and not need what I did not have. But now I am in the world and among its cares and even if I am ill here, there will be someone to look after me and so I do this in order not to destroy the monk in me.'

NICETAS

1. Abba Nicetas said of two brothers that they met with the intention of living together. The first thought within himself, 'If my brother wants something, I will do it,' and the second thought the same, 'I will do the will of my brother.' So they lived many years in great charity. Seeing this, the enemy set out to separate them. He stood at the entrance to the cell, appearing to the one like a dove and to the other like a raven. The first said, 'Do you see that little dove?' The other said, 'It is a raven.' They began to argue and to contradict one another, then they stood up and fought till they drew blood, to the great joy of the enemy; and they separated. After three days they returned and came to their senses and each asked the other's forgiveness. They recognized that each of them had believed the bird to be what he had seen and recognized that their conflict came from the enemy. So they lived to the end without being separated.

·|XII|·

XOIUS

1. A brother asked Abba Xoius, this question, 'If I happen to eat three loaves, is that a lot?' The old man said to him, 'Brother, have you come to the threshing-floor to beat grain?' So he said, 'If I drink three cups of wine, is that a lot?' He said to him, 'If the devil did not exist, it would not be a lot, but since he exists, it is a lot. Wine is alien to monks who live according to God.'

2. One of the Fathers said of Abba Xoius the Theban that one day he went to the mountain of Sinai and when he set out from there, a brother met him, groaning and saying, 'Abba, we are in distress through lack of rain.' The old man said to him, 'Why do you not pray and ask God for some?' The brother said to him: 'We pray, we say litanies and it does not rain.' The old man said to him, 'It is because you do not pray with intensity. Do you want to see that this is so?' Then he stretched his hands towards heaven in prayer and immediately it rained. Seeing this, the brother was filled with fear

and threw himself face downwards on the ground, bending low before him, but the old man fled and the brother told everyone what had happened. When they heard this, they glorified God.

XANTHIAS

1. Abba Xanthias said, 'The thief was on the cross and he was justified by a single word; and Judas who was counted in the number of the apostles lost all his labour in one single night and descended from heaven to hell. Therefore, let no-one boast of his good works, for all those who trust in themselves fall.'

2. Abba Xanthias went up from Scetis to Terenuthis one day. In the place where he rested he was offered a little wine, because of the demands of the journey. When they heard that he was there, some others brought him one possessed by the devil. The devil began to insult the old man, 'You have brought me to this wine-bibber!' The old man did not want to cast him out, but because of the insult he said, 'I have confidence in Christ that I shall not finish this cup before you have gone out.' When the old man began to drink, the devil cried out, saying, 'You are burning me, you are burning me!' and before he had finished the devil went out by the grace of Christ.

3. The same abba said, 'A dog is better than I am, for he has love and he does not judge.'

❖| OMICRON |❖

OLYMPIUS

1 Abba Olympius said this, 'One of the pagan priests came down from Scetis one day and came to my cell and slept there. Having reflected on the monks' way of life, he said to me, "Since you live like this, do you not receive any visions from your God?" I said to him, "No." Then the priest said to me, "Yet when we make a sacrifice to our God, he hides nothing from us, but discloses his mysteries; and you, giving yourselves so much hardship, vigils, prayer and asceticism, say that you see nothing? Truly, if you see nothing, then it is because you have impure thoughts in your hearts, which separate you from your God, and for this reason his mysteries are not revealed to you." So I went to report the priest's words to the old men. They were filled with admiration and said this was true. For impure thoughts separated God from man.'

2. Abba Olympius of the Cells was tempted to fornication. His thoughts said to him, 'Go, and take a wife.' He got up, found some

mud, made a woman and said to himself, 'Here is your wife, now
you must work hard in order to feed her.' So he worked, giving
himself a great deal of trouble. The next day, making some mud
again, he formed it into a girl and said to his thoughts, 'Your wife
has had a child, you must work harder so as to be able to feed her
and clothe your child.' So, he wore himself out doing this, and said
to his thoughts, 'I cannot bear this weariness any longer.' They
answered, 'If you cannot bear such weariness, stop wanting a wife.'
God, seeing his efforts, took away the conflict from him and he was
at peace.

ORSISIUS

1. Abba Orsisius said, 'If an unbaked brick is put in the foundations near to the river, it does not last for a single day, but baked,
it lasts like stone. So the man with a carnal disposition of soul, who
has not been in the fire through fear of God like Joseph, utterly
disintegrates when he accepts a position of authority. For many are
the temptations of those who live among men. It is good for him
who knows his limitations to avoid the weight of being in charge
of anything; but those who are firm in faith remain unmoved. If
anyone wished to speak of the great saint Joseph he would have to
say that he was not worldly. How greatly was he tempted and in
that place where there had not yet been any trace of devotion
towards God? But the God of his Fathers was with him and he
delivered him out of all his trouble and now he is with his Fathers
in the Kingdom of Heaven. Let us, therefore, know our limitations
and let us fight; even so we shall scarcely escape the judgement of
God.'

2. He has also said, 'I think that if a man does not guard his heart
well, he will forget and neglect everything he has heard, and thus
the enemy, finding room in him, will overthrow him. It is like a lamp
filled with oil and lit; if you forget to replenish the oil, gradually
it goes out and eventually darkness will prevail. It is still worse if
a rat happens to get near the lamp and tries to eat the wick; it cannot
do so before the oil is exhausted, but when it sees the lamp not only
without light, but also without heat, it tries to pull out the wick and

it brings the lamp down. If it is earthenware it breaks, but if it is brass, the master of the house will fill it with oil again. In the same way, through the soul's negligence, the Holy Spirit gradually withdraws until his warmth is completely extinguished. Finally the enemy devours the ardour of the soul and wickedness spoils the body, too. But if a man is sound in his attachment to God, and has only been led away through negligence, God, in his mercy, sends his fear to him and the remembrance of punishment and so prepares him to be vigilant and to guard himself with more prudence in the future, until his visitation.'

⬦| PI |⬦

POEMEN (called the Shepherd)

The Sayings attributed to Poemen form one seventh of the whole of the Alphabetical Collection. *It seems probable that this was the nucleus out of which the whole book grew. He figures also in many other Sayings in this book and in other collections. It is not certain that all these Sayings belong to one Poemen, since Poemen, 'the Shepherd', was a common title in Egypt. Nor is it certain which Poemen is meant: there is the Poemen who met Rufinus at Pispir in the 370s, and the Sayings connected with Anthony, Ammonas, Pior, Pambo and Joseph would fit in well with him, as an elder in Scetis in the last decade of the fourth century. He may be the same, or he may not, as the Poemen who left Scetis with his seven brothers in 408, and outlived Arsenius (+449). His contacts were with those closer to the devastation of Scetis, John the Dwarf, Agathon, and Moses. It seems most probable that it is from this group that settled at Terenuthis that this collection comes: it would be appropriate for such a commemoration of the Sayings of the great Old Men to be begun when the first age seemed to have passed.*

The involvement of Poemen with his family is worth noticing: besides his brothers, his mother, his nephew and a child related to him are mentioned. The close ties of Egyptian monks with their families and their villages were constantly having to be broken in favour of the freedom of the desert.

1. While he was still young, Abba Poemen went one day to an old man to ask him about three thoughts. Having reached the old man, he forgot one of the three and went back to his cell. But as he was stretching out his hand to turn the key, he remembered the thought which he had forgotten and leaving the key, he returned to the old man. The old man said to him, 'You come quickly, brother.' He told him, 'At the moment when I was putting out my hand to grasp the key, I remembered the thought which I was trying to find; so I did not open the door, but have retraced my steps.' Now the length of the way was very great and the old man said to him, 'Poemen, Shepherd of the flock, your name will be known throughout Egypt.'

2. Once Paësius, the brother of Abba Poemen, made friends with someone outside his cell. Now Abba Poemen did not want that. So he got up and fled to Abba Ammonas and said to him, 'Paësius, my brother, holds converse with someone, so I have no peace.' Abba Ammonas said to him, 'Poemen, are you still alive? Go, sit down in your cell; engrave it on your heart that you have been in the tomb for a year already.'

3. One day the priests of the district came to the monasteries where Abba Poemen was. Abba Anoub came and said to him, 'Let us invite the priests in today.' But he stood for a long time without giving him any reply, and, quite offended, Abba Anoub went away. Those who were sitting beside Poemen said to him, 'Abba, why didn't you answer him?' Abba Poemen said to them, 'It is not my business, for I am dead and a dead man does not speak.'

4. Before Abba Poemen's group came there, there was an old man in Egypt who enjoyed considerable fame and repute. But when Abba Poemen's group went up to Scetis, men left the old man to go to see Abba Poemen. Abba Poemen was grieved at this and said to his disciples, 'What is to be done about this great old man, for

men grieve him by leaving him and coming to us who are nothing? What shall we do, then to comfort this old man?' He said to them, 'Make ready a little food, and take a skin of wine and let us go to see him and eat with him. And so we shall be able to comfort him.' So they put together some food, and went. When they knocked at the door the old man's disciple answered, saying, 'Who are you?' They responded, 'Tell the abba it is Poemen who desires to be blessed by him.' The disciple reported this and the old man sent him to say, 'Go away, I have no time.' But in spite of the heat they persevered, saying, 'We shall not go away till we have been allowed to meet the old man.' Seeing their humility and patience, the old man was filled with compunction and opened the door to them. Then they went in and ate with him. During the meal he said, 'Truly, not only what I have heard about you is ture, but I see that your works are a hundred-fold greater,' and from that day, he became their friend.

5. One day the magistrate of that district wanted to see Abba Poemen but the old man did not want to see him. So, he seized his sister's son and threw him into prison, under the pretext that he was a criminal saying, 'If the old man comes to intercede for him I will let him go.' Then his sister came to weep at Poemen's door, but he gave her no answer. Then she reproached him in these words, saying, 'Heart of stone, have pity on me, for he is my only son.' But he only said to her, 'Poemen has not brought forth any sons.' At that, she went away. When he heard this, the magistrate sent Poemen this message, 'If you only ask me by a word, I will let him go.' The old man replied, 'Judge him according to the law; if he is worthy of death, put him to death, if not, do what you choose.'

6. One day a brother sinned in a monastery. Now there was an anchorite in the district who had not gone out for a long time. The abba of the monastery went to see him and to give him the news that the brother had sinned. The anchorite said, 'Drive him away.' So the brother left the monastery and he went into a cave and wept there. Now it happened that some brothers were going to see Abba Poemen and they heard him weeping. They entered, found him in great misery and invited him to go to see the old man, but he refused, saying, 'I am going to die here.' So when they reached Abba Poemen's cell they told him about the brother. And he exhorted

them, and he sent them away saying, 'Say to him, Abba Poemen
sends for you.' Then the brother came. Seeing he was in such
distress, Abba Poemen stood up, embraced him and was kind to him
and invited him to eat. Then he sent one of the brethren to the
anchorite, saying, 'For many years I have desired to see you, having
heard of you. But because of our lethargy, we have not yet met.
Now, however, if God wills it and you have the time, give yourself
the trouble of coming here, and we will see one another.' The old
man had never left his cell but when he heard this he said, 'If God
had not inspired the old man, he would not have sent someone to
summon me.' So he got up and went to see Poemen. They embraced
one another with joy and sat down. Abba Poemen said to him, 'Two
men dwelt in one place and someone belonging to each of them
died; the first one, leaving his own dead, went to weep over the
other's.' Hearing these words, the anchorite was filled with compunction and he remembered what he had done and said, 'Poemen,
you have gone up to heaven and I have gone down to the earth.'

7. Many old men came to see Abba Poemen and one day it
happened that a member of Abba Poemen's family came, who had
a child whose face, through the power of the devil, was turned
backwards. The father seeing the number of Fathers present, took
the child and sat down outside the monastery, weeping. Now it
happened that one of the old men came out and seeing him, asked
him, 'Man, why are you weeping?' He replied, 'I am related to Abba
Poemen, and see the misfortune which has overtaken my child.
Though I want to bring him to the old man, we are afraid he does
not want to see us. Each time he hears I am here, he has me driven
away. But since you are with him, I have dared to come. If you will,
Father, have pity on me, take the child inside and pray for him.' So
the old man took the child, went inside and behaved with good
sense. He did not immediately present him to Abba Poemen, but
began with the lesser brethren, and said, 'Make the sign of the cross
over this little child.' Having had him signed by all in turn, he
presented him at last to Abba Poemen. Abba Poemen did not want
to make the sign of the cross over him, but the others urged him,
saying, 'Do as everyone else has done.' So groaning he stood up and
prayed, saying, 'God, heal your creature, that he be not ruled by the
enemy.' When he had signed him, the child was healed immediately
and given back whole to his father.

8. A brother from Abba Poemen's neighbourhood left to go to another country one day. There he met an anchorite. The latter was very charitable and many came to see him. The brother told him about Abba Poemen. When he heard of his virtue, the anchorite wanted to see him. Some time afterwards when the brother had returned to Egypt the anchorite went there to see the brother who had formerly paid him a visit. He had told him where he lived. When he saw him, the brother was astonished and very pleased. The anchorite said to him, 'Please will you be so kind as to take me to Abba Poemen.' So he brought him to the old man and presented him, saying, 'This is a great man, full of charity, who is held in high estimation in his district. I have spoken to him about you, and he has come because he wants to see you.' So Abba Poemen received him with joy. They greeted one another and sat down. The visitor began to speak of the Scriptures, of spiritual and of heavenly things. But Abba Poemen turned his face away and answered nothing. Seeing that he did not speak to him, the other went away deeply grieved and said to the brother who had brought him, 'I have made this long journey in vain. For I have come to see the old man, and he does not wish to speak to me.' Then the brother went inside to Abba Poemen and said to him, 'Abba, this great man who has so great a reputation in his own country has come here because of you. Why did you not speak to him?' The old man said, 'He is great and speaks of heavenly things and I am lowly and speak of earthly things. If he had spoken of the passions of the soul, I should have replied, but he speaks to me of spiritual things and I know nothing about that.' Then the brother came out and said to the visitor, 'The old man does not readily speak of the Scriptures, but if anyone consults him about the passions of the soul, he replies.' Filled with compunction, the visitor returned to the old man and said to him, 'What should I do, Abba, for the passions of the soul master me?' The old man turned towards him and replied joyfully, 'This time, you come as you should. Now open your mouth concerning this and I will fill it with good things.' Greatly edified, the other said to him, 'Truly, this is the right way!' He returned to his own country giving thanks to God that he had been counted worthy to meet so great a saint.

9. One day the chief magistrate of the district seized one of the men of Abba Poemen's village, and everyone came to beg the old

man to go and have him released. He replied, 'Leave me for three days and I will go.' Abba Poemen prayed to the Lord in these words, 'Lord, do not give me this grace, otherwise they will never let me stay in this place.' Then the old man went to intercede with the magistrate, who replied, 'Will you intercede for a brigand, abba?' The old man rejoiced that he had not been granted this grace.

10. They said that one day Abba Poemen and his brethren were making ropes and the work was delayed because they had nothing with which to buy flax. One of their friends told a friendly merchant about this. Now Abba Poemen did not want to receive anything from anyone because of the trouble it causes. But the merchant wanted to do something for the old man, so he pretended to need ropes and brought a camel and took them away. When the brothers came to see Abba Poemen and learned what the merchant had done, they said, intending to praise him, 'Truly, Abba, he has taken them though he did not need them so as to do us a service.' Hearing that he had taken them without needing them, Abba Poemen said to the brother, 'Get up, hire a camel and bring them back, and if you do not bring them back, Poemen will no longer live here with you. I do not want to do wrong to someone who does not need those ropes, lest he should suffer loss by it and take my reward from me.' The brother went away with much labour and brought them back; otherwise the old man would have gone away from them. When he saw the ropes, he rejoiced as though he had found a great treasure.

11. A priest of Pelusia heard it said of some brethren that they often went to the city, took baths and were careless in their behaviour. He went to the *synaxis,* and took the habit away from them. Afterwards, his heart was moved, he repented and went to see Abba Poemen, obsessed by his thoughts. He brought the monastic habits of the brothers and told him all about it. The old man said to him, 'Don't you sometimes have something of the old Adam in you?' The priest said, 'I have my share of the old Adam.' The abba said to him, 'Look, you are just like the brethren yourself; if you have even a little share of the old Adam, then you are subject to sin in the same way.' So the priest went and called the brothers and asked their pardon; and he clothed them in the monastic habit again and let them go.

12. A brother questioned Abba Poemen saying, 'I have committed a great sin and I want to do penance for three years.' The old man said to him, 'That is a lot.' The brother said, 'For one year?' The old man said again, 'That is a lot.' Those who were present said, 'For forty days?' He said again, 'That is a lot.' He added, 'I myself say that if a man repents with his whole heart and does not intend to commit the sin any more, God will accept him after only three days.'

13. He also said, 'The distinctive mark of the monk is made clear through temptations.'

14. He also said, 'Just as the king's body-guard stands always on guard at his side, so the soul should always be on guard against the demon of fornication.'

15. Abba Anoub asked Abba Poemen about the impure thoughts which the heart of man brings forth and about vain desires. Abba Poemen said to him, 'Is the axe any use without someone to cut with it? (Is. 10.15) If you do not make use of these thoughts, they will be ineffectual too.'

16. Abba Poemen also said, 'If Nabuzardan, the head-cook, had not come, the temple of the Lord would not have been burned: (2 Kings 24.8f.) that is to say: if slackness and greed did not come into the soul, the spirit would not be overcome in combat with the enemy.'

17. It was said of Abba Poemen that if he was invited to eat against his will, he wept but he went, so as not to refuse to obey his brother and cause him pain.

18. Abba Poemen also said, 'Do not live in a place where you see that some are jealous of you, for you will not make progress.'

19. Some brothers told Abba Poemen of a brother who did not drink wine. He said, 'Wine is not for monks.'

20. Abba Isaiah questioned Abba Poemen on the subject of impure thoughts. Abba Poemen said to him, 'It is like having a chest full of clothes, if one leaves them in disorder they are spoiled in the course of time. It is the same with thoughts. If we do not do

anything about them, in time they are spoiled, that is to say, they disintegrate.'

21. Abba Joseph put the same question and Abba Poemen said to him, 'If someone shuts a snake and a scorpion up in a bottle, in time they will be completely destroyed. So it is with evil thoughts: they are suggested by the demons; they disappear through patience.'

22. A brother came to see Abba Poemen and said to him, 'I sow my field and give away in charity what I reap from it.' The old man said to him, 'That is good,' and he departed with fervour and intensified his charity. Hearing this, Abba Anoub said to Abba Poemen, 'Do you not fear God, that you have spoken like that to the brother?' The old man remained silent. Two days later Abba Poemen saw the brother coming and in the presence of Abba Anoub said to him, 'What did you ask me the other day? I was not attending.' The brother said, 'I said that I sow my field and give away what I gain in charity.' Abba Poemen said to him, 'I thought you were speaking of your brother who is in the world. If it is you who are doing this, it is not right for a monk.' At these words the brother was saddened and said, 'I do not know any other work and I cannot help sowing the fields.' When he had gone away, Abba Anoub made a prostration and said, 'Forgive me.' Abba Poemen said, 'From the beginning I too knew it was not the work of a monk but I spoke as I did, adapting myself to his ideas and so I gave him courage to increase his charity. Now he has gone away full of grief and yet he will go on as before.'

23. Abba Poemen said, 'If a man has sinned and denies it, saying: "I have not sinned," do not reprimand him; for that will discourage him. But say to him, "Do not lose heart, brother, but be on guard in future," and you will stir his soul to repentance.'

24. He also said, 'Experience is a good thing; it is that which tests a man.'

25. He also said, 'A man who teaches without doing what he teaches is like a spring which cleanses and gives drink to everyone, but it not able to purify itself.'

26. Going into Egypt one day, Abba Poemen saw a woman who was sitting in a tomb and weeping bitterly. He said, 'If all the delights of the world were to come, they could not drive sorrow away from the soul of this woman. Even so the monk would always have compunction in himself.'

27. He also said, 'A man may seem to be silent, but if his heart is condemning others he is babbling ceaselessly. But there may be another who talks from morning till night and yet he is truly silent; that is, he says nothing that is not profitable.'

28. A brother came to see Abba Poemen and said to him, 'Abba, I have many thoughts and they put me in danger.' The old man led him outside and said to him, 'Expand your chest and do not breathe in.' He said, 'I cannot do that.' Then the old man said to him, 'If you cannot do that, no more can you prevent thoughts from arising, but you can resist them.'

29. Abba Poemen said, 'If three men meet, of whom the first fully preserves interior peace, and the second gives thanks to God in illness, and the third serves with a pure mind, these three are doing the same work.'

30. He also said, 'It is written: "As the hart longs for flowing streams, so longs my soul for Thee, O God." (Ps. 42.1) For truly harts in the desert devour many reptiles and when their venom burns them, they try to come to the springs, to drink so as to assuage the venom's burning. It is the same for the monks: sitting in the desert they are burned by the venom of evil demons, and they long for Saturday and Sunday to come to be able to go to the springs of water, that is to say, the body and blood of the Lord, so as to be purified from the bitterness of the evil one.'

31. Abba Joseph asked Abba Poemen, 'How should one fast?' Abba Poemen said to him, 'For my part, I think it better that one should eat every day, but only a little, so as not to be satisfied.' Abba Joseph said to him, 'When you were younger, did you not fast two days at a time, abba?' The old man said: 'Yes, even for three days and four and the whole week. The Fathers tried all this out as they were able and they found it preferable to eat every day, but just a small amount. They have left us this royal way, which is light.'

32. It was said of Abba Poemen that every time he prepared to go to the *synaxis,* he sat alone and examined his thoughts for about an hour and then he set off.

33. A brother asked Abba Poemen, 'An inheritance has been left me, what ought I to do?' The old man said to him, 'Go, come back in three days and I will tell you.' So he returned as it had been decided. Then the old man said, 'What shall I say to you, brother? If I tell you to give it to the church, they will make banquets with it; if I tell you to give it to your relations, you will not receive any profit from it; if I tell you to give it to the poor, you will not do it. Do as you like, it is none of my business.'

34. Another brother questioned him in these words: 'What does, "See that none of you repays evil for evil" mean?' (1 Thess. 5.15) The old man said to him, 'Passions work in four stages—first, in the heart; secondly, in the face; thirdly, in words; and fourthly, it is essential not to render evil for evil in deeds. If you can purify your heart, passion will not come into your expression; but if it comes into your face, take care not to speak; but if you do speak, cut the conversation short in case you render evil for evil.'

35. Abba Poemen said, 'Vigilance, self-knowledge and discernment; these are the guides of the soul.'

36. He also said, 'To throw yourself before God, not to measure your progress, to leave behind all self-will; these are the instruments for the work of the soul.'

37. He also said, 'The victory over all the afflictions that befall you, is, to keep silence.'

38. He also said, 'All bodily comfort is an abomination to the Lord.'

39. He also said, 'Compunction has two sides: it is a good work and a good protection.'

40. He also said, 'If a thought about bodily needs overtakes you, put the matter right at once; and if it comes a second time, put it right again, but the third time, if it presents itself, do not pay any attention to it, for it is not being any use to you.'

41. He also said that a brother questioned Abba Adonias saying, 'What does it mean to become nothing?' The old man said, 'It means to place oneself beneath irrational beings and to know what they are without blame.'

42. He also said, 'If man remembered that it is written: "By your words you will be justified and by your words you will be condemned," (Matt. 12.37) he would choose to remain silent.'

43. He also said, 'The beginning of evil is heedlessness.'

44. He also said that Abba Isidore, the priest of Scetis, spoke to the people one day saying, 'Brothers, is it not in order to endure affliction that we have come to this place? But now there is no affliction for us here. So I am getting my sheepskin ready to go where there is some affliction and there I shall find peace.'

45. A brother said to Abba Poemen, 'If I see something, do you want me to tell you about it?' The old man said to him, 'It is written: "If one gives answer before he hears, it is his folly and shame." (Prov. 18.13) If you are questioned, speak; if not, remain silent.'

46. A brother asked Abba Poemen saying, 'Can a man put his trust in one single work?' The old man said to him that Abba John the Dwarf said, 'I would rather have a bit of all the virtues.'

47. The old man said that a brother asked Abba Pambo if it is good to praise one's neighbour and that the old man said to him, 'It is better to be silent.'

48. Abba Poemen said, 'Even if a man were to make a new heaven and earth, he could not live free of care.'

49. He also said, 'As the breath which comes out of his nostrils, so does a man need humility and the fear of God.'

50. A brother asked Abba Poemen, 'What should I do?' The old man said to him, 'When Abraham entered the promised land he bought a sepulchre for himself and by means of this tomb, he inherited the land.' The brother said to him, 'What is the tomb?' The old man said, 'The place of tears and compunction.'

51. A brother said to Abba Poemen, 'If I give my brother a little bread or something else, the demons tarnish these gifts saying it was

only done to please men.' The old man said to him, 'Even if it is to please men, we must give the brother what he needs.' He told him the following parable, 'Two farmers lived in the same town; one of them sowed and reaped a small and poor crop, while the other, who did not even trouble to sow reaped absolutely nothing. If a famine comes upon them, which of the two will find something to live on?' The brother replied, 'The one who reaped the small poor crop.' The old man said to him, 'So it is for us; we sow a little poor grain, so that we will not die of hunger.'

52. Abba Poemen said that Abba Ammonas said, 'A man can spend his whole time carrying an axe without succeeding in cutting down the tree; while another, with experience of tree-felling brings the tree down with a few blows. He said that the axe is discernment.'

53. A brother asked Abba Poemen, 'How should a man behave?' The old man said to him, 'Look at Daniel: no-one found anything in him to complain about except for his prayers to the Lord his God.'

54. Abba Poemen said, 'The will of man is a brass wall between him and God and a stone of stumbling. When a man renounces it, he is also saying to himself, "By my God, I can leap over the wall." (Ps. 18.29) If a man's will is in line with what is right, then he can really labour.'

55. He also said, 'As the old men were sitting at a meal one day, Abba Alonius got up to serve and when they saw that, they praised him. But he answered absolutely nothing. So one of them said to him privately, "Why don't you answer the old men who are complimenting you?" Abba Alonius said to him, "If I were to reply to them I should be accepting their praises." '

56. He also said, 'Men speak to perfection but they do precious little about it.'

57. Abba Poemen said, 'Just a smoke drives the bees away and also takes the sweetness out of their work, so bodily ease drives the fear of God from the soul and dissipates all its activity.'

58. A brother came to see Abba Poemen in the second week of Lent and told him about his thoughts; he obtained peace, and said

to him, 'I nearly did not come here today.' The old man asked him why. The brother said, 'I said to myself, "Perhaps he will not let me in because it is Lent." ' Abba Poemen said to him, 'We have not been taught to close the wooden door but the door of our tongues.'

59. Abba Poemen said, 'You must flee from sensual things. Indeed, every time a man comes near to a struggle with sensuality, he is like a man standing on the edge of a very deep lake and the enemy easily throws him in whenever he likes. But if he lives far away from sensual things, he is like a man standing at a distance from the lake, so that even if the enemy draws him in order to throw him to the bottom, God sends him help at the very moment he is drawing him away and doing him violence.'

60. He also said, 'Poverty, hardship, austerity and fasting, such are the instruments of the solitary life. It is written, "When these three men are together, Noah, Job, and Daniel, there am I, says the Lord." (cf. Ezek. 14.14) Noah represents poverty, Job suffering and Daniel discernment. So, if these three works are found in a man, the Lord dwells in him.'

61. Abba Joseph said, 'While we were sitting with Abba Poemen he mentioned Agathon as "abba", and we said to him, "He is very young, why do you call him 'abba?' " Abba Poemen said, "Because his speech makes him worthy to be called abba." '

62. A brother came to Abba Poemen one day and said to him, 'What should I do, Father, for I am tempted to fornication? I went to Abba Ibiston and he said to me, "You must not let it stay with you." ' Abba Poemen said to him, 'Abba Ibiston's deeds are in heaven with the angels and he does not realise that you and I remain in fornication. If a monk controls his belly and his tongue and if he lives like an exile, be confident, he will not die.'

63. Abba Poemen said, 'Teach your mouth to say that which you have in your heart.'

64. A brother questioned Abba Poemen saying, 'If I see my brother committing a sin, is it right to conceal it?' The old man said to him, 'At the very moment when we hide our brother's fault, God hides our own and at the moment when we reveal our brother's fault, God reveals ours too.'

65. He said that someone asked Abba Paësius, 'What should I do about my soul, because it is insensitive and does not fear God?' He said to him, 'Go, and join a man who fears God, and live near him; he will teach you, too, to fear God.'

66. He also said, 'If a monk can overcome two things, he can become free from the world.' The brother asked him what these two things were and he said, 'Bodily ease and vain-glory.'

67. Abraham, the disciple of Abba Agathon, questioned Abba Poemen saying, 'How do the demons fight against me?' Abba Poemen said to him, 'The demons fight against you? They do not fight against us at all as long as we are doing our own will. For our own wills become the demons, and it is these which attack us in order that we may fulfil them. But if you want to see who the demons really fight against, it is against Moses and those who are like him.'

68. Abba Poemen said, 'God has given this way of life to Israel: to abstain from everything which is contrary to nature, that is to say, anger, fits of passion, jealousy, hatred and slandering the brethren; in short, everything that is characteristic of the old man.'

69. A brother questioned Abba Poemen saying, 'Give me a word.' And he said to him, 'The Fathers put compunction as the beginning of every action.' The brother said again, 'Give me another word.' The old man replied, 'As far as you can, do some manual work so as to be able to give alms, for it is written that alms and faith purify from sin.' The brother said, 'What is faith?' The old man said, 'Faith is to live humbly and to give alms.'

70. A brother questioned Abba Poemen saying, 'If I see a brother whom I have heard is a sinner, I do not want to take him into my cell, but when I see a good brother I am happy to be with him.' The old man said, 'If you do a little good to the good brother, do twice as much for the other. For he is sick. Now, there was an anchorite called Timothy in a coenobium. The abbot, having heard of a brother who was being tempted, asked Timothy about him, and the anchorite advised him to drive the brother away. Then when he had been driven away, the brother's temptation fell upon Timothy to the point where he was in danger. Then Timothy stood up before God and said, "I have sinned. Forgive me." Then a voice came

which said to him, "Timothy, the only reason I have done this to you is because you despised your brother in the time of his temptation."'

71. Abba Poemen said, 'The reason why we are so greatly tempted is because we do not guard our name and status, as Scripture says. Do we not see that the Saviour gave peace to the Canaanite woman, accepting her as she was? (cf. Matt. 15) And the same for Abigail, because she said to David, "Upon me alone be the guilt," (1 Sam. 25.24) the Lord heard her and loved her. Abigail stands for the soul and David for God. So when the soul accuses herself before the Lord, the Lord loves her.'

72. One day Abba Poemen went with Abba Anoub to the district of Diolcos. Arriving at the cemetery, they saw a woman in great sorrow, weeping bitterly. Standing there they watched her. Going a little further they met someone and Abba Poemen asked him, 'What is this woman weeping so bitterly for?' He said, 'Because her husband is dead and her son and her brother.' Abba Poemen said to the brother, 'I tell you, if a man does not mortify all his carnal desires and acquire compunction like this, he cannot become a monk. Truly the whole of this woman's life and soul are turned to compunction.'

73. Abba Poemen said, 'Do not judge yourself, but live with someone who knows how to behave himself properly.'

74. He said that when a brother went to see Abba John the Dwarf, he offered him that charity of which the apostle speaks, 'Charity suffers long and is kind.' (1. Cor. 13.4)

75. He said of Abba Pambo that Abba Anthony used to say of him, 'Through fearing God, he caused the spirit of God to dwell in him.'

76. One of the Fathers related this about Abba Poemen and his brethren: 'When they were living in Egypt, their mother wanted to see them and was not able to do so. So she took note of the time when they went to church and went to meet them. But when they saw her, they made a detour and closed the door in her face. But she beat on the door and cried with tears and groans, saying, "I must see you, my beloved children!" Hearing her, Abba Anoub went to

Abba Poemen and said to him, "What shall we do with this old woman who is weeping against the door?" From inside where he was standing, he heard her weeping with many groans and he said to her, "Woman, why are you crying out like this?" When she heard his voice, she cried out even more, weeping and saying, "I want to see you, my children. What will happen if I do see you? Am I not your mother? Was it not I who suckled you? So I was troubled when I heard your voice." The old man said to her, "Would you rather see us here or in the age which is to come?" She said to him, "If I do not see you here, shall I see you in the age to come?" He said to her, "If you refrain from seeing us now, you will see us yonder." So she departed full of joy and said, "If I shall see you perfectly yonder, I do not want to see you here." '

77. A brother asked Abba Poemen saying, 'High things, what are they?' The old man said to him, 'Righteousness.'

78. Some heretics came to Abba Poemen one day and began to speak evil of the archbishop of Alexandria suggesting that he had received the laying on of hands from priests. The old man, who had remained silent till then, called his brother and said, 'Set the table, give them something to eat and send them away in peace.'

79. Abba Poemen said that a brother who lived with some other brothers asked Abba Bessarion, 'What ought I to do?' The old man said to him, 'Keep silence and do not always be comparing yourself with others.'

80. He also said, 'Do not give your heart to that which does not satisfy your heart.'

81. He also said, 'If you take little account of yourself, you will have peace, wherever you live.'

82. He also said that Abba Sisoes said, 'There is a kind of shame that contains a culpable lack of fear.'

83. He also said, 'When self-will and ease become habitual, they overthrow a man.'

84. He also said, 'If you are silent, you will have peace wherever you live.'

85. He also said concerning Abba Pior that every day he made a new beginning.

86. A brother asked Abba Poemen, 'If a brother is involved in a sin and is converted, will God forgive him?' The old man said to him, 'Will not God, who has commanded men to act thus, do as much himself and even more? For God commanded Peter to forgive till seventy times seven.' (Matt. 18.22)

87. A brother asked Abba Poemen, saying, 'Is it good to pray?' The old man said that Abba Anthony said, 'This word comes from the mouth of the Lord, who said, "Comfort, comfort my people." ' (Is. 40.1)

88. A brother asked Abba Poemen, 'Can a man keep all his thoughts in control, and not surrender one to the enemy?' And the old man said to him, 'There are some who receive ten and give one.'

89. The same brother put the same question to Abba Sisoes who said to him, 'It is true that there are some who give nothing to the enemy.'

90. There was a great *hesychast* in the mountain of Athlibeos. Some thieves fell upon him and the old man began to cry out. When they heard this the neighbours seized the robbers and took them to the magistrate who threw them into prison. The brothers were very sorry about this and they said, 'It is through us that they have been put in prison.' They got up and went to Abba Poemen to tell him about it. He wrote to the old man saying, 'Consider the first betrayal and where it comes from and then examine the second. In truth, if you had not first failed within, you would not have committed the second betrayal.' On hearing Abba Poemen's letter read (for he was renowned in all the district for not coming out of his cell), he arose, went to the city, got the robbers out of prison and liberated them in public.

91. Abba Poemen said, 'A monk does not complain of his lot, a monk does not return evil for evil, a monk is not angry.'

92. Some old men came to see Abba Poemen and said to him, 'When we see brothers who are dozing at the *synaxis*, shall we rouse them so that they will be watchful?' He said to them, 'For my part

when I see a brother who is dozing, I put his head on my knees and let him rest.'

93. It was said of a brother that he had to fight against blasphemy and he was ashamed to admit it. He went where he heard some great old men lived to see them, in order to open his heart to them but when he got there, he was ashamed to admit his temptation. So he kept going to see Abba Poemen. The old man saw he was worried, and he was sorry he did not tell him what was wrong. So one day he forestalled him and said, 'For a long time you have been coming here to tell me what is troubling you, and when you are here you will not tell me about it, but each time you go away unhappy, keeping your thoughts to yourself. Now tell me, my child, what it is all about.' He said to him, 'The demon wars against me to make me blaspheme God and I am ashamed to say so.' So he told him all about it and immediately he was relieved. The old man said to him, 'Do not be unhappy, my child, but every time this thought comes to you say, "It is no affair of mine, may your blasphemy remain upon you, Satan, for my soul does not want it." Now everything that the soul does not desire, does not long remain,' and the brother went away healed.

94. A brother said to Abba Poemen, 'I see that wherever I go I find support.' The old man said to him, 'Even those who hold a sword in their hands have God who takes pity on them in the present time. If we are courageous, he will have mercy on us.'

95. Abba Poemen said, 'If a man accuses himself, he is protected on all sides.'

96. He said that Abba Ammonas said, 'A man may remain for a hundred years in his cell without learning how to live in the cell.'

97. Abba Poemen said, 'If a man has attained to that which the Apostle speaks of "to the pure, everything is pure," (Titus 1.15) he sees himself less than all creatures.' The brother said, 'How can I deem myself less then a murderer?' The old man said, 'When a man has really comprehended this saying, if he sees a man committing a murder he says, "He has only committed this one sin but I commit sins every day." '

98. A brother put the same question to Abba Anoub, telling him what Abba Poemen had said. Abba Anoub said to him, 'If a man really affirms this saying, when he sees his brother's faults he sees that his integrity exceeds his faults.' The brother said, 'What is integrity?' The old man replied, 'Always to accuse himself.'

99. A brother said to Abba Poemen, 'If I fall into a shameful sin, my conscience devours and accuses me saying: "Why have you fallen?" ' The old man said to him, 'At the moment when a man goes astray, if he says, I have sinned, immediately the sin ceases.'

100. A brother asked Abba Poemen saying, 'Why do the demons persuade my soul to look up to him who is superior to me and make me despise him who is my inferior?' The old man replied, 'About that, the Apostle has this to say: "In a great house there are not only vessels of gold and silver, but also of wood and earthenware; and if anyone purifies himself from what is ignoble, then he will be a vessel for noble use, consecrated and useful to the master of the house, ready for any good work." ' (2 Tim. 2.20–21)

101. A brother asked Abba Poemen, 'Why should I not be free to do without manifesting my thoughts to the old men?' The old man replied, 'Abba John the Dwarf said, "The enemy rejoices over nothing so much as over those who do not manifest their thoughts." '

102. A brother said to Abba Poemen, 'My heart becomes lukewarm when a little suffering comes my way.' The old man said to him, 'Do we not admire Joseph, a young man of seventeen, for enduring his temptation to the end? And God glorified him. Do we not also see Job, how he suffered to the end, and lived in endurance? Temptations cannot destroy hope in God.'

103. Abba Poemen said, 'Life in the monastery demands three things: the first is humility, the next is obedience, and the third which sets them in motion and is like a goad is the work of the monastery.'

104. A brother asked Abba Poemen, 'In the time of my affliction I looked for something from one of the old men which would be useful to me and he gave it me as a free gift. Now if God comes to my aid, ought I in my turn to give it to others as a free gift, or

rather give it back to him who gave it to me?' The old man said to him, 'What is right in the sight of God, is for you to give it back to him, for it is his.' The brother said, 'If I return it to him and he does not want it, but says to me, "Go, give it away however you like as a free gift," what shall I do?' The old man said to him, 'This thing belongs to him, but if it is offered to you spontaneously without your asking for it, it belongs to you. Whether he is a monk or a secular person, if he no longer wants what you ask for and gives it you, then it is right for you, with his knowledge, to give it away in his name as a free gift.'

105. It was said of Abba Poemen that he never wished to speak after another old man, but that he preferred to praise him in everything he had said.

106. Abba Poemen said, 'Many of our Fathers have become very courageous in asceticism, but in fineness of perception there are very few.'

107. One day Abba Isaac was sitting beside Abba Poemen when they heard a cock crow. Abba Isaac said to him, 'Is it possible to hear that here, abba?' He replied, 'Isaac, why do you make me talk? You and those like you hear those noises, but the vigilant man does not trouble about them.'

108. It was said that if one of the brethren came to see Abba Poemen the latter used to send him first to Abba Anoub, because he was older than he. But Abba Anoub would say to them, 'Go to my brother Poemen because it is he who has the gift of speaking.' Whenever Abba Anoub came to sit beside Abba Poemen the latter refused to speak in his presence.

109. A secular man of devout life came to see Abba Poemen. Now it happened that there were other brethren with the old man, asking to hear a word from him. The old man said to the faithful secular, 'Say a word to the brothers.' When he insisted, the secular said, 'Please excuse me, abba; I myself have come to learn.' But he was urged on by the old man and so he said, 'I am a secular, I sell vegetables and do business; I take bundles to pieces, and make smaller ones; I buy cheap and sell dear. What is more I do not know how to speak of the Scriptures; so I will tell you a parable. A man

said to his friends, "I want to go to see the emperor; come with me."
One friend said to him, "I will go with you half the way." Then he
said to another friend, "Come and go with me to the emperor," and
he said to him, "I will take you as far as the emperor's palace." He
said to a third friend, "Come with me to the emperor." He said, "I
will come and take you to the palace and I will stay and speak and
help you to have access to the emperor." ' They asked what was the
point of the parable. He answered them, 'The first friend is asceticism, which leads the way; the second is chastity which takes us to
heaven; and the third is almsgiving which with confidence presents
us to God our King.' The brethren withdrew edified.

110. A brother settled outside his village and did not return there
for many years. He said to the brethren, 'See how many years it is
since I went back to the village, while you often go up there.' This
was told to Abba Poemen and the old man said, 'I used to go back
up there at night and walk all round my village, so that the thought
of not having gone up there would not cause me vain-glory.'

111. A brother said to Abba Poemen, 'Give me a word,' and he
said to him, 'As long as the pot is on the fire, no fly nor any other
animal can get near it, but as soon as it is cold, these creatures get
inside. So it is for the monk; as long as he lives in spiritual activities,
the enemy cannot find a means of overthrowing him.'

112. Abba Joseph said of Abba Poemen that he said, 'This saying
which is written in the Gospel: "Let him who has no sword, sell his
mantle and buy one," (Luke 22.36) means this: let him who is at ease
give it up and take the narrow way.'

113. Some Fathers questioned Abba Poemen saying, 'If we see a
brother in the act of committing a sin, do you think that we ought
to reprove him?' The old man said to them, 'For my part, if I have
to go out and I see someone committing a sin, I pass on my way
without reproving him.'

114. Abba Poemen said, 'It is written: "Give witness of that
which your eyes have seen" (cf. Proverbs 25.8); but I say to you
even if you have touched with your hands, do not give witness. In
truth, a brother was deceived in this respect: he thought he saw his
brother in the act of sinning with a woman; greatly incensed, he

drew near and kicked them (for he thought it was they), saying, "Now stop; how much longer will you go on?" Now it turned out that it was some sheaves of corn. That is the reason why I said to you: even if you touch with your hands, do not reprove.'

115. A brother asked Abba Poemen, 'What shall I do, for fornication and anger war against me?' The old man said, 'In this connection David said: "I will pierce the lion and I will slay the bear" (cf 1 Sam. 17.35); that is to say: I will cut off anger and I will crush fornication with hard labour.'

116. He also said, ' "Greater love hath no man than this that a man lay down his life for his friends." (John 15.13) In truth if someone hears an evil saying, that is, one which harms him, and in his turn, he wants to repeat it, he must fight in order not to say it. Or if someone is taken advantage of and he bears it, without retaliating at all, then he is giving his life for his neighbour.'

117. A brother asked Abba Poemen, 'What is a hypocrite?' The old man said to him, 'A hypocrite is he who teaches his neighbour something he makes no effort to do himself. It is written, "Why do you see the speck that is in your brother's eye, but do not notice the log that is in your own eye, etc." ' (Matt. 7.3–4)

118. A brother questioned Abba Poemen saying, 'What does it mean to be angry with your brother without a cause?' He said, 'If your brother hurts you by his arrogance and you are angry with him because of it, that is getting angry without cause. If he plucks out your right eye and cuts off your right hand, and you get angry with him, you are angry without cause. But if he separates you from God, then be angry with him.'

119. A brother asked Abba Poemen what he should do about his sins. The old man said to him, 'He who wishes to purify his faults purifies them with tears and he who wishes to acquire virtues, acquires them with tears; for weeping is the way the Scriptures and our Fathers give us, when they say "Weep!" Truly, there is no other way than this.'

120. A brother questioned Abba Poemen saying, 'What does it mean to repent of a fault?' The old man said, 'Not to commit it again in future. This is the reason the righteous were called blameless, for they gave up their faults and became righteous.'

121. He also said, 'The wickedness of men is hidden behind their backs.'

122. A brother questioned Abba Poemen, 'What ought I to do about all the turmoils that trouble me?' The old man said to him, 'In all our afflictions let us weep in the presence of the goodness of God, until he shows mercy on us.'

123. The brother asked him, 'What ought I to do about the sterile affections that I have?' He said to him, 'There are men who tire themselves to death involving themselves in the friendships of this world. But keep yourself away from all that and do not get involved in such relationships and they will be transformed of their own accord.'

124. A brother asked Abba Poemen, 'Can a man be dead?' He replied, 'He who is inclined to sin starts to die, but he who applies himself to good will live and will put it into practice.'

125. Abba Poemen said that blessed Abba Anthony used to say, 'The greatest thing a man can do is to throw his faults before the Lord and to expect temptation to his last breath.'

126. Abba Poemen was asked for whom this saying is suitable, 'Do not be anxious about tomorrow.' (Matt. 6.34) The old man said, 'It is said for the man who is tempted and has not much strength, so that he should not be worried, saying to himself, "How long must I suffer this temptation?" He should rather say every day to himself, "Today." '

127. He also said, 'Instructing one's neighbour is for the man who is whole and without passions; for what is the use of building the house of another, while destroying one's own?'

128. He also said, 'What is the good of giving oneself to a trade without seeking to learn it?'

129. He also said, 'Everything that goes to excess comes from the demons.'

130. He also said, 'When a man prepares to build a house, he gathers together all he needs to be able to construct it, and he collects different sorts of materials. So it is with us; let us acquire a little of the virtues.'

131. Some Fathers asked Abba Poemen, 'How could Abba Nisterus bear so well with his discipline?' Abba Poemen said to them, 'If I had been in his place, I would even have put a pillow under his head.' Abba Anoub said, 'And what would you have said to God?' Abba Poemen said, 'I would have said to him: "You have said, 'First take the log out of your own eye, then you will see clearly to take the speck out of your brothers' eye.'"' (Matt. 7.5)

132. Abba Poemen said, 'Because of our need to eat and to sleep, we do not see the simple things.'

133. He also said, 'Many become powerful, but few eminent.'

134. He also said, groaning, 'All the virtues come to this house except one and without that virtue it is hard for a man to stand.' Then they asked him what virtue was, and he said, 'For a man to blame himself.'

135. Abba Poemen often said, 'We do not need anything except a vigilant spirit.'

136. One of the Fathers asked Abba Poemen, 'Who is he who says, "I am a companion of all who fear Thee,"' (Ps. 119.63) and the old man said, 'It is the Holy Spirit who says that.'

137. Abba Poemen said that a brother asked Abba Simon, 'If I come out of my cell and find my brother amusing himself, I amuse myself with him and if I find him in the act of laughing, I laugh with him. Then when I return to my cell, I am no longer at peace.' The old man said to him, 'So, when you come out of your cell and find people laughing or talking you want to laugh and talk with them, and when you return to your cell, you expect to find yourself as you were before?' The brother said, 'What should I do?' The old man replied, 'Be watchful inwardly; be watchful outwardly.'

138. Abba Daniel said, 'We went one day to Abba Poemen and ate together. After we had eaten he said to us, "Go, rest a little, brothers." The brothers went to take a little rest but I wanted to speak to him privately to I went to his cell. When he saw me coming he settled himself as though he were asleep. For that was always the old man's way, to do everything in secret so that no one noticed it.'

139. Abba Poemen said, 'If you have visions or hear voices do not tell your neighbour about it, for it is a delusion in the battle.'

140. He also said, 'The first time flee; the second time, flee; and the third, become like a sword.'

141. Abba Poemen said to Abba Isaac, 'Let go of a small part of your righteousness and in a few days you will be at peace.'

142. A brother came to see Abba Poemen and while several of them were sitting round, he praised a brother for hating evil. Abba Poemen said to the one who had spoken, 'What does it mean to hate evil?' The brother was surprised and found nothing to say in reply. Getting up, he made a prostration before the old man, and said, 'Tell me what hatred of evil is?' The old man said to him, 'Hatred of evil is to hate one's thoughts and to praise one's neighbour.'

143. A brother went to see Abba Poemen and said to him, 'What ought I to do?' The old man said to him, 'Go and join one who says "What do I want?" and you will have peace.'

144. Abba Joseph related that Abba Isaac said, 'I was sitting with Abba Poemen one day and I saw him in ecstasy and I was on terms of great freedom of speech with him, I prostrated myself before him and begged him, saying, "Tell me where you were." He was forced to answer and he said, "My thought was with Saint Mary, the Mother of God, as she wept by the cross of the Saviour. I wish I could always weep like that." '

145. A brother asked Abba Poemen, 'What can I do about this weight which is crushing me?' The old man said to him, 'In ships, small or large, there are tow-ropes which are lashed round the centre when the wind is unfavourable, to draw the small craft slowly along until God sends the wind. When the sailors notice that darkness is falling, then they throw out anchors so that the vessels may not drift away.'

146. A brother asked Abba Poeman about the harm which he was suffering through his thoughts. The old man said to him, 'In this matter it is like a man who has fire on his left and a cup of water on his right. If the fire kindles, he must take water from the cup and extinguish it. The fire is the enemy's seed, and the water is the act of throwing oneself before God.'

147. A brother asked Abba Poemen, 'Is it better to speak or to be silent?' The old man said to him, 'The man who speaks for God's sake does well; but he who is silent for God's sake also does well.'

148. A brother asked Abba Poemen, 'How can a man avoid speaking ill of his neighbour?' The old man said to him, 'We and our brothers are two images; when a man is watchful about himself, and has to reproach himself, in his heart he thinks his brother better than he; but when he appears to himself to be good, then he thinks his brother evil compared to himself.'

149. A brother asked Abba Poemen about *accidie*. The old man said to him, '*Accidie* is there every time one begins something, and there is no worse passion, but if a man recognizes it for what it is, he will gain peace.'

150. Abba Poemen said, 'In Abba Pambo we see three bodily activities; abstinence from food until the evening every day, silence, and much manual work.'

151. He said that Abba Theonas said, 'Even if a man acquires a virtue, God does not grant him grace for himself alone.' He knew that he was not faithful in his own labour, but that if he went to his companion, God would be with him.

152. A brother said to Abba Poemen, 'I want to go to the monastery, and dwell there.' The old man said to him, 'If you want to go the the monastery, you must be careful about every encounter and everything you do, or you will not be able to do the work of the monastery; for you will not have the right even to drink a single cup there.'

153. A brother questioned Abba Poemen saying, 'What ought I to do?' He said, 'It is written, "I confess my iniquity, I am sorry for my sin." ' (Ps. 38.18)

154. Abba Poemen said, 'Fornication and slander, are two thoughts that should never be talked about or pondered in the heart; for if you want to understand them in the heart, it does no good: but if you fight shy of them, you will obtain peace.'

155. Abba Poemen's brethren said to him, 'Let us leave this place, for the monasteries here worry us and we are losing our souls; even

the little children who cry do not let us have interior peace.' Abba Poemen said to them, 'Is it because of voices of angels that you wish to go away from here?'

156. Abba Bitimius asked Abba Poemen, 'If someone has a grievance against me, and I ask his pardon but cannot convince him, what is to be done?' The old man said to him, 'Take two other brothers with you and ask his pardon. If he is not satisfied, take five others. If he is still not satisfied by them, take a priest. If even so he is not satisfied, then pray to God without anxiety, that he may himself satisfy him and do not worry about it.'

157. Abba Poemen said, 'To instruct your neighbour is the same thing as reproving him.'

158. He also said, 'Do not do your own will; you need rather to humble yourself before your brother.'

159. A brother questioned Abba Poemen saying, 'I have found a place where peace is not disturbed by the brethren; do you advise me to live there?' The old man said to him, 'The place for you is where you will not harm your brother.'

160. Abba Poemen said, 'These three things are the most helpful of all: fear of the Lord; prayer; and doing good to one's neighbour.'

161. A brother said to Abba Poemen, 'My body is getting sick, and yet my passions are not getting weaker.' The old man said to him, 'The passions are like thorns.'

162. A brother asked Abba Poemen, 'What ought I to do?' The old man said to him, 'When God is watching over us, what have we got to worry about?' The brother said to him, 'Our sins.' Then the old man said, 'Let us enter into our cell, and sitting there, remember our sins, and the Lord will come and help us in everything.'

163. A brother going to market asked Abba Poemen, 'How do you advise me to behave?' The old man said to him, 'Make friends with anyone who tries to bully you and sell your produce in peace.'

164. Abba Poemen said, 'Teach your mouth to say what is in your heart.'

165. Abba Poemen was asked about impurities and he replied, 'If we are active and very watchful, we shall not find impurities in ourselves.'

166. Abba Poemen said, 'Since Abba Moses and the third generation in Scetis, the brothers do not make progress any more.'

167. He also said, 'A man who stays in his place in life will not be troubled.'

168. A brother asked Abba Poemen, "How should I live in the cell?' He said to him, 'Living in your cell clearly means manual work, eating only once a day, silence, meditation; but really making progress in the cell, means to experience contempt for yourself wherever you go, not to neglect the hours of prayer and to pray secretly. If you happen to have time without manual work, take up prayer and do it without disquiet. The perfection of these things is to live in good company and be free from bad.'

169. A brother asked Abba Poemen, 'If a brother has a little money which belongs to me, do you advise me to ask him for it?' The old man said to him, 'Ask him for it once.' The brother said to him, 'And then what should I do? For I cannot control my thoughts.' The old man said to him, 'Be quiet and do not think about it. But do not distress your brother.'

170. It happened that several Fathers went to the home of a friend of Christ; among them was Abba Poemen. During the meal, meat was served and everyone ate some except Abba Poemen. The old men knew his discretion and they were surprised that he did not eat it. When they got up, they said to him, 'You are Poemen, and yet you behaved like this?' The old man answered, 'Forgive me, my Fathers; you have eaten and no-one is shocked; but if I had eaten, since many brothers come to me, they would have suffered harm, for they would have said Poemen has eaten meat; why should not we eat it ourselves?' So they admired his discernment.

171. Abba Poemen said, 'I say this about myself: I am thrown into the place where Satan is thrown.'

172. He also said to Abba Anoub, 'Turn away your eyes lest they behold vanity; (cf. Ps. 119.37) for licence causes souls to perish.'

173. One day when Abba Poemen was sitting down, Paësius fought with his brother till the blood ran from their heads. The old man said absolutely nothing to them. Then Abba Anoub came in and saw them, he said to Abba Poemen, 'Why have you let the brothers fight without saying anything to them?' Abba Poemen replied, 'They are brothers, and they will make it up again.' Abba Anoub said, 'What do you mean? You saw them behaving like this, and all you say is they will make it up again?' Abba Poemen said to him, 'Try and think that inwardly I was not here to see it.'

174. A brother asked Abba Poemen, 'Some brothers live with me; do you want me to be in charge of them?' The old man said to him, 'No, just work first and foremost, and if they want to live like you, they will see to it themselves.' The brother said to him, 'But it is they themselves, Father who want me to be in charge of them.' The old man said to him, 'No, be their example, not their legislator.'

175. Abba Poemen said 'If a brother comes to visit you and you realise that you have not profited by his visit, search your heart, and discover what you were thinking about before he came, and then you will understand why his visit was useless. If you do this with humility and care, you will be blameless with regard to your neighbour, bearing your own weaknesses. If a man settles somewhere with care, he does not sin for he is in the presence of God. I see that this is how a man acquires the fear of God.'

176. He also said, 'A man who lives with a boy, and is incited by him to no matter what passions of the old man, and yet keeps him with him, that man is like someone who has a field which is eaten up with maggots.'

177. He also said, 'Wickedness does not do away with wickedness; but if someone does you wrong, do good to him, so that by your action you destroy his wickedness.'

178. He also said, 'David, when he was fighting with the lion, seized it by the throat and killed it immediately. If we take ourselves by the throat and by the belly, with the help of God, we shall overcome the invisible lion.'

179. A brother asked Abba Poemen this question, 'What shall I do, because trouble comes to me and I am overwhelmed by it?' The

old man said, 'Violence makes both small and great to be over-thrown.'

180. It was said of Abba Poemen that he dwelt at Scetis with his two brothers, and the younger one was a nuisance to them. So he said to the other brother, 'This lad is making us powerless, let us get up and go away from here.' So they went away and left him. When he saw that they did not come back for a long time, the young brother realized that they were going far away and he began to run after them, crying out. Abba Poemen said, 'Let us wait for our brother, for he is worn out.' When he reached them he bowed to them and said, 'Where are you going? Are you leaving me on my own?' The old man said to him, 'It is because you are a worry to us that we are going away.' He said to them, 'Yes, yes, let us go together wherever you wish.' The old man, seeing his lack of malice, said to his brother, 'Brother, let us go back, for he is not doing this on purpose but it is the devil who is doing it.' So they turned back and went home again.

181. The *hegumen* of a monastery asked Abba Poemen, 'How can I acquire the fear of God?' Abba Poemen said to him, 'How can we acquire the fear of God when our belly is full of cheese and preserved foods?'

182. A brother asked Abba Poemen, 'Abba, there were two men, one a monk and the other a secular. One evening the monk decided to put off the habit the next morning and the secular decided to become a monk. Now both of them died in the night. How will they be judged?' The old man said to him, 'The monk died a monk, the secular died a secular; in fact they died in the state in which they found themselves.'

183. Abba John, who had been exiled by the Emperor Marcian, said, 'We went to Syria one day to see Abba Poemen and we wanted to ask him about purity of heart. But the old man did not know Greek and no interpreter could be found. So, seeing our embarrassment, the old man began to speak Greek, saying, 'The nature of water is soft, that of stone is hard; but if a bottle is hung above the stone, allowing the water to fall drop by drop, it wears away the stone. So it is with the word of God; it is soft and our heart is hard,

but the man who hears the word of God often, opens his heart to the fear of God.'

184. Abba Isaac came to see Abba Poemen and found him washing his feet. As he enjoyed freedom of speech with him he said, 'How is it that others practice austerity and treat their bodies hardly?' Abba Poemen said to him, 'We have not been taught to kill our bodies, but to kill our passions.'

185. He also said, 'There are three things which I am not able to do without: food, clothing and sleep; but I can restrict them to some extent.'

186. A brother said to Abba Poemen, 'I eat a lot of vegetables.' The old man said, 'That does not help you; rather eat bread and a few vegetables, and do not go back to your relations for what you need.'

187. It was said of Abba Poemen that if some old men were sitting with him, speaking of the ancients, and Abba Sisoes was mentioned, he would say, 'Keep silence about Abba Sisoes, for that which concerns him goes beyond what can be said.'

188. He also said, 'Teach your heart to guard that which your tongue teaches.'

189. A brother questioned Abba Poemen, saying, 'I am losing my soul through living near my abba; should I go on living with him?' The old man knew that he was finding this harmful and he was surprised that he even asked if he should stay there. So he said to him, 'Stay if you want to.' The brother left him and stayed on there. He came back again and said, 'I am losing my soul.' But the old man did not tell him to leave. He came a third time and said, 'I really cannot stay there any longer.' Then Abba Poemen said, 'Now you are saving yourself; go away and do not stay with him any longer,' and he added, 'When someone sees that he is in danger of losing his soul, he does not need to ask advice. It is right to ask about secret thoughts and then it is up to the old man to test them; but with visible faults, do not ask; cut them off at once.'

190. Abba Poemen said that Abba Paphnutius was great and he had recourse to short prayers.

191. A brother asked Abba Poemen, 'How should I behave in the place where I live?' The old man said, 'Have the mentality of an exile in the place where you live, do not desire to be listened to and you will have peace.'

192. He also said, 'This voice cries out to a man to his last breath, "Be converted today."'

193. He also said, 'David wrote to Joab, "Continue the battle and you will take the city and sack it." Now the city is the enemy.'

194. He also said, 'Joab said to the people, "Be courageous and let us play the man for our people, and for the cities of our God." (I Chron. 19.13) Now we ourselves are these men.'

195. He also said, 'If Moses had not led his sheep to Midian he would not have seem him who was in the bush.' (cf. Exodus 3. 2–7)

196. A brother came to Abba Poemen and asked, 'How did you come here?' and he told him, 'If I were to die in Scetis with my brothers, I would be willing, and here we are.'

197. He also said, 'If a man understands something and does not practise it, how can he teach it to his neighbour?'

198. He also said, 'A man who lives with a companion ought to be like a stone pillar; hurt him, and he does not get angry, praise him, and he is not puffed up.'

199. He also said, 'A man knows nothing about the powers that are outside him; but if they enter into him, he must fight them and drive them out.'

200. He also said, 'Not understanding what has happened prevents us from going on to something better.'

201. He also said, 'Do not lay open your conscience to anyone whom you do not trust in your heart.'

202. Abba Poemen said, 'If I am in a place where there are enemies, I become a soldier.'

203. Abba Poemen heard of someone who had gone all week without eating and then had lost his temper. The old man said, 'He could do without food for six days, but he could not cast out anger.'

204. Abba Poemen said, 'I will tell you why we have so much difficulty; it is because we do not care about our brother whom Scripture tells us to receive. Moreover we do not remember the woman of Canaan (cf. Matt. 15.22) who followed the Lord crying and begging for her daughter to be cured, and the Lord heard her and gave her peace.'

205. Abba Poemen said, 'If the soul keeps far away from all discourse in words, from all disorder and human disturbance, the Spirit of God will come in to her and she who was barren will be fruitful.'

206. A brother asked Abba Poemen, 'How should those who are in the monastery behave?' The old man said to him, 'Whoever lives in the monastery should see all the brethren as one; he should guard his eyes and his lips; and then he will be at peace without anxiety.'

207. Abba Poemen said this about the son of Shemai, 'His mistake was to justify himself; whoever does that destroys himself.'

208. A brother asked Abba Poemen, 'What can I do about my sins?' and the old man said to him, 'Weep interiorly, for both deliverance from faults and the acquisition of virtues are gained through compunction.'

209. He also said,' Weeping is the way that Scripture and our Fathers have handed on to us.'*

PAMBO

Pambo, born about A.D. 303, was one of the first to join Amoun in Nitria. He was an Egyptian and illiterate, until taught the Scriptures as a monk and ordained priest, in 340. He was invited by Bishop Athanasius to go to Alexandria. With Macarius and Isidore he was counted by Jerome as one of the masters of the desert. Melania met him when she visited Egypt. He died about A.D. 373.

1. There was a monk named Pambo and they said of him that he spent three years saying to God, 'Do not glorify me on earth.' But

*188–209 are additions from J.C.-Guy's text (pp. 29–31).

God glorified him so that one could not gaze steadfastly at him because of the glory of his countenance.

2. Two brethren came to see Abba Pambo one day and the first asked him, 'Abba, I fast for two days, then I eat two loaves; am I saving my soul, or am I going the wrong way?' The second said, 'Abba, every day I get two pence from my manual work, and I keep a little for my food and give the rest in alms; shall I be saved or shall I be lost?' They remained a long time questioning him and still the old man gave them no reply. After four days they had to leave and the priests comforted them saying, 'Do not be troubled, brothers. God gives the reward. It is the old man's custom not to speak readily till God inspires him.' So they went to see the old man and said to him, 'Abba, pray for us.' He said to them, 'Do you want to go away?' They said, 'Yes.' Then, giving his mind to their works and writing on the ground he said, 'If Pambo fasted for two days together and ate two loaves, would he become a monk that way? No. And if Pambo works to get two pence and gives them in alms, would he become a monk that way? No, not that way either.' He said to them, 'The works are good, but if you guard your conscience towards your neighbour, then you will be saved.' They were satisfied and went away joyfully.

3. Four monks of Scetis, clothed in skins, came one day to see the great Pambo. Each one revealed the virtue of his neighbour. The first fasted a great deal; the second was poor; the third had acquired great charity; and they said of the fourth that he had lived for twenty-two years in obedience to an old man. Abba Pambo said to them, 'I tell you, the virtue of this last one is the greatest. Each of the others has obtained the virtue he wished to acquire; but the last one, restraining his own will, does the will of another. Now it is of such men that the martyrs are made, if they persevere to the end.'

4. Athanasius, Archbishop of Alexandria, of holy memory, begged Abba Pambo to come down from the desert to Alexandria. He went down, and seeing an actress he began to weep. Those who were present asked him the reason for his tears, and he said, 'Two things make me weep: one, the loss of this woman; and the other, that I am not so concerned to please God as she is to please wicked men.'

5. Abba Pambo said, 'By the grace of God, since I left the world, I have not said one word of which I repented afterwards.'

6. He also said, 'The monk should wear a garment of such a kind that he could throw it out of his cell and no-one would steal it from him for three days.'

7. Once it happened that Abba Pambo made the journey to Egypt with some brothers. Meeting some lay people who were sitting down, he said to them, 'Stand up, greet the monks, so that you may be blessed, for they speak with God without interruption and their lips are holy.'

8. They said of Abba Pambo that as he was dying, at the very hour of his death, he said to the holy men who were standing near him, 'Since I came to this place of the desert and built my cell and dwelt here, I do not remember having eaten bread which was not the fruit of my hands and I have not repented of a word I have said up to the present time; and yet I am going to God as one who has not yet begun to serve him.'

9. He was greater than many others in that if he was asked to interpret part of the Scriptures or a spiritual saying, he would not reply immediately, but he would say he did not know that saying. If he was asked again, he would say no more.

10. Abba Pambo said, 'If you have a heart, you can be saved.'

11. The priest of Nitria asked him how the brethren ought to live. He replied, 'With much labour, guarding their consciences towards their neighbour.'

12. They said of Abba Pambo that he was like Moses, who received the image of the glory of Adam when his face shone. His face shone like lightening and he was like a king sitting on his throne. It was the same with Abba Silvanus and Abba Sisoes.

13. They said of Abba Pambo that his face never smiled. So one day, wishing to make him laugh, the demons stuck wing feathers on to a lump of wood and brought it in making an uproar and saying, 'Go, go.' When he saw them Abba Pambo began to laugh and the demons started to say in chorus, 'Ha! ha! Pambo has laughed!' But in reply he said to them, 'I have not laughed, but I

made fun of your powerlessness, because it takes so many of you to carry a wing.'

14. Abba Theodore of Pherme asked Abba Pambo, 'Give me a word.' With much difficulty he said to him, 'Theodore, go and have pity on all, for through pity, one finds freedom of speech before God.'

PISTUS

1. Abba Pistus related that which follows: 'We were seven anchorites who went to see Abba Sisoes who lived at Clysma, begging him to give us word. He said to us, "Forgive me, for I am a very simple man. But I have been to Abba Or and to Abba Athre. Abba Or was ill for eighteen years. I made a prostration before him and asked him to give me a word. Abba Or said to me, 'What shall I say to you? Go, and do what you see is right; God comes to him who reproaches himself and does violence to himself in everything.' Abba Or and Abba Athre did not come from the same part of the country, yet until they left their bodies, there was great peace between them. Abba Athre's obedience was great, and great was Abba Or's humility. I spent several days with them, without leaving them for a moment, and I saw a great wonder that Abba Athre did. Someone brought them a little fish and Abba Athre wanted to cook it for the old man. He was holding the knife in the act of cutting up the fish and Abba Or called him. He left the knife in the middle of the fish and did not cut up the rest of it. I admired his great obedience, for he did not say, 'Wait till I have cut up the fish.' I said to Abba Athre, 'Where did you find such obedience?' He said to me, 'It is not mine, but the old man's.' He took me with him, saying, 'Come and see his obedience.' He took the fish, intentionally cooked some of it badly, and offered it to the old man who ate it without saying anything. Then he said to him, 'Is it good, old man?' He replied, 'It is very good.' Afterwards he brought him a little that was well cooked and said, 'Old man, I have spoiled it,' and he replied, 'Yes, you have spoiled it a little.' Then Abba Athre said to me, 'Do you see how obedience is intrinsic to the old man?' I came away

from there and what I have told you, I have tried to practise as far
as I could." '

PIOR

Pior, an early settler in Nitria, lived at first with Anthony the Great.
He was a priest, and became a solitary in Scetis.

1.Blessed Pior worked at harvest-time for someone, and he was
told to go and get his wages. But he put it off till later and returned
to his hermitage. Next year, when the season required it, he went
harvesting, worked strenuously and returned to his hermitage without anyone giving him anything. When the third summer was coming to an end and the old man had completed his usual work, he
went away without taking any payment. But the master of the
harvest, having put his affairs in order, took the wages and went to
the monasteries, in search of the saint. Scarcely had he found him
than he threw himself at his feet, giving him his due and saying, 'The
Lord gave it to me.' But Abba Pior only asked him to take the wages
to the church to the priest.

2. Abba Pior used to walk a hundred paces while he was eating.
Someone asked him why he ate like that, and he said, 'I do not want
to make eating an occupation, but something accessory.' To another
who also asked him the same question, he replied, 'It is so that my
soul should not feel any bodily pleasure in eating.'

3. There was at that time a meeting at Scetis about a brother who
had sinned. The Fathers spoke, but Abba Pior kept silence. Later,
he got up and went out; he took a sack, filled it with sand and
carried it on his shoulder. He put a little sand also into a small bag
which he carried in front of him. When the Fathers asked him what
this meant he said, 'In this sack which contains much sand, are my
sins which are many; I have put them behind me so as not to be
troubled about them and so as not to weep; and see here are the little
sins of my brother which are in front of me and I spend my time
judging them. This is not right, I ought rather to carry my sins in
front of me and concern myself with them, begging God to forgive

me for them.' The Fathers stood up and said, 'Truly, this is the way of salvation.'

PITYRION

1. Abba Pityrion, the disciple of Abba Anthony said, 'If anyone wants to drive out the demons, he must first subdue the passions; for he will banish the demon of the passion which he has mastered. For example, the devil accompanies anger; so if you control your anger, the devil of anger will be banished. And so it is with each of the passions.'

PISTAMON

1. A brother asked Abba Pistamon, 'What should I do? I get worried when I sell my manual work.' The old man replied, 'Abba Sisoes and all the others used to sell their manual work; that is not dangerous in itself. But when you sell it, say the price of each thing just once, then, if you want to lower the price a little, you can do so. In this way you will be at peace.' The brother then said, 'If I can get what I need by one means or another, do you still advise me to take the trouble to do manual work?' The old man replied, 'Even if you do have what you need by other means, do not give up your manual work. Work as much as you can, only do it without getting worried about it.'

PETER THE PIONITE

1. In the Cells they said of Abba Peter the Pionite that he did not drink wine. When he grew old, the brothers prepared a little wine diluted with water for him, and asked him to accept it. But he said, 'To me that is just as bad as spiced wine.' He was passing judgement on himself in his comment about this liquid.

2. A brother said to Abba Peter, the disciple of Abba Lot, 'When I am in my cell, my soul is at peace, but if a brother comes to see

me and speaks to me of external things, my soul is disturbed.' Abba Peter told him that Abba Lot used to say, 'Your key opens my door.' The brother said to him, 'What does that mean?' The old man said, 'When someone comes to see you, you say to him, "How are you? Where have you come from? How are the brethren? Did they welcome you or not?" Then you have opened the brother's door and you will hear a great deal that you would rather not have heard.' The brother said to him, 'That is so. What should a man do, then, when a brother comes to see him?' The old man said, 'Compunction is absolute master. One cannot protect oneself where there is no compunction.' The brother said, 'When I am in my cell, compunction is with me, but if someone comes to see me or I go out of my cell, I do not have it any more.' The old man said, 'That means that you do not really have compunction at all yet. It is merely that you practise it sometimes. It is written in the Law: "When you buy a Hebrew slave, he shall serve six years and in the seventh he shall go free, for nothing. If you give him a wife and she brings forth sons in your house and he does not wish to go because of his wife and children, you shall lead him to the door of the house and you shall pierce his ear with an awl and he shall become your slave for ever." ' (cf. Ex. 21.2–6) The brother said, 'What does that mean?' The old man said, 'If a man works as hard as he can at anything, at the moment when he seeks what he needs, he will find it.' The brother said, 'Please explain this to me.' The old man said, 'The bastard will not remain in anyone's service; it is the legitimate son who will not leave his father.'

3. Abba Peter and Abba Epimachus were said to have been companions at Rhaithou. While they were eating with the community, they were asked to go to the table of the senior brethren. Only Abba Peter would go and that not without difficulty. When they left, Abba Epimachus said to him, 'How did you dare to go to the table of the seniors?' He replied, 'If I had been sitting with you, the brothers would have asked me, as the senior brother, to give the blessing first and as I am older than you, I shall have had to do it. But with the Fathers, I was the youngest of all and the most humble in thought.'

4. Abba Peter said, 'We must not be puffed up when the Lord does something through our mediation, but we must rather thank

him for having made us worthy to be called by him.' He used to say it is good to think about each virtue in this way.

PAPHNUTIUS

Paphnutius, born early in the fourth century was influenced by Anthony the Great and became a disciple of Isidore and of Macarius. He was trained first in a cenobitic monastery, then became a solitary. He was called 'the Buffalo' for his love of solitude. When Cassian visited Egypt, he was head of the four monasteries of the desert.

1. Abba Paphnutius said, 'When I was walking along the road, I happened to lose my way and found myself near a village and I saw some people who were talking about evil things. So I stood still, praying for my sins. Then behold an angel came, holding a sword and he said to me, "Paphnutius, all those who judge their brothers perish by his sword, but because you have not judged, but have humbled yourself before God, saying that you have sinned, your name is written in the book of the living!" '

2. It was said of Abba Paphnutius that he did not readily drink wine. One day he found himself on the road facing a band of robbers who were drinking wine. The captain of the band was acquainted with him and knew that he did not drink wine. Seeing how weary he was, he filled him a cup of wine and holding his sword in his hand he said to him, 'If you do not drink this, I will kill you.' So the old man, knowing that he was fulfilling the commandment of God and in order to win the confidence of the robber, took the cup and drank it. Then the captain asked his forgiveness, saying, 'Forgive me, abba, for I have made you unhappy.' But the old man said, 'I believe that, thanks to this cup, God will have mercy on you now and in the age to come.' Then the robber captain said, 'Have confidence in God that from now on I shall not harm anyone.' So the old man converted the whole band by giving up his own will for the Lord's sake.

3. Abba Poemen said that Abba Paphnutius used to say, 'During the whole lifetime of the old men, I used to go to see them twice

a month, although it was a distance of twelve miles. I told them each of my thoughts and they never answered me anything but this, "Wherever you go, do not judge yourself and you will be at peace." '

4. There was at Scetis with Paphnutius a brother who had to fight against fornication and he said, 'Even if I take ten wives, I shall not satisfy my desire.' The old man encouraged him, saying, 'No, my child, this warfare comes from the demons.' But he did not let himself be persuaded and he left for Egypt to take a wife. After a time it happened that the old man went up to Egypt and met him carrying baskets of shell-fish. He did not recognize him at all, but the other said to him, 'I am so and so, your disciple.' And the old man, seeing him in such disgrace, wept and said, 'How have you lost your dignity and come to such humiliation? No doubt you have taken ten wives?' And groaning, he said, 'Truly I have only taken one, and I have a great deal of trouble satisfying her with food.' The old man said, 'Come back with us.' He said, 'Is it possible to repent, abba?' He said that it was. And leaving everything, the brother followed him and returned to Scetis, and thanks to this experience he became a proved monk.

5. There was a brother who lived in the desert of the Thebaid and the thought crossed his mind, 'Why do you live here in this useless way? Get up and go to the monastery and there you will make progress.' So he went and found Abba Paphnutius and told him about this thought. The old man said to him, 'Go and stay in your cell; make only one prayer in the morning and one in the evening and one at night. When you are hungry, eat, when you are thirsty, drink; when you are tired, sleep. But stay in the cell and take no notice of this thought.' The brother went and found Abba John and told him what Abba Paphnutius had said and Abba John said, 'Don't pray at all, just stay in the cell.' So the brother went and found Abba Arsenius and told him all about it and the old man said to him, 'Do as the others have told you. I have nothing to say but that,' and he went away satisfied.

6. Amma Sarah sent someone to say to Abba Paphnutius, 'Have you really done the work of God by letting your brother be despised?' and Abba Paphnutius said, 'Paphnutius is here with the

intention of doing the work of God, and he has nothing to do with anyone else.'*

PAUL

1. One of the Fathers used to tell of a certain Abba Paul, from Lower Egypt, who lived in the Thebaid. He used to take various kinds of snakes in his hands and cut them through the middle. The brethren made prostration before him saying, 'Tell us what you have done to receive this grace.' He said, 'Forgive me, Fathers, but if someone has obtained purity, everything is in submission to him, as it was to Adam, when he was in Paradise before he transgressed the commandment.'

PAUL THE BARBER

1. Abba Paul the Barber and his brother Timothy lived in Scetis. They often used to argue. So Abba Paul said, 'How long shall we go on like this?' Abba Timothy said to him, 'I suggest you take my side of the argument and in my turn I will take your side when you oppose me.' They spent the rest of their days in this practice.

2. The same Abbas Paul and Timothy, the Barbers, were troubled by the brethren at Scetis. Timothy said to his brother, 'Why do we follow this trade? They do not let us live in peace the whole day long.' But Abba Paul replied, 'The peace of the night is enough for us if our thoughts are watchful.'

PAUL THE GREAT

1. Abba Paul the Great, the Galatian, said, 'The monk who possesses in his cell some small things which he needs and who comes out to busy himself with them, is the plaything of the demons. I have experienced this myself.'

*6 is an addition from J.-C. Guy's text (p. 31).

2. Abba Paul said, 'I am in the slough, sinking in up to my neck and I weep in the presence of God, saying, "Have mercy on me." '

3. It was said of Abba Paul that he spent the whole of Lent eating only one measure of lentils, drinking one small jug of water, and working at one single basket, weaving it and unweaving it, living alone until the feast.

4. Abba Paul said: 'Keep close to Jesus.'*

PAUL THE SIMPLE

1. Blessed Abba Paul the Simple, the disciple of Abba Anthony, told the Fathers that which follows: One day he went to a monastery to visit it and to make himself useful to the brethren. After the customary conference, the brothers entered the holy church of God to perform the *synaxis* there, as usual. Blessed Paul looked carefully at each of those who entered the church observing the spiritual disposition with which they went to the *synaxis*, for he had received the grace from the Lord of seeing the state of each one's soul, just as we see their faces. When all had entered with sparkling eyes and shining faces, with each one's angel rejoicing over him, he said, 'I see one who is black and his whole body is dark; the demons are standing on each side of him, dominating him, drawing him to them, and leading him by the nose, and his angel, filled with grief, with head bowed, follows him at a distance.' Then Paul, in tears, beat his breast and sat down in front of the church, weeping bitterly over him whom he had seen. The brethren, seeing this strange behaviour and the abrupt change which had brought him to tears and compunction, asked him persistently to tell them why he was weeping, fearing lest he were doing it as a sign of accusation against all of them. Then they asked him to go to the *synaxis* with them. But Paul kept apart from them and remained sitting outside, lamenting over him whom he had seen in this state. Shortly after the end of the *synaxis*, as everyone was coming out, Paul scrutinized each one, wanting to know in what state they were coming away. He

*4 is an addition from J.-C. Guy's text (p. 32.).

saw that man, previously black and gloomy, coming out of the church with a shining face and white body, the demons accompanying him only at a distance, while his holy angel was following close to him, rejoicing greatly over him. Then Paul leaped for joy and began to cry out, blessing God, 'O the ineffable loving-kindness and goodness of God!' and he went running up to an elevated place and in a powerful voice he said, 'Come, see the works of the Lord, how terrible they are and worthy of our wonder! Come and see him who wills that all men should be saved and come to the knowledge of the truth! Come, let us bow down and throw ourselves at his feet and let us say, "Only You can take sins away!"' Everyone ran together in haste, wanting to hear what he was saying. When they were all assembled, Paul related what he had seen at the entrance to the church and what had happened afterwards and he asked that man to tell them the reason why God had suddenly bestowed such a change upon him. Then the man whom Paul pointed out told all that had happened to him in front of everyone, saying, 'I am a sinful man; I have lived in fornication for a long time, right up to the present moment; when I went into the holy church of God, I heard the holy prophet Isaiah being read, or rather, God speaking through him: "Wash you, make you clean, take away the evil from your hearts, learn to do good before mine eyes. Even though your sins are as scarlet I will make them white like snow. And if you will, and if you listen to me, you shall eat the good things of the earth." (cf. Is. 1.16–19) And I,' he continued, 'the fornicator, am filled with compunction in my heart because of this word of the prophet and I groan within myself, saying to God, "God, who came into the world to save sinners, that which You now proclaim by the mouth of Your prophet, fulfil in me who am a sinner and an unworthy man." From now on, I give my word, I affirm and promise in my heart that I will not sin any more, but I renounce all unrighteousness and I will serve You henceforth with a pure conscience. Today, O Master, from this time forward, receive me, as I repent and throw myself at Your feet, desiring in future to abstain from every fault.' He continued, 'With these promises, I came out of the church, sure in my soul that I would no longer commit any evil before God.' At these words they all with one voice cried out to God, 'How manifold are thy works, Lord, in wisdom hast thou made them all.' (Ps. 104.24) So, as Christians, having learnt from the holy Scriptures and from holy revelations, let us know the great goodness of God for those who sincerely take refuge in him and who correct their past faults, by repentance, and let us not despair of our salvation. In truth, as it was proclaimed by the prophet Isaiah, God washes those who are dirty with sin, whitens them as wool and as snow and bestows the good things of the heavenly Jerusalem on them; just as, in the prophet Ezekiel, God has sworn by an oath, to satisfy us and not to let us be lost. "For I have no pleasure in the death of anyone says the Lord God; so turn, and live." ' (Ezek. 18.32)

PETER OF DIOS

1. Peter, priest of Dios, when he prayed with others, ought to have stood in front, because he was a priest but because of his humility he stood behind saying, 'This is what is written in the life of Saint Anthony.' He did this without annoying anyone.

✦| RHO |✦

AN ABBA OF ROME
(This is almost certainly Arsenius)

1. There was a monk from Rome who lived at Scetis near the church. He had a slave to serve him. The priest, knowing his bad health and the comfort in which he used to live, sent him what he needed of whatever anyone brought to the church. Having lived twenty-five years at Scetis he had acquired the gift of insight and became famous. One of the great Egyptians heard about him and came to see him, thinking he would find him leading a life of great corporal austerity. He entered and greeted him. They said the prayer and sat down. Now the Egyptian saw he was wearing fine clothing, and that he possessed a bed with a coverlet and a small pillow. He saw that his feet were clean and shod in sandals. Noticing all this, he was shocked, because such a way of life is not usual in that district; much greater austerity is required. Now the old man had the gift of insight and he understood that he was shocked, and so he said to him who served him, 'We will celebrate a feast today

for the abba's sake.' There were a few vegetables, and he cooked them and at the appointed hour, they rose and ate. The old man had a little wine also, because of his illness; so they drank some. When evening came, they recited the twelve psalms and went to sleep. They did the same during the night. On rising at dawn, the Egyptian said to him, 'Pray for me,' and he went away without being edified. When he had gone a short distance, the old man, wishing to edify him, sent someone to bring him back. On his arrival he received him once again with joy and asked him, 'Of what country are you?' He said, 'Egypt.' 'And of what city?' 'I am not a citizen at all.' 'And what was your work in the village?' 'I was a herdsman.' 'Where did you sleep?' He replied, 'In the field.' 'Did you have anything to lie upon?' He said, 'Would I go and put a bed under myself in a field?' 'But how did you sleep?' He said, 'On the bare ground.' The old man said next, 'What was your food in the fields, and what wine did you drink?' He replied, 'Is there food and drink in the fields?' 'But how did you live?' 'I ate dry bread, and, if I found any, green herbs and water.' The old man replied, 'Great hardship! Was there a bath-house for washing in the village?' He replied, 'No, only the river, when we wanted it.' After the old man had learnt all this and knew of the hardness of his former life, he told him his own former way of life when he was in the world, with the intention of helping him. 'I, the poor man whom you see, am of the great city of Rome and I was a great man in the palace of the emperor.' When the Egyptian heard the beginning of these words, he was filled with compunction and listened attentively to what the other was saying. He continued, 'Then I left the city and came to this desert. I whom you see had great houses and many riches and having despised them I have come to this little cell. I whom you see had beds all of gold with coverings of great value, and in exchange for that, God has given me this little bed and this skin. Moreover, my clothes were the most expensive kind and in their stead I wear these garments of no value. Again. at my table there was much gold and instead of that God has given me this little dish of vegetables and a cup of wine. There were many slaves to serve me and see how in exchange for that, God troubles this old man to serve me. Instead of the bath-house, I throw a little water over my feet and wear sandals because of my weakness. Instead of music and lyres, I say the twelve psalms and the same at night; instead of the sins I used to commit I now say my rule of prayer. So then I beg you, abba, do not be shocked at my weakness.' Hearing this, the Egyptian came to his senses and said, 'Woe to me, for after so much hardship in the world, I have found ease; and what I did not have before, that I now possess. While after so great ease, you have come to humility and poverty.' Greatly edified, he withdrew, and he became his friend and often went to him for help. For he was a man full of discernment and the good odour of the Holy Spirit.

2. The same monk used to say that there was a certain old man who had a good disciple. Through narrowmindedness he drove him outside with his sheepskin. The brother remained sitting outside. When the old man opened the door, he found him sitting, and he repented saying, 'O Father, the humility of your patience has over-come my narrowmindedness. Come inside and from now on you are the old man and the father, and I am the younger and the disciple.'

RUFUS

1. A brother asked Abba Rufus, 'What is interior peace, and what use is it?' The old man said, 'Interior peace means to remain sitting in one's cell with fear and knowledge of God, holding far off the remembrance of wrongs suffered and pride of spirit. Such interior peace brings forth all the virtues, preserves the monk from the burning darts of the enemy, and does not allow him to be wounded by them. Yes, brother, acquire it. Keep in mind your future death, remembering that you do not know at what hour the thief will come. Likewise be watchful over your soul.'

2. Abba Rufus said, 'He who remains sitting at the feet of his spiritual father receives a greater reward than he who lives alone in the desert.' He added that one of the Fathers said, 'I have seen four orders in heaven: in the first order is the sick man who gives thanks to God; in the second, the man who observes hospitality and for that reason, gets up to serve; in the third, the man who crosses the desert without seeing anyone; in the fourth, the man who obeys his Father and remains in submission to him for the Lord's sake. The one who was living in submission was wearing a chain of gold and a shield

and had greater glory than the others. I said to him who was guiding me, "Why does the one who is least have more glory than the others?" He answered me, "He who practises hospitality acts according to his own will; but the last one possesses obedience. Having abandoned all his desires, he depends on God and his own Father; it is because of this that he has received more glory than the others." See, my child, how good obedience is when it is undertaken for the Lord. You have partly understood the elements of this virtue, my children. O obedience, salvation of the faithful! O obedience, mother of all the virtues! O obedience, discloser of the kingdom! O obedience opening the heavens, and making men to ascend there from earth! O obedience, food of all the saints, whose milk they have sucked, through you they have become perfect! O obedience, companion of the angels!'

ROMANUS

1. When Abba Romanus was at the point of death, his disciples gathered round him and said, 'How ought we to conduct ourselves?' The old man said to them, 'I do not think I have ever told one of you to do something, without having first made the decision not to get angry, if what I said were not done; and so we have lived in peace all our days.'

⊹I SIGMA I⊹

SISOES

Sisoes was trained as an ascetic with Abba Or in Scetis. He left Scetis after the death of St. Anthony, saying it had become too popular and settled on St. Anthony's mountain for seventy-two years. He found it deserted, which may indicate a time after the Saracen attack there in 357. He received supplies from Pispir by a servant and was in touch with Rhaithou and Clysma.

1. A brother whom another brother had wronged came to see Abba Sisoes and said to him, 'My brother has hurt me and I want to avenge myself.' The old man pleaded with him saying, 'No, my child, leave vengeance to God.' He said to him, 'I shall not rest until I have avenged myself.' The old man said, 'Brother, let us pray.' Then the old man stood up and said, 'God, we no longer need you to care for us, since we do justice for ourselves.' Hearing these words, the brothers fell at the old man's feet, saying, 'I will no longer seek justice from my brother; forgive me, abba.'

2. A brother asked Abba Sisoes saying, 'What should I do? When I go to the church, often there is an *agape* there after the service and they make me stay for it?' The old man said to him, 'It is a difficult question.' Then Abraham, his disciple, said, 'If the gathering takes place on Saturday or Sunday and a brother drinks three cups of wine, is that not a lot?' The old man said, 'If Satan is not in it, it is not much.'

3. Abba Sisoes' disciple said to him, 'Father, you are growing old. Let us now go back nearer to inhabited country.' The old man said to him, 'Let us go where there are no women.' His disciple said to him, 'Where is there a place where there are no women except the desert?' So the old man said, 'Take me to the desert.'

4. Abba Sisoes' disciple often said to him 'Abba, get up, and let us eat.' And he would say to him, 'Have we not eaten, my child?' He would reply, 'No, Father.' The the old man would say, 'If we have not eaten, bring the food, and we will eat.'

5. Abba Sisoes expressed himself freely one day, saying, 'Have confidence: for thirty years I have not prayed to God about my faults, but I have made this prayer to him: "Lord Jesus, save me from my tongue," and until now every day. I fall because of it, and commit sin.'

6. A brother said to Abba Sisoes, 'How is it that the passions do not leave me?' The old man said, 'Their tools are inside you; give them their pay and they will go.'

7. Abba Sisoes was living for a time on the mountain of Abba Anthony, and his disciple was a long time coming, so he did not see anyone for ten months. Now while he was walking on the mountain he met a Pharanite who was hunting wild animals. The old man said to him, 'Where have you come from? And how long have you been here?' He replied, 'Indeed, abba, I have been eleven months on this mountain and I have not seen anyone except you.' Hearing this the old man entered his cell and beat his breast saying, 'Look, Sisoes, you thought you had done something special but you have not even equalled this layman.'

8. There was a liturgy on the mountain of Abba Anthony and they had a small bottle of wine there. One of the old men took a

jug and a cup and offered some to Abba Sisoes. He drank some. A second time, he also accepted some. But when he was offered some a third time, he did not accept it, saying, 'Stop, brother, don't you know that it is of Satan?'

9. One of the brethren went to see Abba Sisoes on Abba Anthony's mountain. While they were talking, he said to Abba Sisoes, 'Have you already reached Abba Anthony's stature, Father?' The old man said to him, 'If I had one of Abba Anthony's thoughts, I should become all flame; but I do know a man, who with difficulty is able to bear Anthony's thoughts.'

10. One of the inhabitants of the Thebaid came to see Abba Sisoes one day because he wanted to become a monk. The old man asked him if he had any relations in the world. He replied, 'I have a son.' The old man said, 'Go and throw him into the river and then you will become a monk. As he went to throw him in, the old man sent a brother in haste to prevent him. The brother said, 'Stop, what are you doing?' But the other said to him, 'The abba told me to throw him in.' So the brother said, 'But afterwards he said do not throw him in.' So he left his son and went to find the old man and he became a monk, tested by obedience.

11. A brother asked Abba Sisoes, 'Did Satan pursue them like this in the early days?' The old man said to him, 'He does this more at the present time, because his time is nearly finished and he is enraged.'

12. Abraham, Abba Sisoes' disciple, was tempted one day by the devil and the old man saw that he had given way. Standing up, he stretched his hands towards heaven, saying, 'God, whether you will, or whether you will not, I will not let you alone till you have healed him,' and immediately the brother was healed.

13. A brother said to Abba Sisoes, 'I am aware that the remembrance of God stays with me.' The old man said to him, 'It is no great thing to be with God in your thoughts, but it is a great thing to see yourself as inferior to all creatures. It is this, coupled with hard work, that leads to humility.'

14. It was said of Abba Sisoes that when he was at the point of death, while the Fathers were sitting beside him, his face shone like

the sun. He said to them, 'Look, Abba Anthony is coming.' A little later he said, 'Look, the choir of prophets is coming.' Again his countenance shone with brightness and he said, 'Look, the choir of apostles is coming,' His countenance increased in brightness and lo, he spoke with someone. Then the old men asked him, 'With whom are you speaking, Father?' He said, 'Look, the angels are coming to fetch me, and I am begging them to let me do a little penance.' The old man said to him, 'You have no need to do penance, Father.' But the old man said to them, 'Truly, I do not think I have even made a beginning yet.' Now they all knew that he was perfect. Once more his countenance suddenly became like the sun and they were all filled with fear. He said to them, 'Look, the Lord is coming and he's saying, "Bring me the vessel from the desert." ' Then there was as a flash of lightening and all the house was filled with a sweet odour.

15. Abba Adelphius, bishop of Nilopolis, went to find Abba Sisoes on the mountain of Abba Anthony. When they were ready to leave, before setting out on their road Abba Sisoes made them eat before morning. Now it was a fast day. As he was setting the table, behold, some brothers came and knocked on the door. He said to his disciple, 'Give them a little to eat, for they are tired.' Abba Adelphius said to him, 'No, don't do that, in case they say that Abba Sisoes eats before morning.' So the old man thought about it and then he said to the brother, 'Go on, give them something.' Now when they saw the food they said, 'Have you visitors, and is that why the old man is eating with you?' The brother replied it was so. They they were very distressed and they said, 'May God forgive you, because you have let the old man eat now. Do you not know that because of this, he will mortify himself for a long time?' Hearing this, the bishop did penance before the old man saying, 'Forgive me, abba, for I reasoned on a human level while you do the work of God.' Abba Sisoes said to him, 'If God does not glorify a man, the glory of men is without value.'

16. Some brothers went to see Abba Sisoes to hear a word from him. But he did not speak to them saying, 'Excuse me.' Seeing his little baskets, the visitors asked his disciple Abraham, 'What do you do with these little baskets?' He said, 'We sell them here and there.' Hearing this the old man said, 'Even Sisoes eats now and then.' By

these words the visitors were greatly helped and they returned with joy, edified by his humility.

17. Abba Ammoun of Rhaithou asked Abba Sisoes, 'When I read the Scriptures, my mind is wholly concentrated on the words so that I may have something to say if I am asked.' The old man said to him, 'That is not necessary; it is better to enrich yourself through purity of spirit and to be without anxiety and then to speak.'

18. A secular who had a son came to see Abba Sisoes on Abba Anthony's mountain. On the way, it happened that his son died. He was not troubled by this but brought him with confidence to the old man and bowed down with his son, as though making prostration, so that he would be blessed by the old man. Then the father stood up, left the child at the old man's feet and went outside. The old man, thinking that the boy was bowing said to him, 'Get up, go outside.' For he did not know that he was dead. Immediately the boy stood up and went out. When he saw it, his father was filled with amazement and went back inside. He bowed before the old man and told him the whole story. When he heard it the old man was filled with regret, for he had not intended that to happen. So the disciple asked the father of the child not to speak of it to anyone before the old man's death.

19. Three old men came to see Abba Sisoes, having heard about him. The first said to him, 'Father, how shall I save myself from the river of fire?' He did not answer him. The second said to him, 'Father, how can I be saved from the gnashing of teeth and the worm which dieth not?' The third said, 'Father, what shall I do, for the remembrance of the outer darkness is killing me?' By way of reply the old man said to them, 'For my part, I do not keep in mind the remembrance of any of these things, for God is compassionate and I hope that he will show me his mercy.' Hearing this, the old men went back offended. But the old man, not wishing to let them go away hurt, said to them, 'Blessed are you, my brothers; truly I envy you. The first speaks of the river of fire, the second of hell and the third of darkness. Now if your spirit is filled with such remembrances, it is impossible for you to sin. What shall I do, then? I who am hard of heart and to whom it has not been granted so much as to know whether there is a punishment for men; no doubt it is

because of this that I am sinning all the time.' They prostrated
themselves before him and said, 'Now we have seen exactly that of
which we have heard tell.'

20. They asked Abba Sisoes, 'If a brother sins, surely he must do
penance for a year?' He replied, 'That is a hard saying.' The visitors
said, 'For six months?' He replied, 'That is a great deal.' They said,
'For forty days?' He said, 'That is a great deal, too.' They said to
him, 'What then? If a brother falls, and the *agape* is about to be
offered, should he simply come to the *agape,* too?' The old man said
to them, 'No, he needs to do penance for a few days. But I trust in
God that if such a man does penance with his whole heart, God will
receive him, even in three days.'

21. When Abba Sisoes went to Clysma one day, some seculars
came to see him. Though they talked a great deal, he did not answer
them by so much as a word. Later, one of them said, 'Why do you
bother the old man? He does not eat; that is why he cannot speak.'
The old man replied, 'For my part, I eat when the need arises.'

22. Abba Joseph asked Abba Sisoes, 'For how long must a man
cut away the passions?' The old man said to him, 'Do you want to
know how long?' Abba Joseph answered, 'Yes.' The the old man
said to him, 'So long as a passion attacks you, cut it away at once.'

23. A brother asked Abba Sisoes of Petra how to live and the old
man said to him, 'Daniel said: do not eat the bread of desires.' (cf.
Dan. 10.3)

24. It was said of Abba Sisoes that when he was sitting in the cell
he would always close the door.

25. One day some Arians came to see Abba Sisoes on Abba
Anthony's mountain and they began to speak against the orthodox
faith. The old man gave them no answer but he called his disciple
and said to him, 'Abraham, bring me the book of Saint Athanasius
and read it.' Then they were silent as their heresy was unmasked and
he sent them away in peace.

26. Abba Ammoun of Rhaithou came to Clysma one day to meet
Abba Sisoes. Seeing that Abba Sisoes was grieved because he had
left the desert, Abba Ammoun said to him, 'Abba, why grieve about

it? What would you do in the desert, now you are so old?' The old man pondered this sorrowfully and said to him, 'What are you saying to me, Ammoun? Was not the mere liberty of my soul enough for me in the desert?'

27. Abba Sisoes was sitting in his cell one day. His disciple knocked on the door and the old man shouted out to him saying, 'Go away, Abraham, do not come in. From now on I have no time for the things of this world.'

28. A brother asked Abba Sisoes, 'Why did you leave Scetis, where you lived with Abba Or and come to live here?' The old man said, 'At the time when Scetis became crowded, I heard that Anthony was dead and I got up and came here to the mountain. Finding the place peaceful I have settled here for a little while.' The brother said to him, 'How long have you been here?' The old man said to him, 'Seventy-two years.'

29. He also said, 'When there is someone who takes care of you, you are not to give him orders.'

30. A brother asked Abba Sisoes, 'If we are walking along the road and the guide leads us astray, ought we to tell him so?' The old man answered, 'No.' Then the brother said, 'Should we let him lead us astray then?' The old man said to him, 'What else? Will you take a stick to beat him? I know some brethren who were walking and the guide misled them the whole night. There were twelve of them and they all knew that they were lost and each one struggled not to say so. When day came and the guide realized that they had lost their way and said to them, "Forgive me, but I am lost," they all said to him, "We knew that but we kept silence." Hearing this he was filled with wonder and said, "Even to the point of death, the brothers control themselves so as not to speak," and he gave glory to God. The length of the road on which they had gone astray was twelve miles.'

31. One day the Saracens came and robbed the old man and his brother. As he was setting off into the desert to find something to eat, the old man found some camel dung and having broken it up, he found some grains of barley in it. He ate a grain and put the other into his hand. His brother came and saw him in the act of eating

and said to him, 'Is this charity, to find food and to eat it along without having called me?' Abba Sisoes said to him, 'I have not wronged you, brother, here is your share which I have kept in my hand.'

32. They said Abba Sisoes the Theban dwelt at Calamon of Arsinoe. Another old man was ill there in the other *lavra* and when he heard of it, Abba Sisoes was very sorry. Now Abba Sisoes used to fast for two days at a time, so there was one day when he did not eat. When he heard about the old man's illness, he said to himself, 'What shall I do? If I go and see him, I am afraid the brethren will compel me to eat, but if I wait until tomorrow, I am afraid he may die. This is what I will do; I will go and I will not eat.' So he went fasting, both fulfilling the commandment of God and yet not relaxing his way of life for the sake of God.

33. One of the Fathers related of Abba Sisoes of Calamon that, wishing to overcome sleep one day, he hung himself over the precipice of Petra. An angel came to take him down and ordered him not to do that again and not to transmit such teaching to others.

34. One of the Fathers asked Abba Sisoes, 'If I am sitting in the desert and a barbarian comes to kill me and if I am stronger than he, shall I kill him?' The old man said to him, 'No, leave him to God. In fact whatever the trial is which comes to a man, let him say, "This has happened to me because of my sins," and if something good comes say, "It is through the providence of God." '

35. A brother asked Abba Sisoes the Theban, 'Give me a word,' and he said, 'What shall I say to you? I read the New Testament, and I turn to the old.'

36. The same brother asked Abba Sisoes of Petra about the saying which Abba Sisoes the Theban had said to him and the old man said, 'I go to sleep in sin and I awaken in sin.'

37. They said of Abba Sisoes the Theban that when the assembly was dismissed he used to flee to his cell and they used to say of him, 'He is possessed by a devil.' But he was really doing the work of God.

38. A brother asked Abba Sisoes 'What shall I do, abba, for I have fallen?' The old man said to him, 'Get up again.' The brother

said, 'I have got up again, but I have fallen again.' The old man said, 'Get up again and again.' So then the brother said, 'How many times?' The old man said, 'Until you are taken up either in virtue or in sin. For a man presents himself to judgement in the state in which he is found.'

39. A brother asked an old man, 'What shall I do, for I am troubled about manual work? I love making ropes and I cannot make them.' The old man said that Abba Sisoes used to say, 'You should not do work which gives you satisfaction.'

40. Abba Sisoes said, 'Seek God, and do not seek where he dwells.'

41. He also said, 'Shame and lack of fear often lead to sin.'

42. A brother asked Abba Sisoes, 'What am I to do?' He said to him: 'What you need is a great deal of silence and humility. For it is written: "Blessed are those who wait for him" (Is. 30.18) for thus they are able to stand.'

43. Abba Sisoes said, 'Let yourself be despised, cast your own will behind your back, and you will be free from care and at peace.'

44. A brother asked Abba Sisoes, 'What shall I do about the passions?' The old man said, 'Each man is tempted when he is lured and enticed by his own desire.' (James 1.14)

45. A brother asked Abba Sisoes to give him a word. He said, 'Why do you make me speak without need? Whatever you see, do that.'

46. One day Abba Abraham, Abba Sisoes' disciple, went away on an errand. During his absence the old man did not wish to be served by anyone else. 'Shall I let any other man, except my brother, get used to me?' He refused till his disciple should return, and put up with the hardship.

47. They said of Abba Sisoes that once when he was sitting down, he cried with a loud voice, 'O misery!' His disciple said to him, 'What is the matter, father?' The old man said to him, 'I seek a man to speak to and I do not find one.'

48. One day Abba Sisoes left Abba Anthony's mountain to go to the outer mountain of the Thebaid and there he stayed. Now there were some Meletians there who lived at Calamon of Arsinoe. Hearing that the old man had come to the outer mountain, some people wished to see him but they said, 'What shall we do because the Meletians are on the mountain. We know that the old man does not suffer harm from them but we are afraid lest, in wanting to meet the old man, we fall into the temptation of the heretics.' So as not to meet the heretics, they did not go to see the old man.

49. This is what they relate about Abba Sisoes when he became ill. The old men were sitting beside him and he spoke to some of them. They said to him, 'What do you see, abba?' He said to them, 'I see beings coming towards me, and I am begging them to leave me a little while so that I may repent.' One of the old men said to him, 'And even if they allow you a respite, can you now profit by it and do penance?' The old man said to him, 'If I am not able to do that, at least I can groan a little over my soul and that is enough for me.'

50. They said of Abba Sisoes that when he came to Clysma he fell ill. While he was sitting with his disciple in his cell, someone knocked on the door. Then the old man understood and said to his disciple, 'Abraham, say to him who is knocking, "I am Sisoes on the mountain and I am Sisoes on my bed."' Hearing this, the one who knocked disappeared.

51. Abba Sisoes, the Theban, said to his disciple, 'Tell me what you see in me and then I will tell you what I see in you.' His disciple said to him, 'You are a good man, but a little hard.' The old man said to him, 'You are good, too, but you are not tough enough.'

52. They said of Abba Sisoes the Theban that he did not eat bread. At the Paschal Feast the brothers bowed to him and invited him to eat with them. He answered them, 'There is only one thing I can do: either I eat bread with you, or else I eat all the dishes you have prepared.' They said to him, 'Eat only bread,' and he did so.

53. If anyone asked Abba Sisoes about Abba Pambo, he would say, 'Pambo was very great in his works.'

54. Abba Sisoes said to a brother, 'How are you getting on?' and he replied, 'I am wasting my time, father.' The old man said, 'If I happen to waste a day, I am grateful for it.'*

SILVANUS

Silvanus, a Palestinian by birth, was the head of a community of twelve disciples in Scetis, among whom was Mark the Calligrapher. The group moved to Sinai in 380, and later went to Syria where they settled in the region of Gaza. They lived in a lavra, *with scattered cells and a central church for worship on Saturday and Sunday. Silvanus died before 414 and was succeeded by his disciple Zacharias.*

1. Abba Silvanus and his disciple Zacharias went to a certain monastery one day. They were given something to eat a little before taking the road and when they got outside his disciple found some water beside the path and wanted to drink. The old man said to him, 'Zacharias, it is a fast today.' The latter said to him, 'But, Father, have we not eaten?' The old man said to him, 'What we have eaten came through charity but, my child, let us keep our own fast.'

2. As Abba Silvanus was sitting with the brethren one day he was rapt in ecstasy and fell with his face to the ground. After a long time he got up and wept. The brethren besought him saying, 'What is it, Father?' But he remained silent and wept. When they insisted on his speaking he said, 'I was taken up to see the judgement and I saw there many of our sort coming to punishment and many seculars going into the kingdom.' The old man was full of compunction and never wanted to leave his cell. If he was obliged to go out, he hid his face in his cowl saying, 'Why should I seek to see this earthly light, which is of no use?'

3. Another time his disciple Zacharias entered and found him in ecstasy with his hands stretched towards heaven. Closing the door, he went away. Coming at the sixth and the ninth hours he found him in the same state. At the tenth hour he knocked, entered, and found him at peace and said to him, 'What has happened today,

---

*53 and 54 are additions from J.-C. Guy's text (p. 33).

Father?' The latter replied, 'I was ill today, my child.' But the disciple seized his feet and said to him, 'I will not let you go until you have told me what you have seen.' The old man said, 'I was taken up to heaven and I saw the glory of God and I stayed there till now and now I have been sent away.'

4. One day while Abba Silvanus was living on the mountain of Sinai his disciple Zacharias went away on an errand and said to the old man, 'Open the well and water the garden.' The old man went out with his face hidden in his cowl, looking down at his feet. Now at that moment a brother came along and seeing him from a distance he observed what he was doing. So he went up to him and said, 'Tell me, abba, why were you hiding your face in your cowl while you watered the garden?' The old man said to him, 'So that my eyes should not see the trees, my son, in case my attention should be distracted by them.'

5. A brother went to see Abba Silvanus on the mountain of Sinai. When he saw the brothers working hard he said to the old man, 'Do not labour for the food which perishes. (John 6.27) Mary has chosen the good portion.' (Luke 10.42) The old man said to his disciple, 'Zacharias, give the brother a book and put him in a cell without anything else.' So when the ninth hour came the visitor watched the door expecting someone would be sent to call him to the meal. When no-one called him he got up, went to find the old man and said to him, 'Have the brothers not eaten today?' The old man replied that they had. Then he said, 'Why did you not call me?' The old man said to him, 'Because you are a spiritual man and do not need that kind of food. We, being carnal, want to eat, and that is why we work. But you have chosen the good portion and read the whole day long and you do not want to eat carnal food.' When he heard these words the brother made a prostration saying, 'Forgive me, abba.' The old man said to him, 'Mary needs Martha. It is really thanks to Martha that Mary is praised.'

6. One day someone asked Abba Silvanus, 'How have you lived, father, in order to become so wise?' He replied, 'I have never let a thought that would bring the anger of God upon me enter my heart.'

7. It was said of Abba Silvanus that he stayed in his cell in secret. He had some small dried peas with which he made a hundred

necklaces to earn his food. Someone came from Egypt with an ass laden with loaves. He knocked and put them down in the cell. Then the old man, taking the necklaces, loaded them on the ass and sent him away.

8. They said of Abba Silvanus that his disciple Zacharias went out without him and, taking some brothers with him, moved the garden fence back to make it larger. When he knew this, the old man took his sheepskin, went out and said to the brothers, 'Pray for me.' When they saw what he was doing they threw themselves at his feet saying, 'Tell us what is the matter, Father.' He said to them, 'I shall not go back inside, nor take off my sheepskin till you have put the fence back where it was at first.' So they moved the fence once again and put it back as it was. So the old man returned to his cell.

9. Abba Silvanus said, 'I am a slave, and my master says to me: "Do your work, and I will feed you; but do not try to find out whence I shall feed you. Do not try to find out whether I have it, or whether I steal it, or whether I borrow it; simply work, and I will feed you." Therefore, when I work, I eat the fruit of my wages; but if I do not work, I eat charity.'

10. He also said, 'Unhappy is the man whose reputation is greater than his work.'

11. Abba Moses asked Abba Silvanus, 'Can a man lay a new foundation every day?' The old man said, 'If he works hard, he can lay a new foundation at every moment.'

12. The Fathers used to say that someone met Abba Silvanus one day and saw his face and body shining like an angel and he fell with his face to the ground. He said that others also had obtained this grace.

SIMON

1. A magistrate came to see Abba Simon one day. When he heard of it, he put on his apron and went out to attend to a palm-tree. When the visitors arrived they called out to him, 'Old man, where

is the anchorite?' He replied, 'There is no anchorite here.' Hearing these words, they went away again.

2. Another time, another magistrate came to visit him. The clergy went on ahead and said to the old man, 'Abba, get ready, for this magistrate has heard of you and is coming for your blessing.' So he said, 'Yes, I will prepare myself.' Then he put on a rough habit and taking some bread and cheese in his hands he went and sat in the doorway to eat it. When the magistrate arrived with his suite and saw him, he despised him and said, 'Is this the anchorite of whom we have heard so much?' and they went away at once.

SOPATRUS

Someone asked Abba Sopatrus, 'Give me a commandment, abba, and I will keep it.' He said to him, 'Do not allow a woman to come into your cell and do not read apocryphal literature. Do not get involved in discussions about the image.* Although this is not heresy, there is too much ignorance and liking for dispute between the two parties in this matter. It is impossible for a creature to understand the truth of it.'

SARMATAS

1. Abba Sarmatas said, 'I prefer a sinful man who knows he has sinned and repents, to a man who has not sinned and considers himself to be righteous.'

2. They said of Abba Sarmatas that on Abba Poemen's advice, he was often alone for forty days. He completed this time as though he had done nothing special. Abba Poemen went to see him and said to him, 'Tell me what you have seen by giving yourself such great hardship.' The other said to him, 'Nothing special.' Abba Poemen said to him, 'I shall not let you go till you tell me.' Then he said, 'I

---

*This refers to the doctrine of the image of God in man, the interpretation of which was a burning issue in the desert.

have discovered one simple thing: that if I say to my sleep, "Go," it goes, and if I say to it, "Come," it comes.'

3. A brother asked Abba Sarmatas, 'My thoughts say to me: "Do not work, but eat, drink and sleep."' The old man said to him, 'When you are hungry, eat; when you are thirsty, drink; when you are drowsy, sleep.' Fortunately another old man came to see the brother and the brother told him what Abba Sarmatas had said. Then the old man said to him, 'This is what the old man said to you: when you are very hungry, and when you are thirsty to the point of not being able to stand it any more, then eat and drink; and when you have watched for a very long time and are drowsy, sleep. This is what the old man was saying to you.'

4. The same brother asked Abba Sarmatas again, 'My thoughts say to me: "Come out and go and see the brethren."' The old man said, 'Do not listen to them about this, but say: "I listened to you before, but I do not want to listen to you this time."'

5. Abba Sarmatas also said, 'If a man does not flee from everything possible, he makes sin inevitable.'*

SERAPION

1. One day Abba Serapion passed through an Egyptian village and there he saw a courtesan who stayed in her own cell. The old man said to her, 'Expect me this evening, for I should like to come and spend the night with you.' She replied, 'Very well, abba.' She got ready and made the bed. When evening came, the old man came to see her and entered her cell and said to her, 'Have you got the bed ready?' She said, 'Yes, abba.' Then he closed the door and said to her, 'Wait a bit, for we have a rule of prayer and I must fulfil that first.' So the old man began his prayers. He took the psalter and at each psalm he said a prayer for the courtesan, begging God that she might be converted and saved, and God heard him. The woman stood trembling and praying beside the old man. When he had completed the whole psalter the woman fell to the ground. Then

*5 is an addition from J.-C. Guy's text (p. 33).

the old man, beginning the Epistle, read a great deal from the apostle and completed his prayers. The woman was filled with compunction and understood that he had not come to see her to commit sin but to save her soul and she fell at his feet, saying, 'Abba, do me this kindness and take we where I can please God.' So the old man took her to a monastery of virgins and entrusted her to the amma and he said, 'Take this sister and do not put any yoke or commandment on her as on the other sisters, but if she wants something, give it her and allow her to walk as she wishes.' After some days the courtesan said, 'I am a sinner; I wish to eat every second day.' A little later she said, 'I have committed many sins and I wish to eat every fourth day.' A few days later she besought the amma saying, 'Since I have grieved God greatly by my sins, do me the kindness of putting me in a cell and shutting it completely and giving me a little bread and some work through the window.' The amma did so and the woman pleased God all the rest of her life.

2. A brother said to Abba Serapion, 'Give me a word.' The old man said to him, 'What shall I say to you? You have taken the living of the widows and orphans and put it on your shelves.' For he saw them full of books.

3. Abba Serapion said, 'When the soldiers of the emperor are standing at attention, they cannot look to the right or left; it is the same for the man who stands before God and looks towards him in fear at all times; he cannot then fear anything from the enemy.'

4. A brother went to find Abba Serapion. According to his custom, the old man invited him to say a prayer. But the other, calling himself a sinner and unworthy of the monastic habit, did not obey. Next Abba Serapion wanted to wash his feet, but using the same words again, the visitor prevented him. Then Abba Serapion made him eat and he began to eat with him. Then he admonished him saying, 'My son, if you want to make progress stay in your cell and pay attention to yourself and your manual work; going out is not so profitable for you as remaining at home.' When he heard these words the visitor was offended and his expression changed so much that the old man could not but notice it. So he said to him, 'Up to now you have called yourself a sinner and accused yourself of being unworthy to live, but when I admonished you lovingly, you were

extremely put out. If you want to be humble, learn to bear generously what others unfairly inflict upon you and do not harbour empty words in your heart.' Hearing this, the brother asked the old man's forgiveness and went away greatly edified.

SERINUS

1. They said of Abba Serinus that he used to work hard and always ate two small loaves. Abba Job, his companion and himself a great ascetic, went to see him and said, 'I am careful about what I do in the cell, but when I come out I do as the brothers do.' Abba Serinus said to him, 'There is no great virtue in keeping to your regime in your cell, but there is if you keep it when you come out of your cell.'

2. Abba Serinus said, 'I have spent my time in harvesting, sewing and weaving, and in all these employments if the hand of God had not sustained me, I should not have been fed.'

SPYRIDON

1. It was said of Spyridon that he took care of his flock of sheep with such great holiness that he was judged worthy to be a shepherd of men too. He was called to the episcopate of one of the cities of Cyprus named Trimithuntes. Although he was charged with the episcopate, because of his great humility he pastured his sheep too. Now in the middle of the night some robbers came to the sheepfold secretly and tried to steal the sheep. But God, who saves the shepherd, saved the sheep also. Through an invisible power, the robbers found themselves bound to the sheepfold. Now at daybreak the shepherd comes to his sheep, and when he came and found the robbers with their hands behind their backs he understood what had happened. He said a prayer and released the robbers, then reprimanded them, and admonished them at length to give themselves henceforth to hardship and righteous suffering and no longer to live

unrighteously. Then he freed them and gave them a ram, adding with a good grace, 'So that you do not have the appearance of having watched in vain.'

2. It was also said of him that he had a young daughter who shared her father's devotion and whose name was Irene. One of their acquaintances entrusted her with an ornament of great price. For greater safety she hid the treasure in the earth but shortly after, she departed this life. After a time, he who had made the deposit came. Not finding the girl he applied to her father, Abba Spyridon, at first demanding, then imploring. The old man grieved for the loss suffered by him who had made the deposit, so he went to his daughter's tomb and begged God to show him, before the time, the resurrection promised her. He was not disappointed of his hope for immediately his daughter appeared alive to her father and named the place where the treasure lay and immediately she disappeared. So taking up the deposit, the old man returned it to its owner.

SAIUS

1. It was said that Abba Saius and Abba Moue lived together. Abba Saius was very obedient, but he was very rigid. To test him, the old man said to him, 'Go and steal.' Through obedience Abba Saius went to steal from the brethren, giving thanks to the Lord in everything. Abba Moue took the things and returned them secretly. Now once when they were on the road, Abba Saius was overcome with weakness and the old man left him there exhausted and went to say to the brethren, 'Go and carry Saius, because he is lying there helpless.' So they went and brought him in.

SARAH

1. It was related of Amma Sarah that for thirteen years she waged warfare against the demon of fornication. She never prayed that the warfare should cease but she said, 'O God, give me strength.'

2. Once the same spirit of fornication attacked her more insistently, reminding her of the vanities of the world. But she gave herself up to the fear of God and to asceticism and went up onto her little terrace to pray. Then the spirit of fornication appeared corporally to her and said, 'Sarah, you have overcome me.' But she said, 'It is not I who have overcome you, but my master, Christ.'

3. It was said concerning her that for sixty years she lived beside a river and never lifted her eyes to look at it.

4. Another time, two old men, great anchorites, came to the district of Pelusia to visit her. When they arrived one said to the other, 'Let us humiliate this old woman.' So they said to her, 'Be careful not to become conceited thinking to yourself: "Look how anchorites are coming to see me, a mere woman." ' But Amma Sarah said to them, 'According to nature I am a woman, but not according to my thoughts.'

5. Amma Sarah said, 'If I prayed God that all men should approve of my conduct, I should find myself a penitent at the door of each one, but I shall rather pray that my heart may be pure towards all.'

6. She also said, 'I put out my foot to ascend the ladder, and I place death before my eyes before going up it.'

7. She also said, 'It is good to give alms for men's sake. Even if it is only done to please men, through it one can begin to seek to please God.'

8. Some monks of Scetis came one day to visit Amma Sarah. She offered them a small basket of fruit. They left the good fruit and ate the bad. So she said to them, 'You are true monks of Scetis.'

9. She also said to the brothers, 'It is I who am a man, you who are women.'*

SYNCLETICA

1. Amma Syncletica said, 'In the beginning there are a great many battles and a good deal of suffering for those who are advanc-

*9 is an addition from J.-C. Guy's text (p. 34).

ing towards God and afterwards, ineffable joy. It is like those who wish to light a fire; at first they are choked by the smoke and cry, and by this means obtain what they seek (as it is said: "Our God is a consuming fire" [Heb. 12.24]): so we also must kindle the divine fire in ourselves through tears and hard work.'

2. She also said, 'We who have chosen this way of life must obtain perfect temperance. It is true that among seculars, also, temperance has the freedom of the city, but intemperance cohabits with it, because they sin with all the other senses. Their gaze is shameless and they laugh immoderately.'

3. She also said, 'Just as the most bitter medicine drives out poisonous creatures so prayer joined to fasting drives evil thoughts away.'

4. She also said, 'Do not let yourself be seduced by the delights of the riches of the world, as though they contained something useful on account of vain pleasure. Worldly people esteem the culinary art, but you, through fasting and thanks to cheap food, go beyond their abundance of food. It is written: "He who is sated loathes honey." (Prov. 27.7) Do not fill yourself with bread and you will not desire wine.'

5. Blessed Syncletica was asked if poverty is a perfect good. She said, 'For those who are capable of it, it is a perfect good. Those who can sustain it receive suffering in the body but rest in the soul, for just as one washes coarse clothes by trampling them underfoot and turning them about in all directions, even so the strong soul becomes much more stable thanks to voluntary poverty.'

6. She also said, 'If you find yourself in a monastery do not go to another place, for that will harm you a great deal. Just as the bird who abandons the eggs she was sitting on prevents them from hatching, so the monk or the nun grows cold and their faith dies, when they go from one place to another.'

7. She also said, 'Many are the wiles of the devil. If he is not able to disturb the soul by means of poverty, he suggests riches as an attraction. If he has not won the victory by insults and disgrace, he suggests praise and glory. Overcome by health, he makes the body ill. Not having been able to seduce it through pleasures, he tries to overthrow it by involuntary sufferings. He joins to this, very severe

illness, to disturb the faint-hearted in their love of God. But he also destroys the body by very violent fevers and weighs it down with intolerable thirst. If, being a sinner, you undergo all these things, remind yourself of the punishment to come, the everlasting fire and the sufferings inflicted by justice, and do not be discouraged here and now. Rejoice that God visits you and keep this blessed saying on your lips: "The Lord has chastened me sorely but he has not given me over unto death." (Ps. 118.18) You were iron, but fire has burnt the rust off you. If you are righteous and fall ill, you will go from strength to strength. Are you gold? You will pass through fire purged. Have you been given a thorn in the flesh? (2 Cor. 12.1) Exult, and see who else was treated like that; it is an honour to have the same sufferings as Paul. Are you being tried by fever? Are you being taught by cold? Indeed Scripture says: "We went through fire and water; yet thou has brought us forth to a spacious place." (Ps. 66.12) You have drawn the first lot? Expect the second. By virtue offer holy words in a loud voice. For it is said: "I am afflicted and in pain." (Ps. 69.29) By this share of wretchedness you will be made perfect. For he said: "The Lord hears when I call him." (Ps. 4.3) So open your mouth wider to be taught by these exercises of the soul, seeing that we are under the eyes of our enemy.'

8. She also said, 'If illness weighs us down, let us not be sorrowful as though, because of the illness and the prostration of our bodies we could not sing, for all these things are for our good, for the purification of our desires. Truly fasting and sleeping on the ground are set before us because of our sensuality. If illness then weakens this sensuality the reason for these practices is superfluous. For this is the great asceticism: to control oneself in illness and to sing hymns of thanksgiving to God.'

9. She also said, 'When you have to fast, do not pretend illness. For those who do not fast often fall into real sicknesses. If you have begun to act well, do not turn back through constraint of the enemy, for through your endurance, the enemy is destroyed. Those who put out to sea at first sail with a favourable wind; then the sails spread, but later the winds become adverse. Then the ship is tossed by the waves and is no longer controlled by the rudder. But when in a little while there is a calm, and the tempest dies down, then the

ship sails on again. So it is with us, when we are driven by the spirits who are against us; we hold to the cross as our sail and so we can set a safe course.'

10. She also said, 'Those who have endured the labours and dangers of the sea and then amass material riches, even when they have gained much desire to gain yet more and they consider what they have at present as nothing and reach out for what they have not got. We, who have nothing of that which we desire, wish to acquire everything through the fear of God.'

11. She also said, 'Imitate the publican, and you will not be condemned with the Pharisee. Choose the meekness of Moses and you will find your heart which is a rock changed into a spring of water.'

12. She also said, 'It is dangerous for anyone to teach who has not first been trained in the "practical" life. For if someone who owns a ruined house receives guests there, he does them harm because of the dilapidation of his dwelling. It is the same in the case of someone who has not first built an interior dwelling; he causes loss to those who come. By words one may convert them to salvation, but by evil behaviour, one injures them.'

13. She also said, 'It is good not to get angry, but if this should happen, the Apostle does not allow you a whole day for this passion, for he says: "Let not the sun go down." (Eph. 4.25) Will you wait till all your time is ended? Why hate the man who has grieved you? It is not he who has done the wrong, but the devil. Hate sickness but not the sick person.'

14. She also said, 'Those who are great athletes must contend against stronger enemies.'

15. She also said, 'There is an asceticism which is determined by the enemy and his disciples practice it. So how are we to distinguish between the divine and royal asceticism and the demonic tyranny? Clearly through its quality of balance. Always use a single rule of fasting. Do not fast four or five days and break it the following day with any amount of food. In truth lack of proportion always corrupts. While you are young and healthy, fast, for old age with its

weakness will come. As long as you can, lay up treasure, so that when you cannot, you will be at peace.'

16. She also said, 'As long as we are in the monastery, obedience is preferable to asceticism. The one teaches pride, the other humility.'

17. She also said, 'We must direct our souls with discernment. As long as we are in the monastery, we must not seek our own will, nor follow our personal opinion, but obey our fathers in the faith.'

18. She also said, 'It is written, "Be wise as serpents and innocent as doves." (Matt. 10.16) Being like serpents means not ignoring attacks and wiles of the devil. Like is quickly known to like. The simplicity of the dove denotes purity of action.'

19. Amma Syncletica said, 'There are many who live in the mountains and behave as if they were in the town, and they are wasting their time. It is possible to be a solitary in one's mind while living in a crowd, and it is possible for one who is a solitary to live in the crowd of his own thoughts.'

20. She also said, 'In the world, if we commit an offence, even an involuntary one, we are thrown into prison; let us likewise cast ourselves into prison because of our sins, so that voluntary remembrance may anticipate the punishment that is to come.'

21. She also said, 'Just as a treasure that is exposed loses its value, so a virtue which is known vanishes; just as wax melts when it is near fire, so the soul is destroyed by praise and loses all the results of its labour.'

22. She also said, 'Just as it is impossible to be at the same moment both a plant and a seed, so it is impossible for us to be surrounded by worldly honour and at the same time to bear heavenly fruit.'

23. She also said, 'My children, we all want to be saved, but because of our habit of negligence, we swerve away from salvation.'

24. She also said, 'We must arm ourselves in every way against the demons. For they attack us from outside, and they also stir us up from within; and the soul is then like a ship when great waves break over it, and at the same time it sinks because the hold is too

full. We are just like that: we lose as much by the exterior faults we commit as by the thoughts inside us. So we must watch for the attacks of men that come from outside us, and also repel the interior onslaughts of our thoughts.'

25. She also said, 'Here below we are not exempt from temptations. For Scripture says, "Let him who thinks that he stands take heed lest he fall." (1 Cor. 10.12) We sail on in darkness. The psalmist calls our life a sea and the sea is either full of rocks, or very rough, or else it is calm. We are like those who sail on a calm sea, and seculars are like those on a rough sea. We always set our course by the sun of justice, but it can often happen that the secular is saved in tempest and darkness, for he keeps watch as he ought, while we go to the bottom through negligence, although we are on a calm sea, because we have let go of the guidance of justice.'

26. She also said, 'Just as one cannot build a ship unless one has some nails, so it is impossible to be saved without humility.'

27. She also said, 'There is grief that is useful, and there is grief that is destructive. The first sort consists in weeping over one's own faults and weeping over the weakness of one's neighbours, in order not to destroy one's purpose, and attach oneself to the perfect good. But there is also a grief that comes from the enemy, full of mockery, which some call *accidie*. This spirit must be cast out, mainly by prayer and psalmody.'*

*19–27 are additions from J.-C. Guy's test (pp. 33–5).

⋄| TAU |⋄

TITHOES

1. It was said of Abba Tithoes that when he stood up to pray, if he did not quickly lower his hand, his spirit was rapt to heaven. So if it happened that some brothers were praying with him, he hastened to lower his hands so that his spirit should not be rapt and he should not pray for too long.

2. Abba Tithoes used to say, 'Pilgrimage means that a man should control his own tongue.'

3. A brother asked Abba Tithoes, 'How should I guard my heart?' The old man said to him, 'How can we guard our hearts when our mouths and our stomachs are open?'

4. Abba Matoes used to say of Abba Tithoes, 'No-one can ever speak against him, for like pure gold in the balance, so is Abba Tithoes.'

5. Abba Tithoes was sitting at Clysma one day, thinking and pondering and he said to his disciple, 'Water the palm-trees, my son.'

The latter said to him, 'But we are at Clysma, abba.' The old man said, 'What am I doing at Clysma? Take me to the mountain again.'

6. One day when Abba Tithoes was sitting down, a brother happened to be beside him. Not realizing this, he began to groan, without thinking that the brother was beside him for he was in ecstasy. Afterwards he made a prostration before him and said to him, 'Forgive me, brother; I have not yet become a monk, since I groaned in front of you.'

7. A brother asked Abba Tithoes, 'Which way leads to humility?' The old man said, 'The way of humility is this: self-control, prayer, and thinking yourself inferior to all creatures.'

TIMOTHY

1. Abba Timothy the priest said to Abba Poemen, 'There is a woman who commits fornication in Egypt and she gives her wages away in alms.' Abba Poemen said, 'She will not go on committing fornication, for the fruit of faith is appearing in her.' Now it happened that the mother of the priest Timothy came to see him and he asked her, 'Is that woman still living in fornication?' She replied, 'Yes and she has increased the number of her lovers, but also the numbers of her alms.' And Abba Timothy told Abba Poemen. The latter said, 'She will not go on committing fornication.' Abba Timothy's mother came again and said to him, 'You know that sinner? She wanted to come with me so that you might pray over her.' When he heard this, he told Abba Poemen and he said to him, 'Go and meet her.' When the woman saw him and heard the word of God from him, she was filled with compunction and said to him weeping, 'From today forward I shall cling to God and resolve not to commit fornication any more.' She entered a monastery at once and was pleasing to God.

❖⊦ UPSILON ⊦❖

HYPERECHIUS

1. Abba Hyperechius said, 'As the lion is terrible to wild asses, so is the experienced monk to desires.'

2. He also said, 'Fasting is a check against sin for the monk. He who discards it is like a rampaging stallion.' (cf. Jer. 5.8)

3. He also said, 'He who does not control his tongue when he is angry, will not control his passions either.'

4. He also said, 'It is better to eat meat and drink wine and not to eat the flesh of one's brethren through slander.'

5. He also said, 'It was through whispering that the serpent drove Eve out of Paradise, so he who speaks against his neighbour will be like the serpent, for he corrupts the soul of him who listens to him and he does not save his own soul.'

6. He also said, 'A monk's treasure is voluntary poverty. Lay up treasure in heaven, brother, for there are the ages of quiet and bliss without end.'

7. He also said, 'Let your thoughts be ever in the kingdom of heaven and soon you will possess it as an heritage.'

8. He also said, 'Obedience is the best ornament of the monk. He who has acquired it will be heard by God, and he will stand beside the crucified with confidence, for the crucified Lord became obedient unto death.' (cf. Phil. 2.8)

❖| PHI |❖

PHOCAS

1. Abba Phocas of the monastery of Abba Theognius of Jerusalem used to say, 'When I used to live in Scetis, there was an Abba James in the Cells, a young man, whose father according to the flesh was at the same time his spiritual father. Now the Cells had two churches: one of the Orthodox, which he used to attend, and another of the Monophysites. Since Abba James had the grace of humility, everyone loved him, both the members of the Church and the Monophysites. The Orthodox used to say to him, "Abba James, take care lest the Monophysites deceive you and draw you to their communion." Likewise the Monophysites said to him, "Abba James, you ought to realize that by being in communion with the partisans of the doctrine of the two natures, you are endangering your soul for they are Nestorians and subvert the truth." Abba James, who was a simple man, found himself caught between the two sides and in his distress he went and prayed to God. He hid himself in a withdrawn cell, outside the *lavra*, and put on his garments of burial,

as though preparing himself for death. For the Egyptian fathers have the custom of keeping the cloak and cowl in which they took the holy habit until their death, only wearing them on Sundays for the Holy Communion and taking them off immediately afterwards. Going into this cell then, praying to God, and persevering in fasting, he fell on the ground and remained lying there. Later he said he had experienced many things in these days because of the demons, especially in thought. When forty days had passed, he saw a little child coming towards him joyfully, who said to him, "Abba James, what are you doing here?" Immediately illuminated and drawing strength from his contemplation. he said to him, "Master, you know my difficulty. One side says to me, 'Do not leave the Church,' while the others say to me, 'The partisans of the two natures are deceiving you.' I, in my distress, not knowing what to do, have come to this point." The Lord answered him, "You are very well where you are." Immediately on hearing these words, he found himself at the doors of the holy church of the Orthodox adherents of the Synod.'

2. Abba Phocas also said, 'When he came to Scetis, Abba James was strongly attacked by the demon of fornication. As the warfare pressed harder, he came to see me and told me about it, saying to me, "Tomorrow, I am going to such and such a cave but I entreat you for the Lord's sake, do not speak of it to anyone, not even my father. But count forty days and when they are fulfilled do me the kindness of coming and bringing me holy communion. If you find me dead, bury me, but if you find me still alive, give me holy communion." Having heard this, when the forty days were fulfilled, I took holy communion and a whole loaf with a little wine and went to find him. As I was drawing near to the cave I smelt a very bad smell which came from its mouth. I said to myself, "The blessed one is at rest." When I got close to him, I found him half dead. When he saw me he moved his right hand a little, as much as he could, asking me for the holy communion with his hand. I said to him, "I have it." He wanted to open his mouth but it was fast shut. Not knowing what to do, I went out into the desert and found a piece of wood and with much difficulty. I opened his mouth a little. I poured in a little of the body and the precious blood, as much as he could take of them. Through this participation in the holy

communion he drew strength. A little while after, soaking some crumbs of ordinary bread, I offered them to him and after a time, some more, as much as he could take. So, by the grace of God, he came back with me a day later and walked as far as his own cell, delivered, by the help of God, from the harmful passion of fornication.'

FELIX

1. Some brothers who had some seculars with them, went to see Abba Felix and they begged him to say a word to them. But the old man kept silence. After they had asked for a long time he said to them, 'You wish to hear a word?' They said, 'Yes, abba.' Then the old man said to them, 'There are no more words nowadays. When the brothers used to consult the old men and when they did what was said to them, God showed them how to speak. But now, since they ask without doing that which they hear, God has withdrawn the grace of the word from the old men and they do not find anything to say, because there are no longer any who carry their words out.' Hearing this, the brothers groaned, saying, 'Pray for us, abba.'

PHILAGRIUS

1. There was one of the saints named Philagrius who dwelt in the desert of Jerusalem and worked laboriously to earn his own bread. While he was standing in the market place to sell his manual work, someone dropped a purse with a thousand pieces of money. The old man, finding it, stayed where he was, saying, 'Surely he who has lost it will come back.' He did come back weeping. Taking him aside privately, the old man gave it to him. But the other gripped him, wanting to give him a share. The old man would not agree to this at all and the other began to cry out, 'Come and see what the name of God has done.' The old man fled secretly and left the city in order not to be honoured.

PHORTAS

1. Abba Phortas said, 'If God wants me to live, he knows how to deal with me; but if he does not wish it, what is the good of living?' Though he was bedridden, he did not accept anything from anyone. But he used to say, 'Suppose one day someone brings me something and it is not brought for the love of God, not only have I nothing to give him in return, but he will not receive a recompense from God, because he did not bring it for God's sake; thus the donor will suffer a wrong. It is necessary that those who are consecrated to God and look only to him, should be so well disposed that they do not consider anything as an injury, not even if someone wrongs them ten thousand times.'

✦| CHI |✦

CHOMAS

1. It was said of Abba Chomas that at the point of death he said to his sons, 'Do not dwell with heretics, and do not have anything to do with rulers, then your hands will not be opened to gather together, but open to give.'

CHAEREMON

Chaeremon, a very early settler in Nitria, had his cell forty miles from the church and twelve miles from the central water supply.

1. They said that Abba Chaeremon's cave was forty miles from the church and ten miles from the marsh and water. So when he took his manual work to his cave, he took with him two goatskin bottles, one beside the other, and he sat there, leading a quiet life.

⋄|PSI|⋄

PSENTHAISIUS

1. Abba Psenthaisius, Abba Surus and Abba Psoius used to agree in saying this, 'Whenever we listened to the words of our Father, Abba Pachomius, we were greatly helped and spurred on with zeal for good works; we saw how, even when he kept silence, he taught us by his actions. We were amazed by him and we used to say to each other, "We thought that all the saints were created as saints by God and never changed from their mother's womb, not like other men. We thought that sinners could not live devoutly, because they had been so created. But now we see the goodness of God manifested in our father, for see, he is of pagan origin and he has become devout; he has put on all the commandments of God. Thus even we also can follow him and become equal to the saints whom he himself has followed. Truly it is written: 'Come unto me, all you who labour and are heavy laden, and I will give you rest.' (Matt. 11.28) Let us die, then, and let us live with him, because he has brought us to God in the right way." '

⬧| OMEGA |⬧

OR

*Or, one of the early monks in Nitria, associated with Theodore and Sisoes,
died about A. D. 390.*

1. It was said of Abba Or and Abba Theodore that as they were
building a cell out of clay, they said to one another, 'If God should
visit us now, what should we do?' Then, weeping, they left the clay
there and each of them went back into his cell.

2. They said of Abba Or that he never lied, nor swore, nor hurt
anyone, nor spoke without necessity.

3. Abba Or said to his disciple Paul, 'Be careful never to let an
irrelevant word come into this cell.'

4. Paul, Abba Or's disciple, went to buy some reeds one day. He
ascertained that others had been before him and had paid deposits.
But Abba Or never paid deposits for anything at all, but paid the

full price at the proper time. So his disciple went in search of palm-branches somewhere else. Then a farmer said to him, 'Someone has given me a deposit, but he has not come. So why don't you take these palm-branches.' He took them and he went back to the old man and told him all this. The old man clapped his hands and said, 'Or is not going to work this year.' He did not allow the palm-branches to come inside his cell, but waited for them to be taken to where they belonged.

5. Abba Or said, 'If you see that I am thinking adversely about someone, know that he is thinking in the same way about me.'

6. In Abba Or's neighbourhood there was a villager named Longinas, who gave a great deal away in alms. He asked one of the Fathers who came to see him to take him to Abba Or. The monk went to the old man and praised the villager, saying that he was good and gave many alms. The old man thought about this and then said, 'Yes, he is good.' Then the monk began to beg him, saying, 'Abba, let him come and see you.' But the old man answered, 'Truly, there is no need for him to cross this valley in order to see me.'

7. Abba Sisoes asked Abba Or, 'Give me a word,' and he said to him, 'Do you trust me?' He replied that he did. Then he said to him, 'Go, and what you have seen me do, do also.' Abba Sisoes said to him, 'Father, what have I seen you do?' The old man said, 'In my own opinion, I put myself below all men.'

8. It was said of Abba Or and Abba Theodore, that they laid good foundations, and at all times gave thanks to God.

9. Abba Or said, 'The crown of the monk is humility.'

10. He also said, 'He who is honoured and praised beyond his merits, will suffer much condemnation, but he who is held as of no account among men will receive glory in heaven.'

11. He gave this counsel, 'Whenever you want to subdue your high and proud thoughts, examine your conscience carefully: Have you kept all the commandments? Have you loved your enemies and been kind to them in their misfortunes? Have you counted yourself to be an unprofitable servant and the worst of all sinners? If you find you have done all this, do not therefore think well of yourself as

if you had done everything well but realize that even the thought of such things is totally destructive.'

12. This was what he taught: In all temptation, do not complain about anyone else, but say about yourself, 'These things happen to me because of my sins.'

13. He used to say this, 'Do not speak in your heart against your brother like this: "I am a man of more sober and austere life than he is," but put yourself in subjection to the grace of Christ, in the spirit of poverty and genuine charity, or you will be overcome by the spirit of vain-glory and lose all you have gained. For it is written in the Scriptures: "Let him who stands take heed lest he fall." (1 Cor. 10.12) Let your salvation be founded in the Lord.'

14. He propounded this saying, 'If you are fleeing, flee from men; or the world and the men in it will make you do many foolish things.'

15. He also said, 'If you have spoken evil of your brother, and you are stricken with remorse, go and kneel down before him and say: "I have spoken badly of you; let this be my surety that I will not spread this slander any further." For detraction is death to the soul.'

Glossary

ACCIDIE: despondency, depression, listlessness, a distaste for life without any specific reason.

AGAPE: the primary meaning is 'love'. In the Apophthegmata it is also used to mean the meal taken in common after the celebration of the Liturgy. The Agape can, however, also refer to the Liturgy itself. It is also used in these writings to mean a love-gift, or a loan.

APATHEIA: the state of being unmoved by passion; this involves control of the passions rather than their destruction.

APOPHTHEGM: the memorable saying of an 'old man'. 'Give me a word' is a key phrase in the desert tradition. The 'word' is not an explanation or a consoling suggestion; it is a word given in order to create life and bring the one who receives it to God and salvation. It is a word that is truly life-giving if it is not discussed or argued over, but simply received and integrated into life. These apophthegms were always given to individuals to fit their own needs and circumstances and this should be remembered when using a collection such as this.

CELL: a hut or cave where the monk lives alone or with a disciple. These buildings were scattered about the desert out of earshot of each other. A group of such cells is called a lavra.

CENOBIUM: a monastery where monks or nuns live the common life.

HESYCHIA: stillness, quiet, tranquillity. This is the central consideration in the prayer of the desert Fathers. On the external level is signifies an individual living as a solitary; on a deeper level it is not merely separation from noise and speaking with other people, but the possession of interior quiet and peace. Thus it is possible to use the term of many who do not actually live the hermit life. It means more specifically guarding the mind, constant remembrance of God, and the possession of inner prayer. Hesychasm is the general term and hesychast is the noun used to describe the person seeking to follow this way of prayer.

METANOIA: repentance, interior sorrow for sin. It also means the action by which such sorrow is expressed, usually a prostration. It is also used of a deep bow which is a means of greeting someone with respect. It has in later writings the meaning of conversion of life, and particularly the conversion of monastic life.

MELOTE: sheepskin. A monastic cloak made of sheepskin, also used as a blanket for the monk to sleep on. It could be used for carrying a monk's few possessions.

OLD MAN: *Geron* in Greek, *Pater* in Latin (hence *'gerontikon'* or *'paterikon'* for collections of the Sayings of Old Men). It is the name given to monks who are recognized as being spiritually gifted.

SYNAXIS: the liturgical office said by monks in common, usually on Saturday and Sunday. It is also used here of the individual rule of prayer which a solitary follows.

WORK: used in the Apophthegmata in two senses: either as manual labour, or as spiritual exertion. These two are seen as one, but the idea of interior 'work' predominates for the monk.

Chronological Table for Early Egyptian Monasticism

249–51	Persecution by the Emperor Decius.
c. 251	Anthony the Great born.
c. 292	Pachomius born.
303	Edict of Persecution
c. 315	Amoun begins his monastic life.
c. 320	Pachomius founds a community at Tabennisi.
324	Constantine sole emperor.
325	Council of Nicea.
328	Athanasius, Archbishop of Alexandria.
c. 330	The two Macarii in Egypt.
337	Death of Constantine, as a Christian.
c. 340	Floruit Pambo in Scetis.
	The foundation of the Cells.
	Also in Egypt: Sisoes, John the Dwarf, Paphnutius, Isidore the Priest, Pior, Carion and his son Zacharias.

c. 343   Rufinus and Jerome born.

346   Death of Pachomius.

356   Death of Anthony. Sisoes settles on the Mountain of Anthony sometime later.

357   Athanasius writes the *Life of Anthony*.

361   Julian the Apostate, Emperor.

362   Athanasius exiled.

367   Epiphanius, bishop in Cyprus.

370   Basil, Bishop of Caesarea, writes his *Rules*.

373   Death of Athanasius.

373–5   Rufinus and Melania visit Egypt.
Death of Pambo.

376   Euthymius born.

379   Death of Basil.

381   Council of Constantinople.

383   Evagrius in Nitria and at the Cells.

385   Jerome in Bethlehem.

c. 390   Death of Macarius the Egyptian.

391   Destruction of pagan temples. Floruit John of Lycopolis.

394   Arsenius to Scetis.

398   John Chrysostom, Bishop of Constantinople.

399   Death of Evagrius. Archbishop Theophilus opposes Anthropomorphism and condemns Origenism.

400   John Cassian in Constantinople.

407–8   First devastation of Scetis, Moses and his Companions killed.
Poemen and his brothers, Joseph, Theodore, Agathon, etc. leave Scetis.

407   Death of John Chrysostom.
At Gaza, Silvanus with Mark the Calligrapher, makes a settlement.
At Enaton, Lucius, Lot and Longinus.

410   Sack of Rome by Alaric.

c. 412   Rufinus' Version of the *History of the Monks of Egypt* complete.
Death of Rufinus.

419–20   Palladius' *Lausiac History* written.

421–6   Cassian writes the *Institutes* and *Conferences*.

431   Council of Ephesus.
434   Second devastation of Scetis.
       Arsenius goes to Troë.
c. 439   Saba born.
449   Death of Arsenius.
451   Council of Chalcedon.
455   Sack of Rome by the Vandals.
459   Death of Simeon Stylites.
       Daniel becomes a Stylite.
c. 480   Birth of St. Benedict of Nursia.

Select Bibliography

A. Texts of the *Apophthegmata*

Alphabetical Collection. J. P. MIGNE, *Patrologia Cursus Completus, Series Graeca, vol. 65,* cols. 71–440, Paris, 1868. Supplemented by J. C. GUY in *Recherches sur la Tradition Grecque des Apophthegmata Patrum,* Subsidia hagiographica no. 36. Brussels, 1962.

Anonymous Sayings. Partially published by Nau, *Revue de l'Orient Chrétien,* vols. 12–14 (1907–9), 17–18 (1912–13).

Systematic Collection. Unpublished in Greek. A Latin version by Pelagius and John printed in J. P. MIGNE, *Patrologia Latina, vol. 73,* cols. 851–1052. Also JOSÉ GERALDUS FREIRE, *A versao latina por Pascasio de Dume dos Apophthegmata Patrum.* Coimbra, 1971.

B. Translations of the *Apophthegmata*

Alphabetical Collection. French translation. J.-C. GUY, *Les Apophthegmes des Pères du Désert,* Begrolles, 1966.

Anonymous Sayings. Translation into French of the text published by Nau, op. cit., also in J.-C. GUY, *Les Apophthegmata des Pères du Désert,*

Begrolles, 1966. English translation, BENEDICTA WARD, *The Wisdom of the Desert Fathers*, SLG Press, 1975.

Systematic Collection. French translation J. DION and G. OURY, *Les Sentences des Pères du Désert: Les Apophthegmes des Peres (Recension de Pelage et Jean)*, Solesmes, 1966. Also, L. REGNAULT, *Les Sentences des Pères du Désert: nouveau recueil*, Solesmes, 1970.

Syriac Apophthegmata. English translation WALLIS BUDGE, *The Wit and Wisdom of the Christian Fathers of Egypt*, Oxford, 1934.

Selections from the Apophthegmata in English. OWEN CHADWICK, *Western Asceticism*, SCM PRESS, 1958. THOMAS MERTON, *The Wisdom of the Desert*, Sheldon Press, 1973. HELEN WADDELL, *The Desert Fathers*, Constable & Co., 1936.

C. Other Ancient Sources

ATHANASIUS, *Opera Omnia*, J. P. MIGNE, *Patroligia Graeca, vols 25–28*. *The Life of Saint Anthony*, translated into English by MEYER, Ancient Christian Writers, vol. 10, 1950.

BASIL THE GREAT, *Opera Omnia*, J. P. MIGNE, *Patrologia Graeca, vols. 29–32*. *The Longer and the Shorter Rules*, translated into English by W. K. LOWTHER CLARKE, *The Ascetic Works of Saint Basil*, SPCK, 1925. Also SISTER M. MONICA WAGNER, *Saint Basil, Ascetical Works*, Washington, 1962.

BARSANUFIUS and JOHN. *Correspondence of Barsanufius and John*, edited by NIKODEMUS, Venice, 1816. French translation L. RÉGNAULT, *La Correspondance de Barsanuph et Jean*, Solesmes, 1971. Partly translated into English by DERWAS CHITTY, Barsanufius and John, Athens, 1960.

JOHN CASSIAN, *Opera Omnia*, J. F. MIGNE, *Patrologia Latina, vols. 49–50*. *Institutes*, edition with French translation by J.-C. GUY, Sources Chrétiennes, vol. 109, Paris, 1965. *Conférences*, edition with French translation by E. PICHERY, Sources Chrétiennes, vols. 105–7, Paris, 1964–5. English translation, EDGAR GIBSON, 1894, reissued Eerdmans, USA, 1973. New English translations of *Institutes* and *Conférences* to be published by Cistercian Publications, USA.

DAWES and BAYNES, *Three Byzantine Saints*, Blackwell, 1948; this is a translation of the *Life of Daniel the Stylite*, *The Life of Theodore of Studion*, and the *Life of John the Almsgiver*.

DOROTHEUS OF GAZA, *Opera Omnia*, J. P. MIGNE, *Patrologia Graeca, vol. 88*, cols. 1611–1842. Edition with French translation, L. RÉGNAULT and DE PRÉVILLE, *Dorothée de Gaza, Oevres Spirituelles*, Sources Chrétiennes, vol. 92, Paris, 1963. Also, L. RÉGNAULT,

Maîtres Spirituels au Desert de Gaza, Barsanuphe, Jean et Dorothée, Solesmes, 1967.

EVAGRIUS PONTICUS, *Opera Omnia,* J. P. MIGNE, *Patrologia Graeca, vol. 40,* cols. 1213–86. Edition with French translation by A. C. GUILLAUMONT, *Evagre le Pontique, traite practique ou le moiné,* Sources Chrétiennes, vols. 170–1, Paris, 1971. English translation of *Praktikos and Chapters on Prayer,* JOHN EUDES BAMBERGER, OCSO, Cistercian Publications, USA, 1970.

Historia Monachorum in Aegypto, Latin version of Rufinus, J. P. MIGNE, *Patrologia Latina, vol. 21,* cols. 387–462. Edition with French translation, A. J. FESTUGIÈRE, Subsidia hagiographica no. 34. Brussels, 1961.

JEROME, *Opera Omnia,* J. P. MIGNE, *Patrologia Latina, vols. 22–30.*

JOHN CLIMACUS, *Opera Omnia,* J. P. MIGNE, *Patrologia Graeca, vol. 88,* cols. 596–1210. English translaion *The Ladder of the Divine Ascent,* L. MOORE and M. HEPPELL, Faber and Faber, 1959.

JOHN MOSCHUS, *Patrum Spirituale,* J. P. MIGNE, *Patrologia Graeca, cols. 2851–3116.* Edition with French translation by R. DE JOURNEL, Sources Chretiennes, vol. 12, Paris, 1946.

MAXIMUS THE CONFESSOR, *Opera Omnia,* J. P. MIGNE, *Patrologia Graeca, vols. 90–1.* See L. THUNBERG, *Microcosm and Mediator,* Lund, 1965, with full bibliography.

PACHOMIUS. *S. Pachomii Vitae graecae,* ed. HALKIN, Subsidia hagiographica, no. 19. Brussels, 1932. *Les Vies coptes de S. Pachome et de ses premiers successeurs,* edition with French translation by LEFORT, Louvain, 1934. French translation of the *Vita Prima of Pachomius,* A.-J. FESTUGIÈRE, *Les Moines d'Orient,* vol. 4. Paris, 1965.

PALLADIUS. *The Lausiac History.* Edited by CUTHBERT BUTLER, Cambridge, 1898–1904. English translation R. T. MEYER, *Ancient Christian Writers,* vol. 34, Washington, 1965. Also W. LOWTHER CLARKE, SPCK, 1918.

SOZOMEN. *Historia Ecclesiastica,* edited by J. HUSSEY, 2 vols. Oxford, 1860.

D. Some Modern Related Works

LOUIS BOUYER, *La Vie de S. Antoine, Essai sur la Spiritualité du monachism primatif.* S. Wandrille, 1950.

W. BOUSSET, *Apophthegmata,* Tübingen, 1932.

PETER BROWN, *The World of Late Antiquity,* London, 1971. Also, 'The Rise and Function of the Holy Man in Late Antiquity', *Journal of Roman Studies,* vol. lxi, pp. 80–101, 1971.

OWEN CHADWICK, *John Cassian*, CUP, 1950.

DERWAS CHITTY, *The Desert a City*, Oxford, 1966. Also, *Seven Letters of Saint Anthony*, translated with introduction by DERWAS CHITTY, SLG Press, 1975.

J.-C. GUY, *Recherches sur la Tradition Grecque des Apophthegmata Patrum*, Subsidia hagiographica, vol. 36. Brussels, 1962.

E. R. HARDY, *Christian Egypt*, New York, 1952.

H. G. EVELYN WHITE, *The Monasteries of the Wadi 'n Natrun*, vol. 2, *The History of the Monasteries of Nitria and Scetis*, New York, 1932.

ARMAND VEILLEUX, *La Liturgie dans le cénobitism pachômien au quatrième siècle*, Studia Anselmiana, vol, 57, Rome, 1968.

A. VOOBUS, *A History of Asceticism in the Syrian Orient*, vol. 2. Louvain, 1960.

See also a collection of relevant essays published in *Eastern Churches Review*, vol. 6, no. i, 1974, Clarendon Press.

General Index

Index of People and Places

(Names in large type indicate the sections of sayings of a Monk in this book, with numbers for them in italic.)

[265]

CISTERCIAN PUBLICATIONS INC.
Kalamazoo, Michigan

TITLES LISTING
THE CISTERCIAN FATHERS SERIES

Texts and Studies
in the
Monastic Tradition

Temporarily out of print   † *Forthcoming*

THE CISTERCIAN STUDIES SERIES

MONASTIC TEXTS

CHRISTIAN SPIRITUALITY

MONASTIC STUDIES

CISTERCIAN STUDIES

Temporarily out of print   † *Forthcoming*

Eight Chapters on Perfection and Angel's Song
  (Walter Hilton)
Creative Suffering (Iulia de Beausobre)
Bringing Forth Christ. Five Feasts of the Child
  Jesus (St Bonaventure)
Gentleness in St John of the Cross

Distributed in North America only for Fairacres Press.

DISTRIBUTED BOOKS

St Benedict: Man with An Idea (Melbourne Studies)
The Spirit of Simplicity
Benedict's Disciples (David Hugh Farmer)
The Emperor's Monk: A Contemporary Life of
  Benedict of Aniane
A Guide to Cistercian Scholarship (2nd ed.)

*North American customers may order
through booksellers or directly
from the publisher:*

Cistercian Publications
WMU Station
Kalamazoo, Michigan 49008
(616) 383-4985

*Cistercian monks and nuns have been
living lives of prayer & praise, meditation &
manual labor since the twelfth century.
They are part of an unbroken tradition
which extends back to the fourth century
and which continues today in the Catholic
church, the Orthodox churches, the
Anglican communion, and, most recently,
in the Protestant churches.*

*Share their way of life and their search for
God by reading Cistercian Publications.*

*A complete catalogue of texts-in-
translation and studies on early,
medieval, and modern Christian
monasticism is available at no cost
from Cistercian Publications.*